DIET AND NUTRITION

DIET AND NUTRITION

By

Suresh Gopalani

2008

CYBER TECH PUBLICATIONS
4264/3, Ansari Road, Daryaganj, New Delhi-110002 (India)
Ph.: 011-23244078. Fax: 011-23280028
E-Mail: cyberpublicationsdelhi@yahoo.com

DIET AND NUTRITION

Suresh Gopalani

First Edition 2008

Reprint 2024

Published by :

G.S. Rawat for **Cyber Tech Publications**
4264/3, Ansari Road, Daryaganj, New Delhi-110002 (India)
Ph.: 011-23244078. Fax: 011-23280028
E-Mail: cyberpublicationsdelhi@yahoo.com

Printed at : **Amit Enterprises**, Maujpur, Delhi, (9810878184)

Preface

General public is of the opinion that the physicians play an important role in providing dietary advice, and physicians appreciate their responsibility with regard to nutrition. Dealing with food, diet, and nutrition in the family practice setting-what individuals eat, how this influences their health status, and in what way food habits can be changed-is a meeting point of medical, behavioral, communication, epidemiologic, and nutritional perspectives.

An important aspect of individual nutritional guidance is the background of the target group. In family medicine, a high-risk approach is generally promoted: care is focused on those at highest need who will benefit most from it. Unhealthy food habits are most likely in people with a persistent adverse lifestyle, but this is the group least likely to change. The effect size should, in other words, be related to the population under care. The same is true of the economically disadvantaged. Nutrition is linked to the so-called prevention paradox: effects of interventions may be small or even nonexistent on an individual level but be highly advantageous on a population level.

Nutrition education and communication methods, like diet and nutrition approaches themselves, must be evidence based. That means we need to know the relative efficacies of the different methods and to understand how they work.

In the present work an endeavour has been made in the same direction, it is hopefully anticipated that the readers will derive benefit and information regarding the balanced diet and live a healthy life.

—Author

Contents

1

Nutrition Ecology

INTRODUCTION

Nutrition ecology is an interdisciplinary scientific discipline that incorporates the entire food chain as well as its interactions with health, the environment, society, and the economy. The food chain includes production, harvesting, preservation, storage, transport, processing, packaging, trade, distribution, preparation, composition, and consumption of food, as well as disposal of all waste materials along the food path.

Nutrition ecology has many roots, some of which go back to antiquity. The introduction of systematic agriculture (slash and burn cultivation) and domestication of animals (food rivals) has markedly affected our environment. One early example of the consequences of systematic agriculture is the Greek invasions of other countries as a consequence of their increasing meat consumption, which required them to acquire more farmland for fodder production. Another example is the deforestation for farmland and for building purposes, which began thousands of years ago and has continued to this day. Both the Torah and the Bible mention environmental issues numerous times. The impact of systematic agriculture on the environment was discussed by Thomas Aquinas (1224-1274), Jean-Jacques Rousseau (1712-1778), and Henry David Thoreau (1817-1862). At the end of the 19th century, Jacob von Uexkuell (1864-1944) founded the science of ecology.

Industrialized agriculture was introduced in the 19th century and rapidly took command of all aspects of life, with striking social, economic, and environmental consequences.

Reactions to these developments led to the formation of the Sierra Club in North America and to the Reform Movement in Central Europe in the second half of the 19th century. People migrated from urban to rural areas to dwell in unpolluted regions and to grow their own food. Economic and social reforms were proposed and practiced. Some of these included a vegetarian lifestyle. Another reaction to industrialized agriculture was organic farming, which was initiated by the anthroposophists in 1924 and started to flourish in the 1970s. At that time, a number of organizations were established that raised concerns about the environment and food quality [e.g, the Club of Rome (1968), Greenpeace (1971), World Watch Institute (1975), the Green Party (1980)]. At the same time, literature on the negative influence of industrialized agriculture appeared by Rachel Carson, Frances Moore-Lappe (2), Dennis Meadows, Joan Gussow, and Ralph Nader. These authors discussed the dramatic effects of industrialization and industrialized agriculture on the environment, health, society, and the economy.

ORIGIN OF THE TERM

The term nutrition ecology was coined in 1986 by a group of nutritionists at the University of Giessen, Germany. Nutrition ecology as an interdisciplinary scientific discipline is a holistic concept that considers all links in the nutrition system, with the aim of sustainability. Thus, nutrition ecology describes a new field of nutrition sciences that deals with the local and global consequences of food production, processing, trade, and consumption. Nutrition ecology goes beyond econutrition, which is limited to the interactions of nutrition and environment. Nutrition ecology goes further than the older concept of ecology of food and nutrition, which is limited to the eating patterns of indigenous and aboriginal populations.

At present, nutrition sciences are dominated by health aspects of food and, in part, by food quality. Recommendations are based primarily on physiologic and toxicologic considerations. The implications of our current nutrition system are more complex and go beyond nutrient content and contamination with pathogens and contaminants. To avoid ecologic damage caused by the nutrition system and to attain nutrition security for the world population, additional aspects need to be incorporated. The necessity of taking a more holistic view for a sustainable development is underlined by the current crises in the nutrition system, as discussed at the World Food Summit in June 2002.

DIMENSIONS OF NUTRITION ECOLOGY

As is typical for an interdisciplinary discipline, nutrition ecology deals with a wide range of issues, including research, teaching, and public actions. A broad view of the entire nutrition system covers subject matters such as total food quality, ecologic balances, and life cycle assessments; the influences of nutrition systems on climate, world nutrition, and food prices; and a comparison of different diets and agricultural, environmental, and consumer policies. Basically, there are four dimensions of nutrition ecology: health, the environment, society, and the economy.

To maintain or retain good health, the consumption of an individually optimal diet is recommended. The term preventative diet has been used recently to underline the possibility of avoiding nutrition-based diseases. The aggregate of most studies suggests that the consumption of plant-derived foods (grains, vegetables, fruits, legumes, nuts) should be increased and that the intake of animal-derived foods (meat products, dairy products, and eggs) should be reduced. This principle applies particularly to sedentary individuals. Plant foods should be consumed when they are as fresh as possible, should be minimally processed, and should be eaten partly as raw food.

The nutrition system influences the environment, which in turn determines the quality of food. The environmental impact of food production is determined by the agricultural method used. Conventional farming methods rely on extensive use of natural resources and result in higher levels of food contamination. In contrast, the environmental impact of organic farming is lower. Organic farming practices include controlling pests naturally, rotating crops, and applying legume plants as manure, in contrast to the use of synthetic pesticides and fertilizers in conventional farming. In integrated farming, organic and conventional methods are combined, resulting in an intermediate environmental impact. To reduce the environmental impact of the nutrition system, organic farming needs to be supported globally. In addition, foods should be minimally processed, packaged, and transported.

The nutrition system is closely related to society, including the responsibility for food purchasing and meal preparation, as well as the social implications of the family meal. Furthermore, the interactions between food consumption habits and lifestyle, as well as the social conditions and the wages of people working in the nutrition system, need to be considered. Additional social aspects include the import and export of agricultural and other products and the influence of this trade on people in developing countries.

On a worldwide basis, the major factor driving food consumption patterns is the financial situation of countries, different population groups, and influential individuals. Transportation and processing of food are carried out under the premise that money can be earned. In private households, the food budget is a determining factor in the choice of foods. From a holistic point of view, the food price should include all costs caused by the nutrition system, especially environmental damage (internalization of external costs).

These 4 dimensions of nutrition ecology are of equal importance for achieving a sustainable nutrition system. On this basis, the various aspects of food and nutrition are taken into account. What eating pattern best serves the holistic and sustainable aspects of nutrition ecology? From all we know, a vegetarian diet comes closest to fulfilling the demands and to minimizing damage to the 4 dimensions.

Contribution of Vegetarian Diets

Vegetarians have many reasons not to eat the flesh of animals. In addition to religious beliefs, there are health-based, ecologic, ethical, and philosophical reasons. When the ecologic damage caused by industrial animal production is examined, certain aspects need to be considered. On average, land requirements for meat-protein production are 10 times greater than for plant-protein production. About 40% of the world's grain harvest is fed to animals. Half of this grain would be more than enough to feed all hungry people of our planet. Animal manure, which is produced in huge amounts by industrial agriculture, causes high levels of potentially carcinogenic nitrates in drinking water and vegetables. Animal production requires considerable energy and water resources and leads to deforestation, overgrazing, and overfishing.

One solution to the problems caused by industrial animal production is a vegetarian lifestyle. The positive ecologic effects achieved by vegetarianism can be enhanced by avoiding processed and packaged foods and by choosing seasonally available and locally produced organic foods. In this way, support is given to subsistence and family farming, the securing of employment, and global food security. In addition to these socioeconomic benefits, the caging of animals as well as their transportation over long distances and finally slaughtering them can be avoided, thus fulfilling ethical concerns.

Sustainability

The four dimensions of nutrition ecology are the basis for sustainable nutrition behavior. The term sustainability was introduced in the 17th century by forestry experts in Germany to call attention to the fact that only the amount of trees that would grow back in a given time should be harvested. Presently, sustainability describes development that fulfills current global needs without diminishing the possibility of future generations to meet their own needs.

From a nutritional point of view, sustainability also deals with the fair distribution of food through ecologic and preventive eating behavior. To achieve sustainability, a comprehensive rethinking of common values is needed to attain a new understanding of the quality of life. The question as to the adequate amount of food needs to be addressed at all social levels with the goal of achieving nutrition security for all. To fulfill the demands concerning ecologic, economic, social, and health compatibility, the following 7 principles have been formulated: (1) food should be predominantly plant derived, (2) food should originate from organic farming, (3) food should be produced regionally and seasonally, (4) food should be minimally processed, (5) food should be ecologically packaged, (6) food trade should be fair, and (7) food should be tastefully prepared. These principles have been derived from guidelines of wholesome nutrition described elsewhere. A diet based on these principles has a scientific basis, is socially acceptable, is economically feasible, is culturally desired, is practicable, and has a high degree of sustainability.

There are only a limited number of long-term trials on sustainability. In one project, 3 apple production systems-organic farming, integrated farming, and conventional farming-were compared. The yields were nearly equal, but the organic production system showed not only the best apple quality but also the best soil quality and the least detrimental environmental impact. Therefore, the organic production system had the best environmental sustainability. The economic sustainability is given, since the market price was highest for the organic apples. The authors of this report question the sustainability of conventional farming systems because of escalating production costs, heavy reliance on nonrenewable resources, reduced biodiversity, water contamination, soil erosion, and health risks to farmworkers caused by pesticide use. Another study carried out over 21 y showed that although the crop yield was 20% lower in the organic systems, the input of fertilizer and energy was reduced by 34-53% and the pesticide input by 97%. Enhanced soil fertility and higher biodiversity found in organic plots were due to compost-and legume-based crop rotations.

Biodiversity is also the basis of food variety. Apart from the promotion of breast-feeding, the recommendation to eat a variety of foods is the most internationally agreed-upon dietary guideline. Biodiversity also protects against climate and pestilence disasters. In addition, biodiversity serves increasingly as the basis for new pharmaceuticals.

CONCLUSIONS

Nutrition ecology has the goal of attaining sustainability of food and nutrition security worldwide. To achieve this goal, professionals involved in the nutrition system must inform the public about the principles of nutrition ecology. In this manner, people can be motivated to practice sustainable eating behaviour.

Nutrition ecology is also a question of personal priorities. Interested and well-informed consumers will be able to weigh the arguments and make the necessary decisions. The vision of a sustainable future depends upon individuals who feel responsible for the environment and health. One of the most effective ways to achieve the goals of nutrition ecology, including healthy and sustainable food choices, is a vegetarian lifestyle.

SOIL RESEARCH PROGRAMS

Soil science is highly diverse. It covers all aspects of the structure and function of the surface few meters of terrestrial ecosystems. Soil science also interfaces with many other scientific disciplines. At Oregon State University, we have chosen to concentrate on five disciplinary areas within soil science: The following paragraphs give a brief description of each of these areas, provide some examples of current research, and identify faculty who do research in these areas.

Soil Biology

Research in soil biology is centered on the organisms that inhabit the soil, the processes they mediate, and how these organisms and processes are influenced by the soil environment. Soil biology is an important part of current issues such as sustainability of terrestrial ecosystems, soil quality, biodiversity, biodegradation, waste management, and climate change; as well as more traditional issues of nutrient cycling and plant-microbe interactions.

Peter Bottomley studies soil microbial ecology, the Rhizobium-legume symbiosis, and xenobiotic degradation. Richard Dick works on soil enzymes, microbial diversity, soil quality and C sequestration. David Myrold studies nitrogen cycling, the use of stable isotopes in soil science, and the Frankia-actinorhizal plant symbioses. Jennifer Parke studies rhizosphere ecology, biological control of plant diseases, and the soil ecology of plant pathogens and human pathogens.

In October, 1999 we established a Microbial Observatory at the H.J. Andrews Experimental Forest with the support of a grant from the National Science Foundation.

Soil Chemistry

Research in soil chemistry focuses on the chemical composition of soils and the chemical reactions that take place at soil surfaces and within the soil solution. Soil chemistry is important for understanding the formation of soils, the fate and reactivity of organic and inorganic pollutants, and availability of plant nutrients, all of which are relevant to current issues of water quality and climate change. John Baham studies the redox reactions of hydric soils, the chemistry of soil formation, and phosphorus availability. Van Volk is interested in using plants as phytoaccumulators of metals, such as nickel, and their application in biomining.

Soil Fertility

Research in soil fertility concentrates on the ability of soils to provide adequate amounts of essential nutrients to plants and environmentally sound management of fertilizers. Research ranges from very basic to applied in nature, and has application to both agronomic production and environmental quality. Neil Christensen studies interactions between soil fertility and plant pathology, plant nutrition, and nitrogen nutrition of crops. John Hart is an extension specialist who optimizes fertilizer recommendations and studies the fertilizer requirements of a diverse array of crops, such as cranberries, mint, and sweet corn. Dan Sullivan does research on environmentally sound utilization of wastes as soil amendments and sources of plant nutrients.

Soil Landscape Relationships

Research on soil landscape relationships includes the study of pedogenic processes, the description and mapping of soils, and the application of soils information. Understanding soil formation and applying soils information is vital to current issues such as land use, wetlands delineation, water quality, and regional-to global-scale models of biogeochemical processes. Jay Noller studies soil across landscapes and through time to constrain regional and global scale evolutionary pathways of ecosystems. Herb Huddleston is an extension specialist who studies hydric soils and use of soils information in GIS applications. Implications of Long-Term Land Use and Land Cover Change on Cyprus: A Holocene History of Soil Erosion and Conservation

Soil Physics

Research on soil physics emphasizes the physical properties of soil and the transport of energy, water, solutes, and gases. Soil physics is important to proper soil and agronomic management, related to issues of tillage, erosion, irrigation, and drainage; it also plays a central role in environmental problems, such as water quality and climate change. Larry Boersma does research on plant-water relations, water transport, and modeling soil physical processes. Rich Roseberg is located at Medford and studies water use. Benno Warkentin does research on groundwater quality. Don Wysocki is located at Pendleton and studies soil management in dryland wheat systems. Maria Dragila does research in water transport, preferential flow and pore scale processes.

2

Basic Nutrition

INTRODUCTION

Many people worry that when they stop eating meat and fish, they might be in danger of some nutritional deficiency. This is not the case as all the nutrients you need can easily be obtained from a vegetarian diet. In fact research shows that in many ways a vegetarian diet is healthier than that of a typical meat-eater.

Nutrients are usually divided into five classes: carbohydrates, proteins, fats (including oil), vitamins and minerals. We also need fibre and water. All are equally important to our well-being, although they are needed in varying quantities, from about 250g of carbohydrate a day to less than two micrograms of vitamin B12.

Carbohydrate, fat and protein are usually called macro-nutrients and the vitamins and minerals are usually called micro-nutrients.

Most foods contain a mixture of nutrients (there are a few exceptions, like pure salt or sugar) but it is convenient to classify them by the main nutrient they provide. Still, it is worth remembering that everything you eat gives you a whole range of essential nutrients.

Meat supplies protein, fat, some B vitamins and minerals (mostly iron, zinc, potassium and phosphorous). Fish, in addition to the above, supplies vitamins A, D, and E, and the mineral iodine. All these nutrients can be easily obtained by vegetarians from other sources, as this Information Sheet shows.

PROTEIN

Women need about 45g of protein a day (more if pregnant, lactating or very active), men need about 55g (more if very active). Evidence suggests that excess protein contributes to degenerative diseases. Vegetarians obtain protein from:

- Nuts: hazels, brazils, almonds, cashews, walnuts, pine kernels etc.
- Seeds: sesame, pumpkin, sunflower, linseeds.
- Pulses: peas, beans, lentils, peanuts.
- Grains/cereals: wheat (in bread, flour, pasta etc), barley, rye, oats, millet, maize (sweetcorn), rice.
- Soya products: tofu, tempeh, textured vegetable protein, veggieburgers, soya milk.
- Dairy products: milk, cheese, yoghurt (butter and cream are very poor sources of protein).
- Free range eggs.

You have may have heard that it is necessary to balance the complementary amino acids in a vegetarian diet. This is not as alarming as it sounds. Amino acids are the units from which proteins are made. There are 20 different ones in all. We can make many of them in our bodies by converting other amino acids, but eight cannot be made, they have to be provided in the diet and so they are called essential amino acids.

Single plant foods do not contain all the essential amino acids we need in the right proportions, but when we mix plant foods together, any deficiency in one is cancelled out by any excess in the other. We mix protein foods all the time, whether we are meat-eaters or vegetarians. It is a normal part of the human way of eating. A few examples are beans on toast, muesli, or rice and peas. Adding dairy products or eggs also adds the missing amino acids, eg macaroni cheese, quiche, porridge.

It is now known that the body has a pool of amino acids so that if one meal is deficient, it can be made up from the body's own stores. Because of this, we don't have to worry about complementing amino acids all the time, as long as our diet is generally varied and well-balanced. Even those foods not considered high in protein are adding some amino acids to this pool.

CARBOHYDRATE

Carbohydrate is our main and most important source of energy, and most of it is provided by plant foods. There are three main types: simple sugars, complex carbohydrates or starches and dietary fibre.

The sugars or simple carbohydrates can be found in fruit, milk and ordinary table sugar. Refined sources of sugar are best avoided as they provide energy without any associated fibre, vitamins or minerals and they are also the main cause of dental decay.

Complex carbohydrates are found in cereals/grains (bread, rice, pasta, oats, barley, millet, buckwheat, rye) and some root vegetables, such as potatoes and parsnips. A healthy diet should contain plenty of these starchy foods as a high intake of complex carbohydrate is now known to benefit health.

The unrefined carbohydrates, like wholemeal bread and brown rice are best of all because they contain essential dietary fibre and B vitamins.

The World Health Organisation recommends that 50-70% of energy should come from complex carbohydrates. The exact amount of carbohydrate that you need depends upon your appetite and also your level of activity. Contrary to previous belief a slimming diet should not be low in carbohydrates. In fact starchy foods are very filling relative to the number of calories that they contain.

DIETARY FIBRE

Dietary fibre or non-starch polysaccharide (NSP), as it is now termed, refers to the indigestible part of a carbohydrate food. Fibre can be found in unrefined or wholegrain cereals, fruit (fresh and dried) and vegetables. A good intake of dietary fibre can prevent many digestive problems and protect against diseases like colon cancer and diverticular disease.

FATS AND OILS

Too much fat is bad for us, but a little is necessary to keep our tissues in good repair, for the manufacture of hormones and to act as a carrier for some vitamins. Like proteins, fats are made of smaller units, called fatty acids. Two of these fatty acids, linoleic and linolenic acids, are termed essential as they must be provided in the diet. This is no problem as they are widely found in plant foods.

Fats can be either saturated or unsaturated (mono-unsaturated or poly-unsaturated). A high intake of saturated fat can lead to a raised blood cholesterol level and this has been linked to heart disease. Vegetable fats tend to be more unsaturated and this is one of the benefits of a vegetarian diet. Mono-unsaturated fats, such as olive oil or peanut oil, are best used for frying as the poly-unsaturated fats, like sunflower or safflower oil are unstable at high temperatures. Animal fats (including butter and cheese) tend to be more saturated than vegetable fats, with the exception of palm oil and coconut oil.

VITAMINS

Vitamin is the name for several unrelated nutrients that the body cannot synthesise either at all, or in sufficient quantities. The one thing they have in common is that only small quantities are needed in the diet. The main vegetarian sources are listed below:

Vitamin A (or beta carotene): Red, orange or yellow vegetables like carrots and tomatoes, leafy green vegetables and fruits like apricots and peaches. It is added to most margarines.

B Vitamins: This group of vitamins includes B1 (thiamin), B2 (riboflavin), B3 (niacin), B6 (pyridoxine), B12 (cyanocobalmin), folate, pantothenic acid and biotin.

All the B vitamins except B12 occur in yeasts and whole cereals (especially wheat germ), nuts & seeds, pulses and green vegetables.

Vitamin B12 is the only one that may cause some difficulty as it is not present in plant foods. Only very tiny amounts of

B12 are needed and vegetarians usually get this from dairy produce and free range eggs. It is sensible for vegans and vegetarians who consume few animal foods to incorporate some B12 fortified foods in their diet. Vitamin B12 is added to yeast extracts, soya milks, veggieburgers and some breakfast cereals.

Vitamin C: Fresh fruit, salad vegetables, all leafy green vegetables and potatoes.

Vitamin D: This is vitamin is not found in plant foods but humans can make their own when skin is exposed to sunlight. It is also added to most margarines and is present in milk, cheese and butter. These sources are usually adequate for healthy adults. The very young, the very old and anyone confined indoors would be wise to take a vitamin D supplement especially if they consume very few dairy products.

Vitamin E: Vegetable oil, wholegrain cereals, eggs.

Vitamin K: Fresh vegetables, cereals and bacterial synthesis in the intestine.

MINERALS

Minerals perform a variety of jobs in the body. Details of the some of the most important minerals are listed below:

Calcium: Important for healthy bones and teeth. Found in dairy produce, leafy green vegetables, bread, tap water in hard water areas, nuts and seeds (especially sesame seeds), dried fruits, cheese. Vitamin D helps calcium to be absorbed.

Iron: Needed for red blood cells. Found in leafy green vegetables, wholemeal bread, molasses, eggs, dried fruits (especially apricots and figs), lentils and pulses. Vegetable sources of iron are not as easily absorbed as animal sources, but a good intake of vitamin C will enhance absorption.

Zinc: Plays a major role in many enzyme reactions and the immune system. Found in green vegetables, cheese, sesame and pumpkin seeds, lentils and wholegrain cereals.

Iodine: Present in vegetables, but the quantity depends on how rich the soil is in iodine. Dairy products also have plenty of iodine. Sea vegetables are a good source of iodine for vegans.

CALCIUM

Calcium is the most abundant mineral in the human body. Of the body's total calcium, about 99% is in the bones and teeth where it plays a structural role. The remaining 1% is present in body tissues and fluids where it is essential for cell metabolism, muscle contraction and nerve impulse transmission.

Functions

The main function of calcium is structural. The skeleton of a young adult male contains about 1.2 kg of calcium. There is continuous movement of calcium between the skeleton and blood and other parts of the body. This is finely controlled by hormones. Metabolites of Vitamin D are important in this, increasing reabsorption of calcium by bones.

Calcium also plays a role in cell biology. Calcium can bind to a wide range of proteins altering their biological activity. This is important in nerve impulse transmission and muscle contraction. Calcium is also needed for blood clotting, activating clotting factors.

Vitamin D is needed for absorption of dietary calcium and so calcium deficiency may be linked with rickets in children. In adults, calcium deficiency may lead to osteomalacia (softening of bones). This may be related to repeated pregnancy with lengthy breast feeding.

Osteoporosis can be due to calcium deficiency. This involves loss of calcium from the bones and reduced bone density. This causes bones to be brittle and liable to fracture. Bone loss occurs with age in all individuals. This usually occurs after 35-40 years and involves the shrinking of the skeleton. Bone loss is greatest in women following the menopause. This is due to reduced levels of the hormone, oestrogen. Postmenopausal women are particularly at risk from osteoporosis.

Some research has indicated vegetarian women are at less risk of osteoporosis than omnivorous women. This is thought to be due to animal protein increasing calcium loss from bones. However, other research has found no difference between vegetarians and omnivores.

The risk of osteoporosis may be altered by factors other than diet. Lack of exercise, being underweight, smoking and alcohol can all increase the risk.

A low level of calcium in the blood and tissues can cause hypocalcaemia. This involves sensations of tingling and numbness and muscle twitches. In severe cases muscle spasms may occur. This is called tetany. It is more likely to be due to a hormonal imbalance in the regulation of calcium rather than a dietary deficiency.

Excess calcium in the blood can cause nausea, vomiting and calcium deposition in the heart and kidneys. This usually results from excessive doses of vitamin D and can be fatal in infants.

DIETARY SOURCES

Calcium is present in a wide range of foods. Dairy products, leafy green vegetables, nuts and seeds (almonds, brazils, sesame seeds), tofu, and dried fruit are all good sources of calcium for vegetarians. Most flour is fortified with calcium carbonate so cereals can also be a good source. Hard water may also provide calcium. Meat is a very poor source of calcium.

Calcium balance can be affected by a range of other factors. Vitamin D is essential for absorption of calcium from the gut. This is because calcium is transported into the body by a special carrier protein which requires vitamin D for its synthesis.

A number of substances can inhibit the absorption of calcium. Phytic acid, found in bran, whole cereals and raw vegetables is one of these. Uronic acid, a component of dietary fibre, and oxalic acid, found in certain fruits and vegetables can also bind calcium. However, diets habitually high in these acids are not thought to have a major effect on calcium absorption. Saturated fats can also lessen calcium absorption.

Calcium is lost in the faeces, urine and sweat. Calcium loss is roughly equal to dietary calcium in adults. Calcium loss is reduced if dietary calcium is low. Adaptation to both high and low calcium intakes occur. Reduced intake leads to increased efficiency of absorption. In infants and children calcium is retained for new bone growth. Calcium is also lost during lactation in breast milk.

Sources of Calcium (single servings)					
Good Sources		Fair Sources		Poor sources	
Tofu (60g or 2oz)	304 mg	Brown bread (2 slices)	70 mg	Spaghetti, boiled (100g or 3½oz)	7 mg
Cheddar cheese (slice, 40g)	288 mg	Brazil nuts (9 nuts, 30g)	54 mg	Brown rice (190g or 8oz)	7 mg
Cows milk (0.3 pint)	234 mg	Dried apricots (8 apricots)	46 mg	-	-
Spinach, boiled (130g or 5oz)	208 mg	French beans, boiled (100g)	41 mg	-	-
Dried figs (4 figs)	168 mg	Cottage cheese (45g or 1½oz)	33 mg	-	-
Soya cheese (slice, 40g)	180 mg	Sesame seeds (15g or ½oz)	20 mg	-	-
Chick peas, boiled (200g or 8oz)	92 mg	-	-	-	-
Baked beans (200g or 8 oz)	90 mg	-	-	-	-
Broccoli, boiled (95g or 3½oz)	72 mg	-	-	-	-

Required Intakes

The old Recommended Daily Amounts (RDAs) have now been replaced by the term Reference Nutrient Intake (RNI). The RNI is the amount of nutrient which is enough for at least 97% of the population.

Nutrient intakes for calcium, mg/day.

Age	RNI	Age	RNI
0 to 12 months	525 mg	11 to 18 years, male	1000 mg
1 to 3 years	350 mg	11 to 18 years, female	800 mg
4 to 6 years	450 mg	19 + years	700 mg
7 to 10 years	550 mg	Breast feeding women	1250 mg

During pregnancy, calcium absorption from the gut increases and no additional calcium is generally needed. Pregnant adolescents are an exception to this, having particularly high calcium needs.

Breast feeding women need an extra 550 mg of calcium. A lactating women can lose up to 300 mg a calcium/day in breast milk.

Calcium absorption decreases with age so it is important the elderly have adequate dietary calcium.

Meal Plan

Sample one day's meal plan to meet the RNI of 700 mg for an adult					
Breakfast		Lunch		Evening meal	
Muesli	114 mg	2 slices of brown bread toast	140 mg	Tofu (60g) with broccoli (95g)	376 mg
Soya milk, unfortified	15 mg	Baked beans (200g or 8oz)	90 mg	Brown rice, boiled (165g)	7 mg
Total calcium intake - 742 mg					

FATS AND CHOLESTEROL

Fats provide a concentrated source of energy in the diet. The building blocks of fats are called fatty acids. These can be either saturated, monounsaturated or poly-unsaturated. Foods rich in saturated fats are usually of animal origin. Vegetable fats are generally unsaturated.

Saturated fat raises the level of cholesterol in the blood. Cholesterol is present in animal foods but not plant foods. It is essential for metabolism but is not needed in the diet as our bodies can produce all that is needed. Raised blood cholesterol is associated with an increased risk of heart disease.

Fats and oils are essentially the same. Fats tend to be solid at room temperature whilst oils are liquid. The term lipids include both fats and oils.

Structure and Functions

Fats consist of fatty acids and glycerol. Nearly all the fats in our bodies and in foods are triglycerides, being made up of three fatty acid molecules to one glycerol molecule. There are about 16 different fatty acids commonly present in foods. The nature of fat depends on its constituent fatty acids.

Fats can be classed as either saturated, monounsaturated or polyunsaturated. This depends on the type of chemical bonds present in the fatty acid. If a fatty acid has all the hydrogen atoms it can hold it is termed saturated. However, if some of the hydrogen atoms are absent and the usual single bond between carbon atoms has been replaced by a double bond, then it is unsaturated. If there is just one double bond then it is monounsaturated. If there is more than one then it is polyunsaturated. Most fats contain a proportion of each of these three basic types of fatty acid but are generally described according to which type predominates.

Saturated fats tend to be animal fats and are solid at room temperature. Butter, lard, suet and meat fat are saturated fats. Unsaturated fats are liquid at room temperature. They are usually of plant origin, though fish oils may also be high in polyunsaturated fatty acids. Plant oils may be hardened by the addition of hydrogen atoms, converting double bonds to single bonds. This process is known as hydrogenation. Hydrogenated vegetable oils are often present in margarine and other processed foods.

Fats have a number of important functions in the body. As well as being a concentrated source of energy, fats act as carriers for fat-soluble vitamins A, D, E and K. Fats are also essential for the structure of cell membranes and are precursors of many hormones.

Essential Fatty Acids

Two fatty acids are termed essential fatty acids. These are linoleic acid and a-linolenic acid. These must be present in the diet as the body is unable to make them itself. They are widely present in plant oils such as sunflower, rapeseed and soyabean oils.

Linoleic acid is converted into the body to arachidonic acid from which prostoglandins and other vital compounds are made. Because of this conversion, arachidonic acid is not an essential fatty acid as was once believed. a-Linolenic acid is converted to eicosapentanoic acid (EPA) which is important in proper nerve function. EPA is present in fish oils and is claimed to be beneficial in reducing the symptoms of arthritis and the risk of heart disease. For this reason, fish oils are sometimes used therapeutically. Plant oils containing large amounts of a-linolenic acid can be used as an alternative by vegetarians. Linseeds and linseed oil are particularly rich sources of a-linolenic acid.

Cholesterol

Cholesterol belongs to the sterol group of fats. It is present in all animal tissues but is absent from plants. Cholesterol is essential as a component of cell membranes and a precursor of bile acids and certain hormones. The body can make its own cholesterol and so a dietary source is not required.

Cholesterol is transported in to various proteins. These complex molecules are called lipoproteins. There are four main types of lipoprotein involved in cholesterol transport. The most commonly refer red to are low density lipoprotein (LDL) and high density lipoprotein (HDL).

Cholesterol may form plaques on artery walls if levels in the blood are too high. This can lead to atherosclerosis. Because of this high blood cholesterol is linked with heart disease. It is the LDL cholesterol which has been linked to heart disease. HDL cholesterol may help protect against the risk of heart disease.

The amount of dietary cholesterol is not clearly linked to levels of cholesterol in the blood. Blood cholesterol is more closely related to the amount of saturated fat in the diet, saturated fat raising blood cholesterol. Unsaturated fats are not thought to raise blood cholesterol and may indeed lower levels.

Trans Fatty Acids

Unsaturated fatty acids can exist in two different geometric forms. These are called the cis and trans forms. Unsaturated fatty acids exist naturally in the cis form. During food manufacturing processes these cis fatty acids may be changed to trans fatty acids. Hydrogenation of margarine causes this to occur. It has been suggested that trans fatty acids can increase the risk of heart disease.

Free Radicals

Free radicals are highly reactive molecules which have been linked to both heart disease and cancer. A number of factors, including alcohol, stress and environmental pollutants can increase the generation of free radicals in the body. Polyunsaturated fats can also generate free radicals, especially when exposed to heat or sunlight. Because of this it is suggested that vegetable oils should be stored out of direct sunlight.

Mono-unsaturated olive oil is less vulnerable to free radical generation and so is a better choice for frying.

Anti-oxidants such as vitamins A, C and E offer protection against free radicals. Fresh fruit and vegetables are rich in these anti-oxidants.

Dietary Sources

Saturated fats are nearly always from animal foods. Meat, eggs and dairy products all contain saturated fats. Lard and suet are saturated fats. Coconut oil and palm oil are vegetable sources of saturated fats. Olive oil is a monounsaturated fat. Polyunsaturated fats are usually from plant sources.

The ratio of polyunsaturated to saturated fats in the diet is often called the P:S ratio.

Cholesterol is present in all animal foods but not plant foods. Egg yolks and high-fat dairy products are high in cholesterol.

Required Intakes

Currently it is believed that around 42% of energy in the typical British diet is from fat. Dietary advice is to reduce this. The COMA (Committee on Medical Aspects of Food Policy) report advocated that no more than 35% of daily energy requirement should come from fat whilst the NACNE (National Advisory Committee on Nutritional Education) paper recommends a reduction to no more than 30%. Special emphasis is placed on reducing the amount of saturated fat in the diet.

Vegetarian diets tend to be lower in fat than omnivore diets. However, vegetarians consuming dairy products and processed foods high in fat may still be consuming too much. Advice to vegetarians is to keep fat intake to a minimum, avoid high fat dairy products and processed foods containing dairy fats and hydrogenated vegetable fats, and to use olive oil for cooking purposes.

CEREALS

All too often, cereal products are thought of as nothing more than starchy fillers, and indeed, when you consider how some commercial products like cakes and biscuits and breakfast cereals are made from over-refined grains with nearly all the nutrients except the starch extracted, and then loaded with fat, sugar, artificial flavourings etc., you might be forgiven for thinking that's true. But go back to the original, unrefined grains and you have a wealth of nutrients in a small package. Grains have been the staple foods of many civilisations for thousands of years. Wheat, barley, oats and rye in Europe, maize in America, quinoa in South America, rice in the East, and millet in Africa.

Nutrition: Cereals are seeds of plants, usually members of the grass family but there are a few exceptions. They are annuals, that is they have to be planted every year and at the end of the summer, when they have produced ripe seeds, they die down. Like all seeds, cereals are very nutritious because they contain all the nutrients the embryo plant needs to start growing. Unrefined cereals are valuable sources of proteins, carbohydrates, B vitamins and also contain some fat, iron, vitamin E and trace minerals and are a very good source of fibre in the diet. Some cereals (wheat, barley, rye and oats) contain the protein gluten, which is essential for leavened bread-making. Without sufficient gluten, bread will not rise. People suffering from gluten intolerance or coeliac disease must avoid any cereal containing gluten. In some parts of the world unleavened (unrisen) bread is eaten r the staple cereal is made into noodles or pasta. They are usually cheap to buy and are a valuable source of variety in the vegetarian diet.

Storage: Keep in airtight containers in a cool, dark, dry place. Whole grains can be stored for up to 2 years; flaked, cracked grains and flours should be used within 2-3 months of purchase.

Sprouting: Whole grains can be sprouted, which greatly enhances their nutritional value, e.g. wheat grains, raw buckwheat and barley.

Cooking: Cereals can be used in other ways, besides being ground into flour for bread, cakes etc. Whole grains can be added to stews and casseroles, or cooked until soft. Cracked or kibbled grains are cut or broken pieces of whole grains e.g. kibbled wheat and bulgur wheat. Meal, a coarse kind of flour, can be used to make porridge, thicken soups or mixed with wheat flour to add interesting flavours and textures to ordinary breads, biscuits, muffins etc. Whole grains should be washed thoroughly. Boil the required amount of water, add the washed grain, stir once, put a tight-fitting lid on the pan and simmer for the required cooking time or until the liquid is absorbed. Turn off the heat and leave to stand for 5 minutes before removing the lid.

Barley

Barley grows in a wider variety of climatic conditions than any other cereal. It used to be a very important source of direct human food, but its use has diminished over the last 250 years, replaced by wheat, and it is now used almost exclusively as animal feed or for making beer and whisky. It contains gluten, so barley flour can be made into bread. More usually found in the shops as whole or pot barley, or polished pearl barley, it is also possible to buy barley flakes or kernels. The whole barley is more nutritious with 100g providing 10.5g protein, 2.1g fat, 69.3g carbohydrate, 4g fibre, 50mg folic acid, 6mg iron and 50mg calcium. It can be cooked on its own (1:3 parts water for 45-60 minutes) as a pleasant alternative to rice, pasta or potatoes, or added to stews. Malt extract is made from sprouted barley grains.

Buckwheat (Gluten Free)

Buckwheat is not a true cereal as it is not a member of the grass family, instead being related to sorrels and docks. If you look at docks closely, you can see that the seeds, though smaller, have the same distinctive triangular shape. Buckwheat, a native of central Asia, is now grown in Europe, N America and the former USSR countries, but it is still not widely used in Britain. 100g of buckwheat provides 11.7g protein, 3.9mg iron and it is very high in calcium with 114mg per 100g. Available raw the seeds are greenish-pink, or roasted (known as kasha) the seeds are darker reddish-brown. It can be cooked (1:2 parts water for 6 minutes, leave to stand for 6 minutes) and served like rice or you can add it to stews and casseroles. Buckwheat flour can be added to cakes, muffins, pancakes etc. where it imparts a distinctive flavour. Look out too for buckwheat spaghetti, soba.

Corn or Maize (Gluten Free)

Maize is the principal food plant of America and was unknown in other parts of the world until Columbus reached America in 1492. It was grown by the Maya, Inca and Aztec civilisations, and by various North American Indian tribes and now has spread to Canada, USSR, Italy, Spain, Egypt, India and South Africa. It is used for human food, animal feed and as a source of raw materials for industry. 100g maize gives 9g protein. Fresh maize is often available (sweet corn, corn on the cob) but remember that nutritional values will be lower because less concentrated. We most often see maize as cornflakes or popcorn, but cornmeal or polenta is available and can be added to soup, pancakes, muffins etc. Tortillas are made from maize meal, as are quite a lot of snack foods. Do not confuse cornmeal with highly refined corn starch/flour, used for thickening.

Millet (Gluten Free)

Millet is the name applied to a variety of grasses first cultivated in Asia or Africa. It is a staple crop in Africa because it is drought resistant and keeps well. 100g millet provides 9.9g protein, and 6.8mg iron (higher than other cereals). Millet makes a delicious alternative to rice but the tiny seeds need to be cracked before they will absorb water easily, so they should be first sauteed with a little vegetable oil for 2-3 minutes until some are seen to crack, then add water with care (1:3 parts), bring to the boil and simmer for 15-20 minutes until fluffy. Millet flakes can be made into porridge or added to muesli and millet flour is available, sometimes also made into pasta.

Oats

Oats are thought to have originated in Western Europe and may originally have appeared as a weed in barley and so got spread with the barley. They're now grown in many parts of the world including N W Europe, the former USSR countries, North America, Canada, Australia and China. Used mostly as animal feed, they are very nutritious. In fact, as they are usually inexpensive to buy, they can be a real boon to people trying to get a good diet on a low budget. 100g oats gives 13g protein, 55mg calcium (more than any other cereal except buckwheat), and 4.6mg iron. Available as groats (whole grains with the husks removed) but more usually as various grades of oatmeal, rolled oats or jumbo oat flakes. Oat groats need cooking for 45 minutes in 1:3 parts water. All forms can be used to make porridge, combined with ground nuts to make a roast or added to stews. Oatmeal is low in gluten so can't be used to make a loaf, but can be mixed with wheat flour to add flavour and texture to bread, muffins, pancakes etc.

Quinoa (Gluten Free)

Quinoa is an ancient crop which fed the Central American Aztec Indians for thousands of years, and which has recently been cultivated in Britain. Unlike most grains, it does not belong to the grass family, but is a relative of the garden weed called Fat Hen. It is very nutritious, containing between 13-14% protein with a good amino acid composition but has no gluten so it cannot be used for bread-making. Instead, it is cooked for 15 minutes in 1:3 parts water and served as a side dish or may be used in risotto, pilaff, vegetable stuffings etc.

Rice (Gluten Free)

Rice is one of the world's most important crops. It originated in Asia but is now grown throughout the humid, sub-tropical regions. It differs from most other cereals in requiring land that is submerged in water to grow, though some varieties do grow in upland areas. Rice is a good source of carbohydrate but doesn't have quite as much protein as some other cereals (6.5g per 100g). Unpolished rice (i.e. wholegrain/brown rice) is a good source of B vitamins too.

There are three basic kinds in culinary terms: long, medium and short grain. Long used traditionally in savoury dishes, short in dessert cooking, although this varies across the globe and it is really a matter of personal preference. Long wholegrain rice needs to cook in 1:2 parts water for 35-40 minutes. Rice flour is available but because of the lack of gluten, it cannot be used to make a yeasted loaf but can be used for cakes, biscuits and pancakes. Rice flakes (brown and white) can be added to muesli or made into a milk pudding or porridge.

Wild Rice

Wild rice is not a rice at all but an American grass used as an important food by the Indians and early settlers. Difficulty in harvesting makes it expensive; but the colour, a purplish black and its subtly nutty flavour make it a good base for a special dish and it can be economically mixed with other rices, but may need pre-cooking as it takes 45-50 minutes to cook in 1:3 parts of water.

Rye

Rye is the least important cereal crop and is usually only grown where conditions are relatively unfavourable and other cereals don't do well. It probably originated in S W Asia, but the name occurs in Northern European languages, which suggest early cultivation in that area. It is very hardy and so grows in temperate and cool regions and at high altitudes, and is very tolerant of poor soil fertility. It is the only cereal apart from wheat and barley that has enough gluten to make a yeasted loaf, but it has less gluten than wheat, so rye bread is denser. It is more usual to mix rye flour with wheat flour. Rye grains should be cooked in 1:3 parts water for 45-60 minutes. Kibbled rye is often added to granary-type loaves. You can also add rye to stews and rye flakes are available, which can be used in muesli. 100g of rye gives 9.4g protein.

Spelt

Spelt is closely related to common wheat, originating in the Middle East, and has been popular for decades in Eastern Europe. Higher in protein than wheat, it appears to have a different molecular structure, appearing to cause less problems than wheat for some sufferers of grain allergies. It has an intense nutty, wheaty flavour. The flour is excellent for breadmaking and spelt pasta is becoming more widely available.

Wheat

This is the most familiar cereal used in Britain today, it is used for bread, cakes, biscuits, pastry, breakfast cereals and pasta. All the present varieties of wheat seem to be derived from a hybrid wild wheat that grew in the Middle East 10,000 years ago. Over 30,000 varieties are said to be in cultivation. Wheat can be grown in a very wide range of climatic conditions but is most successful in temperate zones including the UK, North America, Southern Russia and South West Australia.

Nutritionally, 100g whole wheat provide 14g protein, 2.2g fat, 69.1g carbohydrate, 2.3g fibre, 3.1mg iron, 36mg calcium. Wheat grains, also called wheat berries, can be eaten whole, cooked in 1:3 parts of water for 40-60 minutes, they have a satisfying, chewy texture. Cracked or kibbled wheat is the dried whole grains cut by steel blades. Bulgur wheat, made from the whole grains steamed before cracking, only needs rehydrating by soaking in boiling water or stock. Couscous is the steamed, dried and cracked grains of durum wheat and is more refined than bulgur. Soak in 2 parts of water/stock to rehydrate, traditionally it is steamed after soaking. Strong wheat flour (high gluten content) is required for yeasted breadmaking and puff pastry. Plain flour is used for general cooking including cakes and shortcrust pastry. Wheat flakes are used for porridge, muesli and flapjacks. Wheat germ is an excellent source of nutrients, especially vitamin E.

3

Food Allergy and Intolerance

DEFINITIONS AND CAUSES

Food allergy is often mistaken for food intolerance. It is important to note that allergy is only one of a number of possible reasons for food intolerance. Food intolerance can be defined as a condition where particular adverse effects occur after eating a particular food or food ingredient. Genuine food intolerance is different from psychologically based food aversion, where a person strongly dislikes a food and believes that a food produces a particular reaction.

A genuine food allergy is when a specific immune reaction occurs in the body in response to consuming a particular food. Allergies often run in families, and people who are allergic to some foods may also be allergic to other environmental factors, such as house dust, animal fur and pollen.

A true allergic response involves an altered or abnormal tissue reaction to an antigen. An antigen can be a protein, a substance bound to a protein, a food additive or less commonly, a polysaccharide. The antigen combines with an antibody and produces an immune response, which results in cell damage and the release of histamine. The immune system plays an essential role in our bodies in protecting us from the invasion of harmful substances. An allergy occurs when the mechanism operates inappropriately in response to a harmless substance such as a particular food protein.

Food intolerances, other than allergies, can occur for a variety of reasons including:

NON ALLERGIC HISTAMINE RELEASE

The signs are very similar to an allergy and include headache, swelling, urticaria, vomiting and diarrhoea. A substance called histamine is released (it is also released in true allergic reactions) in response to foods such as shellfish or strawberries.

METABOLIC DEFECTS

A lack or deficiency of enzymes responsible for the digestion of food can cause many types of food intolerance. For example, a deficiency in lactase, the enzyme responsible for digesting milk, causes intolerance to milk.

Coeliac disease is a gut intolerance to a protein found in wheat, called gluten, it would not be considered an allergy. The symptoms of coeliac disease are controlled by following a gluten-free diet. It is unknown exactly why or how gluten harms the gut, although it is now thought to be an abnormal immunological response rather than an enzyme deficiency. It is still not considered to be a food allergy in the true sense of the definition.

PHARMACOLOGICAL EFFECTS

Some food substances can act like drugs, particularly if taken in large quantities. The most familiar of these substances is caffeine, found in tea, coffee, chocolate and cola drinks. A large intake of caffeine can cause tremor, migraine and palpitations. Other pharmacologically active substances found in food include histamine, tyramine, tryptamine and serotonin, which may be consumed in foods such as red wine, cheese, yeast extract, avocados and bananas. In susceptible people, these foods can trigger urticaria, facial flushing and headaches.

FOOD INTOLERANCE OF UNKNOWN ORIGIN

Reactions can be provoked by many foods and food products which we cannot be clear about. They may or may not be allergic reactions. Food additives, particularly tartrazine and sodium benzoate, can provoke urticaria, rhinitis and asthma. Yeasts can provoke a number of reactions in some people, particularly skin disorders.

COMMON CAUSES OF FOOD INTOLERANCE

The most common food intolerances, in order of frequency are milk, eggs, nuts, fish/shellfish, wheat/flour, chocolate, artificial colours, pork/bacon, chicken, tomato, soft fruit, cheese and yeast.

Whilst not all food intolerances are related to meat and dairy products, it can be seen from the above list that vegetarians, and particularly vegans, will suffer less from food intolerance because they already eliminate some of the most common causes of intolerance.

SYMPTOMS

The most common symptoms of allergy include asthma, gastro-intestinal symptoms (nausea, vomiting, and diarhhoea), eczema, urticaria (hives), rhinorrhea (heavy discharge from the nose), and angio-oedema (swelling of the blood vessels). Other more long-term symptoms include can depression, anxiety, fatigue, migraine, sleeplessness and hyperactivity in children.

TREATMENT

As it is sometimes quite difficult to distinguish between a genuine food allergy and a food intolerance, treatment is often similar. The first step is to diagnose the food intolerance. This should not be done without medical supervision as some reactions to food intolerance can be dangerous.

Sometimes the cause of a particular food intolerance is obvious, by the immediate effect that occurs on eating a particular food. In this case the treatment is simply to avoid that particular food. In most cases the suspected food is more difficult to track down. A diary kept of foods eaten and symptoms experienced can sometimes help detect the offending food or foods. Other factors such as the weather, menstrual cycles and difficult relationships can affect the symptoms. Sometimes simple exclusion diets are advised where record keeping suggests a particular food may be the cause. So, for example, milk, egg or wheat may be avoided to see if symptoms improve.

Other more restrictive diets may be advised, which only include a limited amount of foods which rarely cause a reaction.

These diets are usually called exclusion diets. The idea of an exclusion diet is to identify an allergy or intolerance, by limiting the food to a very small choice, checking for symptoms and then very gradually introducing test foods to see if there is a reaction. An exclusion diet should not be followed without sound nutritional advice. You can seek the help and advice of The Vegetarian Society if you have any problems with your vegetarian or vegan diet, relating to diagnosis or treatment of a food allergy or intolerance.

DEFINITIONS

A vegetarian is someone living on a diet of grains, pulses, nuts, seeds, vegetables and fruits with or without the use of dairy products and eggs. A vegetarian does not eat any meat, poultry, game, fish, shellfish or crustacea, or slaughter by-products.

TYPES OF VEGETARIAN

Lacto-ovo-vegetarian: Eats both dairy products and eggs. This is the most common type of vegetarian diet.

Lacto-vegetarian: Eats dairy products but not eggs.

Vegan: Does not eat dairy products, eggs, or any other animal product.

STUMBLING BLOCKS

Many foods contain ingredients derived from the slaughter of animals. Gelatine is made from animal ligaments, tendons, bones etc which have been boiled in water. It is often found in confectionery, low fat spreads and desserts, and other dairy products. The term animal fat refers to carcass fat and may be present in a wide range of foods, including biscuits, cakes, and margarines. Suet and lard are types of animal fats. Certain food additives (E numbers) may be derived from animal sources.

Cheese is often made with rennet extracted from the stomach lining of slaughtered calves. Vegetarian cheese is made with rennet from a microbial source. The Vegetarian Society has an information sheet listing ingredients which may be unsuitable for vegetarians.

Many vegetarians that eat eggs will eat only free-range eggs. This is due to moral objections to the battery farming of hens. The Vegetarian Society only endorses products containing eggs if the eggs are certified as free-range.

PRACTICES IN CATERING

Vegetarians dining out will expect work surfaces and chopping boards, utensils and all other kitchen equipment and facilities to be either kept separate from those used for non-vegetarian food preparation, or cleaned thoroughly before vegetarian food preparation.

Caterers should also ensure that fryers, grills and griddles used for preparing non-vegetarian products are thoroughly cleaned. Fryers must be filled with fresh, uncontaminated oil before vegetarian food is cooked.

The Society recommend that caterers keep a separate set of utensils for the preparation and serving of vegetarian meals.

GLUTEN-FREE DIET

A gluten-free diet is essential for people who have coeliac disease or dermatitis herpetiformis (a gluten induced skin sensitivity). Some people may choose to follow a gluten-free diet for other reasons, although these two diseases are the only ones where a gluten-free diet is considered medically imperative.

Gluten is a mixture of proteins found in some cereals, particularly wheat. It is the gliadin component of gluten which is responsible for coeliac disease. A gluten-free diet is not the same as a wheat-free diet, and some gluten-free foods are not wheat free. Despite a good deal of research, it is unknown how or exactly why gluten harms the gut. It is now considered likely that coeliac disease involves an abnormal immunologic response, rather than an enzyme deficiency as was suggested in the past.

The Vegetarian Society believes that a gluten-free diet is compatible with vegetarianism. Some doctors and The Coeliac Society advise against a vegetarian or vegan diet for coeliacs because they believe it may make your diet too complicated and this could mean it is difficult to comply with. There are no known medical or nutritional reasons why you should not be a vegetarian or vegan coeliac, although the gluten-free aspects of your diet must be the priority for your own health and well-being.

It is possible to follow a gluten-free vegan diet, although you must be extra careful to ensure that your diet is nutritionally adequate. It is essential that you seek the advice of a sympathetic dietitian if you want to follow a vegan gluten-free diet.

Vegetarians may initially find it difficult to establish what foods they can and cannot have. This Information Sheet is designed to help.

A gluten-free diet involves the complete avoidance of all foods made from or containing wheat, rye, barley and usually, oats. Some doctors say oats may be permitted, although The Coeliac Society advise against the inclusion of oats in a gluten-free diet.

The Coeliac Society publishes a list of gluten-free manufactured products in a booklet which is updated every year. You can check with The Vegetarian Society if you are unsure whether any particular foods on this list are suitable for vegetarians or vegans. Some manufacturers use the gluten-free symbol on their label.

A wide range of specially manufactured gluten-free foods such as, bread, bread mix, pasta, biscuits, cakes, crispbread and flour are prescribable under the NHS. Some groups of people are exempt from prescription charges, children, pregnant women and pensioners in particular. If you are not exempt, it works out economical to buy a "season ticket" type prescription. Some gluten-free products, such as chocolate biscuits, are considered luxuries and are not prescribable, although they can be bought from the chemist.

Nutritional Advice

Coeliac disease leads to severe damage of the gut surface, which can be completely reversed by following a gluten-free diet. Shortly after the diagnosis of coeliac disease, you need to be extra careful to ensure you have a nutritionally adequate diet, as you may have been suffering from malabsorption of nutrients.

Protein

Some gluten-free flours are low in protein, because they have had the gluten removed, which is itself a protein. Specially manufactured, prescribed gluten-free flours usually have milk protein added. Vegetarians can get protein from nuts & seeds, pulses, the non-gluten containing cereals, soya products, milk, cheese and free range eggs. Make sure some protein is included in each meal, and practice protein complementation with the vegetable proteins, for example, combine a nut or pulse dish with a suitable cereal.

Protein is especially important to a growing child, it is essential to seek the advice of your dietitian if you are bringing up a child on a gluten-free vegetarian or vegan diet.

Anaemia

Following diagnosis, many coeliacs sufferers are anaemic. This is usually due to iron deficiency, although it could also be due to folic acid or vitamin B12 deficiency. Your doctor may prescribe an iron supplement for you until your digestive system is back to normal and can absorb iron again.

To ensure a good intake of iron include pulses, lentils, nuts and green vegetables daily in your diet. Avoid drinking tea with meals and instead have fruit juice, which helps the absorption of iron because it contains vitamin C.

Going Vegetarian

If you are already a vegetarian or vegan and are advised to follow a gluten-free diet, you do not need to abandon your vegetarianism. If you are recently diagnosed and would like to become vegetarian or vegan, do give your digestive system time to recover before making major changes to your diet, after all, you have a lot to think about in getting used to a gluten-free diet. When you have stabilised, you can gradually change to a vegetarian diet.

Do contact The Vegetarian Society if you have any problems, when making the change to a vegetarian way of living. Also, do contact us if you have any difficulties with health professionals, who are sceptical about your following a vegetarian diet. Once coeliac disease has been diagnosed, it is recommended that you follow a gluten-free diet for life.

Vegetarian Gluten-Free and Gluten Containing Foods		
Food	**Gluten Free**	**Gluten Containing**
Cereals, flours, cakes & biscuits	Arrowroot, buckwheat, corn/maize, potato flour, rice, rice bran, rice flour, sago, tapioca, soya, soya bran, soya flour.	Wheat, wholemeal, wholewheat & wheatmeal flour, wheat bran, barley, rye, rye flour, pasta, noodles, semolina, All baked foods made from wheat, rye, semolina, barley & pearl barley.
Dairy products & eggs	Eggs, milk, cream, butter, cheese, curd cheese, coffee whiteners, soya products	Some yoghurts (eg muesli yoghurt), some cheese spreads
Puddings	Tapioca, sago, rice, custard.	Semolina, sponge pudding, pastry, pies, wafers.
Beverages	Tea, coffee, herb tea, fizzy drinks, fruit squash, cocoa, marmite, most alcoholic drinks.	Barley based drinks, barley fruit drinks, malted drinks, beer.
Fruit & vegetables	All fruits & vegetables, unless with certain sauces or cooked with gluten containing foods	
Nuts, seeds & pulses	All, except certain brands of baked beans and beans with a gluten containing sauce	
Preserves & confectionary	Jam, marmalade, sugar, honey, treacle, molasses, golden syrup, some brands of chocolate & sweets.	Confectionary containing flour, some brands of lemon curd
Soups & sauces	Gluten-free if thickened with a suitable flour. Many manufactured sauces, stock cubes, and soups contain gluten	
Miscellaneous	Salt, pepper, vinegar, herbs & spices, tamari, yeast, most food colourings and essences.	Some pepper compounds, shoyu, ready-mix spices, some seasoning powders, certain brands of mustard. Certain medicines may contain gluten.

INFANT DIET

Weaning Vegetarian Babies

Taking the first steps in bringing your child up as a vegetarian isn't difficult. Remember that the nutritional requirements of a small baby are high, needing proportionally more protein, calcium and most other nutrients than at any other time of life. It is now widely recognised by bodies such as the British Medical Association, that a vegetarian diet can provide all the nutrients needed for growing infants.

Bringing up your child as a vegetarian, you will want to get them used to the vegetarian food groups: cereals, beans, nuts and seeds, dairy and soya produce, fruit and vegetables. Your baby may reject stronger-tasting foods, such as broccoli, cauliflower and cabbage, at six months but may like them several months later.

It is quite safe to bring up your baby as a vegan, with no animal foods at all, as long as you make sure that plenty of nutrient-rich foods are included. Vegan babies need good sources of calcium, vitamin B12, vitamin D and protein.

Weaning is a gradual process that begins when you start to replace milk with solid foods. Infants should not be given solid foods before the age of four months except on the advise of a health professional.

A mixed diet should be offered by the age of six months, as soon thereafter babies will need a source of iron in their diet as breast or formula milk can no longer provide enough. Especially if there is a family history of allergies, when you begin weaning your baby, introduce one food at a time and leave a few days between each new food. This way, you will be able to tell if your baby is allergic or sensitive to any particular food.

Stages of Weaning

Before 6 Months

Before the age of four months babies can't properly digest any foods other than breast or formula milk, which remains by far the most important source of nutrition beyond the age of six months. Current recommendations are not to begin the weaning process before the age of six months, however babies can be introduced to solids before the age of six months, particularly if they seem hungry after their breast feed, on the advice of a Health Professional.

Do not give wheat, oats, milk, nuts, eggs or citrus fruit if you decide to start weaning before the age of six months.

6-7 Months

Start by introducing one teaspoon of pureed fruit or baby rice mixed with breast or formula milk after a milk feed or in the middle if this works best for your baby. Take care that the food is adequately cooled. The nutrition of the food is not so important initially as milk still supplies all the baby's needs.

Other foods to try initially are:

- Puréed vegetables, such as potatoes, carrot or courgette
- Puréed fruit, such as banana, cooked apple or pear
- Baby rice, corn meal, sago or millet can all be given as a thin porridge.

As the weeks go on milk remains the most important food in your baby's diet, but you can gradually increase the number of times solid food is given from once to twice a day. Try mashed lentils with some added vegetable oil and a wider variety of fruit and vegetables such as avocado and green vegetables.

7-8 Months

Most babies will by now be regularly eating solids although milk is a large part in their diets. In particular solid foods now provide an important source of iron. You can puree or sieve family foods to give variety, as long as they do not contain added salt.

Try introducing tofu and mashed lentils if your baby is not already eating them. Dairy foods (yoghurt and cheese) can be introduced after six months, as can eggs as long as they are hard-boiled, though some experts recommend avoiding all dairy products and eggs until 12 months old.

8-12 Months

Your baby will gradually be able to cope with lumpier foods. Foods from the family table can be given as long as they do not contain salt. Well cooked and mashed peas and beans can be introduced from around 8 months. They are difficult to digest and so can cause problems if introduced earlier. Avoid sweet biscuits and rusks. Try introducing pieces of peeled apple, raw carrot or crusts of bread. When your baby is able to chew pieces of fruit, sandwiches and toast can become normal everyday foods. By the age of 12 months your baby should be enjoying three meals a day. Many companies produce baby foods suitable for vegetarians but it's quick and easy to prepare your own food for your baby. If you buy shop bought food, always check the ingredients label and look out for The Vegetarian.Society's Seedling symbol to be absolutely sure that it is totally vegetarian.

Important Nutrients

Iron

This is an important nutrient during weaning, as milk is a very poor source of iron. Babies are born with their own store of iron but this will be depleted by six months. Although iron is less easily absorbed from non-animal sources, there are plenty of good vegetable sources.

Iron-rich foods suitable for babies after six months include: puréed apricots, molasses, refined lentils, cereals, well mashed beans and green vegetables. avoid cereals that are very high in fibre as these may inhibit iron absorption. Vitamin C aids absorption of iron from plant foods and so it helps to give sources of these nutrients together. Vitamin C is found in frozen, fresh or juiced fruit and vegetables.

Calcium

Breast or formula milk contains all the calcium your baby needs initially. Good sources of calcium for the later weaning stages include cow's and fortified soya milk, cheese, green vegetables, wholemeal bread, beans, lentils, ground almonds, sesame paste and tofu.

Protein

Because babies are growing rapidly they require more protein than adults compared to their body weight. Breast or formula milk will provide the major source of protein for the first eight months. A variety of foods should be given each day so the baby obtains the right balance of amino acids. For example if a baby has toast, lentils and yoghurt during a day that would give a good balance.

Energy

Babies between the age of 6 and 12 months require 700 to 1000 calories a day, so they need concentrated sources of energy. Babies and young children do not have the capacity to eat large quantities of food and so they need small and frequent meals. Their diet should not contain too many foods that are bulky or watery. Make sure your baby has some concentrated energy foods like lentils with vegetable oil, avocado, cheese or smooth nut butter. Sugar is not a good source of energy for babies.

Vitamin B12

Vitamin B12 is made by micro-organisms and is found mostly in animal foods. Very young babies will get all the vitamin B12 they need from formula or breast milk. Later, vegetarian babies should obtain enough of this vitamin from dairy products and eggs. Vegan babies will need vitamin B12 from fortified foods such as some soya milks, low salt yeast extract or veggie burgers.

Vitamin D

Vitamin D is found in dairy products, eggs and fortified foods like margarine and some breakfast cereals, and can be made by the action of sunlight on the skin. It is found exclusively in animal foods so vegan babies may need a vitamin D supplement. Breast or formula milk should provide all the vitamin D needed initially.

Fibre

A diet too high in fibre will fill up a child before their nutritional needs have been met and can interfere with absorption of minerals, such as zinc, iron and calcium, so refined bran must not be added to a young child's diet. If you think your baby is constipated give extra fluid such as water or diluted fruit juices.

Milk

Babies under two should not be given semi-skimmed and children under five should not be given skimmed milk because skimmed milk lacks the fat soluble vitamins A and D and young children need the energy from fat. Soya milks should be specially formulated for babies if they are used instead of breast milk and should be fortified if used as an alternative to cow's milk for young children. It is recommended that if avoiding animal milk products, soya formula be used up to the age of 2 years.

Salt and Sugar

These should be avoided in the diet of babies and young children. A baby's kidneys are not mature enough to cope with too much salt, and sugary foods and drinks are a prime cause of tooth decay. Sugar gives calories without any associated vitamins or minerals. In addition, a baby who is encouraged to develop a sweet tooth may have problems with obesity in later life.

Nuts

Whole or chopped nuts and seeds are not suitable for children under five because of the danger of choking, but they can be used if finely ground, for example in cooking or smooth nut spread. However many experts suggest avoiding nut products altogether in a small child's diet due to the risk of allergies developing. If there is a history of allergies or other atopic diseases in a family it is certainly best to avoid any nuts, especially peanuts, until at least three years. The pregnant or breastfeeding mother should also avoid peanuts if there is a history of allergies in the family.

Quorn and Textured Vegetable Protein

Quorn products are a useful addition to the diet of young children, but it should not be relied on as the sole or major source of protein since it is relatively low in calories and high in fibre so may satisfy the child's appetite before they have taken in enough energy. Textured vegetable protein may be difficult for young babies to digest, and its salt content must be watched.

Further Information

Even with the help of this Info Sheet and the growing scientific evidence that a vegetarian diet is a healthy option, you may experience resistance from health professionals, family or friends about bringing up your baby as a vegetarian. Contact The Vegetarian Society for help in solving any problems or answering your questions.

PREGNANCY

Preconception

The health of a mother and baby is influenced not only by diet during pregnancy but also by diet before conception. Eating a healthy diet before pregnancy will give your body a good store of nutrients for the baby to draw on during pregnancy. The foetus is most susceptible to nutritional imbalance during the first few months of pregnancy because this is the time of most rapid development.

If the lady is very underweight or overweight, she should try to achieve an acceptable weight for her height by a sensible and well-balanced diet.

If she uses to take the contraceptive pill, it is a good idea to come off and use an alternative method of contraception a few months before conceiving. This is because the pill can alter levels of some nutrients, particularly vitamin B6, folate and zinc. Ensure that she have a well balanced diet with plenty of fresh fruit, vegetables (especially green vegetables) and wholegrain cereals. Try to avoid fatty foods, sweets, biscuits and cakes.

Now is the time to make other healthy lifestyle changes and so stop smoking, cut down on alcohol and drinks containing caffeine such as tea, coffee and cola. Try a barley drink such as Barley Cup, or herb and fruit teas instead.

If the lady find that she is pregnant before she have had time to think about preconception, then don't worry, there is still plenty of time to make healthy changes to the diet.

Pregnancy is a time when good nutrition is vital, for vegetarians and non-vegetarians alike. It is a time of readjustment as well as growth. The nine months are divided up into three divisions of three months each called trimesters. Many women experience changes in mood, activity and appetite with the different stages of pregnancy. There is no truth in the old saying that pregnancy means eating for two.

The extra energy needed is only 200-300 calories a day for nine months. This is equivalent to two slices of bread with margarine or a jacket potato with baked beans or cheese. Some women do feel a lot more hungry than this and if they are gaining weight at the right rate, they should eat according to their appetite.

0-3 Months

Women usually feel different and may experience tiredness as well as a feeling of sickness particularly in the morning. Calorie needs are only about 100kcal more in the early stages of pregnancy and some women do not experience much increase in appetite until the end of this period.

3-6 Months

Appetite usually increases after the first three months and this period requires about 300-400kcal extra calories a day. Extra calorie needs should be met by cereals, pulses, nuts and seeds, dairy products (unless vegan) and starchy vegetables such as potatoes.

6-9 Months

The baby is maturing now and this is a time for easing up on activity and preparing for the birth. The baby takes up a lot of space and may press on the stomach, reducing the capacity for food. Many women feel they need to eat small meals more frequently at this stage.

Normal weight gain during pregnancy is about 22 to 28 pounds or one and a half to two stones (10-12.5kg). Weight gain often slows down during the last few months of pregnancy.

Exercise

It is a good idea to do some form of exercise during pregnancy. Antenatal clinics normally advise on appropriate exercise. Swimming or gentle yoga are often recommended.

Nutrients

Fluid

You may find that you are more thirsty during pregnancy. This is natural as fluid intake should increase. Never allow yourself to become over thirsty and include plenty of fresh water, dilute fruit juices, milk (soya or cow's) and herb teas. Drinks containing caffeine (tea, coffee and cola) should be limited and alcohol should be avoided altogether if possible.

Protein

Increased protein needs in pregnancy are usually met simply by the extra calories from more foods. Protein can be found in milk, cheese, eggs, soya milk, tofu, cereals, nuts and pulses. A normal variety of these foods will provide adequate protein.

Intake of dairy products and eggs should not increase dramatically. Some people believe that excessive amounts may sensitise the baby in the womb to allergies towards these foods.

Iron

The need for iron is increased during pregnancy, especially during the later stages. Anaemia, due to iron deficiency, is common in pregnancy whether you are vegetarian or not. Vegetarians should be especially careful to include plenty of iron in their diet as vegetable sources are not as well absorbed.

Good vegetarian sources of iron can be found in wholegrain cereals, pulses, green vegetables and dried fruits. Iron absorption is increased if taken with a good source of vitamin C, which can be found in fresh fruit and vegetables. Tea contains tannin which can inhibit iron absorption and should not be taken an hour before or after a meal.

Many doctors routinely prescribe iron tablets for pregnant women. Iron tablets may not be needed unless a blood test demonstrates anaemia. Iron levels normally decrease during pregnancy as the blood becomes more dilute. Some women prefer to take a natural iron supplement, such as Floridix, which is available from health food stores.

Calcium and Vitamin D

The body needs extra calcium during pregnancy, especially in the later stages, to enable the baby's bones to develop. Calcium absorption from the gut is more efficient during pregnancy and this should provide enough to meet requirements. Vegans and vegetarian women who consume few dairy products need to be particularly careful to ensure adequate calcium in the diet. Some vegan women, especially if they intend to breast-feed, may decide on a calcium supplement as a wise precaution, although with a good vegetable intake of calcium, it may not be necessary. Good sources of calcium include green vegetables, almonds, sesame seeds or tahini, cow's milk, tofu, cheese, yoghurt, wholegrain cereals and pulses. Vitamin D is essential for calcium absorption and can be obtained from sunlight, margarine and dairy products.

Folate

Folate is one of the B vitamins needed in increased amounts during pregnancy. Research has shown that a deficiency of folate during pregnancy can lead to birth defects. Vegetarians should not be at risk as the best sources of this vitamin are green leafy vegetables, fruit, peanuts, yeast extract and wholegrain cereals.

Vitamin B12

Vitamin B12 is essential to the growth and development of your baby. If adequate amounts of dairy products, eggs and fortified yeast extract are included in your diet, then you should have enough vitamin B12. It is especially important for vegans to include a reliable source of vitamin B12 in the diet during pregnancy. Some vegan foods, such as certain brands of soya milk, margarine and soya products are fortified with this vitamin. If the vitamin B12 in your diet is unreliable, then a supplement is recommended.

WHAT FOODS AND HOW MUCH?

For example, a cereal serving can be two small slices of bread, a portion of pasta or a large potato. A fruit serving is equivalent to one whole piece and a vegetable serving is about

3.5oz (100g). A large portion of nutloaf could be counted as a cereal and a nut serving. If you are gaining weight normally, the size of a serving can be based on appetite.

It is a good idea to avoid sweets, cakes, sugar and soft drinks as these provide extra calories without giving much in the way of nutrients.

During pregnancy over-the-counter medicines and tablets should be avoided unless prescribed by your doctor. A vitamin and mineral supplement should not be needed if a good balanced vegetarian diet is followed, but will not cause any harm if taken as a precaution.

Food Group	Servings / day	Provides
Cereals (wheat, oats, rice, barley, rye etc.)	Four	Energy, protein, fibre, calcium, B vitamins, iron, zinc
Pulses (beans, chick peas, lentils etc.)	One - two	Protein, fibre, energy
Nuts & seeds (almonds, peanuts, nutbutters, sesame seeds etc.)	One - two (small servings)	Energy, protein, fat, calcium
Fruit & vegetables; Leafy greens, Red & yellow vegetables, Fresh fruit, Dried fruit	Four - five	Iron, calcium, folate, Vitamin A, Vitamin C
Dairy products & Soya products (soya milk, tofu etc.)	Three - four	Protein, calcium, vitamin B12
Vegetable oils & fats	Two (small servings)	Energy, vitamins A, D (margarine & butter) & E (vegetable oils)
Yeast extract & other Vitamin B12 fortified foods	One	Vitamin B12

General Advice

Morning Sickness

Studies show that about three quarters of all women experience nausea and vomiting during pregnancy. Nausea normally occurs in the first few months although it can last throughout pregnancy. Morning sickness can be relieved by having a dry biscuit or toast before getting up. Avoiding long intervals between meals helps, as nausea often occurs at the same time as hunger. Starchy foods, such as bread and potatoes, should be eaten regularly as they help maintain blood sugar level and fill the stomach, helping to relieve the sickness.

Food Safety

Pregnant women are advised to avoid soft cheeses such as Brie and mould ripened cheese such as Stilton, because of the risk of listeria. Cottage cheese or hard cheeses, such as Cheddar should be used instead.

Even free range eggs have been found to contain Salmonella. Raw or lightly cooked eggs should be avoided.

Heartburn

Heartburn is very common in the later stages of pregnancy. It can be prevented by avoiding large meals and instead choosing small frequent meals or snacks. It can help to sit up very straight when eating and avoid activity just after a meal. Spicy and fatty foods, fizzy drinks and citrus fruits can make the problem worse.

Constipation

During pregnancy, the digestive system absorbs nutrients more efficiently and this can contribute to constipation. Iron tablets often make the problem worse. Constipation can be relieved by increasing fluid intake and including plenty of wholegrain cereals, pulses, fruits and vegetables in the diet.

Food Cravings and Aversions

Many women experience altered taste preferences during pregnancy which vary considerably. Some experience very strong cravings for particular foods such as fruit, salad vegetables, nuts, starchy foods or chocolate. Aversions to fatty foods, alcohol, tea and coffee are also common.

A healthy vegetarian diet can provide you with all the nutrients you need during your pregnancy and give your baby the best possible start in life.

Iron

Iron is an essential component of haemoglobin, transporting oxygen in the blood to all parts of the body. It also plays a vital role in many metabolic reactions. Iron deficiency can cause anaemia resulting from low levels of haemoglobin in the blood. Iron deficiency is the most widespread mineral nutritional deficiency both in Britain and worldwide.

Functions

Iron is essential for the formation of haemoglobin, the red pigment in blood. The iron in haemoglobin combines with oxygen and transports it through the blood to the body's tissues and organs. The body contains between 3.5 and 4.5g of iron, 2/3 of which is present in haemoglobin. The remainder is stored in the liver, spleen and bone-marrow. A small amount is present as myoglobin, which acts as an oxygen store in muscle tissue.

Iron deficiency can lead to anaemia. Iron stores in the body become depleted and haemoglobin synthesis is inhibited. Symptoms of anaemia include tiredness, lack of stamina, breathlessness, headaches, insomnia, loss of appetite and pallor. All these symptoms are associated with decreased oxygen supply to tissues and organs. Iron also plays an important role in the immune system, people with low iron levels having lowered resistance to infection. Research has also shown iron deficiency to be associated with impaired brain function, and iron deficiency in infants can result in impaired learning ability and behavioural problems. Iron deficiency is the most prevalent nutritional problem both in Britain and worldwide. It has been stated that 2/3 of children and women of child-bearing age in developing countries suffer from iron deficiency, 1/3 suffering from severe deficiency and anaemia. In developed countries, between 10-20% of child-bearing age women are said to be anaemic. Iron is the least plentiful nutrient in the typical British diet and anaemia is fairly common in the UK.

Dietary Sources

Dietary iron exists in two different forms. Haem iron only exists in animal tissues, whilst in plant foods iron is present as non-haem iron. In a mixed omnivore diet around 25% of dietary iron is non-haem iron. Non-haem iron is less easily absorbed by the body than is haem iron. The amount of iron absorbed from various foods ranges from around 1 to 10% from plant foods and 10 to 20% from animal foods.

The absorption of iron is influenced by other constituents of a meal. Phytates, oxalates and phosphates present in plant foods can inhibit absorption, as can tannin in tea. Fibre may also inhibit absorption. Vitamin C greatly increases the absorption of non-haem iron. Foods rich in vitamin C include citrus fruits, green peppers, and fresh leafy green vegetables. Citric acid, sugars, amino acids and alcohol can also promote iron absorption. Iron absorption can also be influenced by the amount of iron in the diet. Lowered levels of iron in the diet result in improved absorption.

Good sources of iron for vegetarians include wholegrain cereals and flours, leafy green vegetables, blackstrap molasses, pulses such as lentils and kidney beans, and some dried fruits.

Sources of Iron (single servings)					
Good sources		**Fair sources**		**Poor sources**	
Chick peas (200g or 7oz)	6.2 mg	Egg, boiled	1.3 mg	Banana (120g or 4¼oz)	0.48 mg
Bran flakes (45g or 1½oz)	5.3 mg	Avocado (75g or 2¾oz)	1.1 mg	Yoghurt (150g or 5½oz)	0.36 mg
Spinach, boiled (100g or 3½oz)	4.0 mg	Asparagus (125g or 4¾oz)	1.1 mg	Cow's milk (½ pint)	0.14 mg
Baked beans (225g or 8oz)	3.2 mg	1 slice wholemeal bread (40g)	1.0 mg	Hard cheese (30g or 1oz)	0.12 mg
Black treacle (35g or 1¼oz)	3.2 mg	Broccoli, boiled (100g or 3½oz)	1.0 mg	Margarine (7g or ¼oz)	0.02 mg
Muesli (60g or 2¼oz)	2.76mg	Brown rice (200g or 7oz)	0.9 mg		
4 Dried figs (60g or 2oz)	2.1 mg	Peanut butter (20g or ½oz)	0.5 mg		
8 Dried apricots (50g or 1¾oz)	2.1 mg				

Despite iron from plant foods being less readily absorbed research has shown that vegetarians are no more likely to suffer from iron deficiency than non-vegetarians. Draper & Wheeler (1989) have stated there is no indication of increased prevalence of iron deficiency amongst vegetarians. Anderson (1981) found the iron status of long-term vegetarian women to be adequate, despite a high intake of fibre and phytate.

Required Intakes

The old Recommended Daily Amounts (RDA's) have now been replaced by the term Reference Nutrient Intake (RNI). The RNI is the amount of nutrient which is enough for at least 97% of the population.

Nutrient Intakes for Iron, mg/day

Age	RNI	Age	RNI
0 to 3 months	1.7 mg	Men 11-18 yrs	11.3 mg
4 to 6 months	4.3 mg	Men 19 + yrs	8.7 mg
7 to 12 months	7.8 mg	Women 11-49 yrs	14.8 mg
1 to 3 yrs	6.9 mg	Women 50 + yrs	8.7 mg
4 to 6 yrs	6.1 mg	-	-
7 to 10 yrs	8.7 mg	-	-

In women of child-bearing age, loss of iron from menstruation of blood adds considerably to iron need. These losses can be highly variable. Around 10% of women of child-bearing age will need more iron than is indicated. In men, post-menopausal women, and children iron is efficiently conserved by the body. Iron in haemoglobin is recycled and the amount of iron lost from the body is very small. Infants and children need extra iron to increase blood volume and muscle tissue. Extra iron is also required during pregnancy and breast feeding.

Meal Plan

Sample one day's meal plan to meet the RNI of 14.8 mg for a women aged 11 to 49 years					
Breakfast		**Lunch**		**Evening meal**	
Bowl of muesli with milk	2.76mg	2 slices of wholemeal bread	2.0 mg	Brown rice (200g or 7oz)	0.94mg
1 slice of toast	1.0 mg	Peanut butter (20g or ¾oz)	0.5 mg	Chick peas (200g or 7oz)	6.2 mg
-	-	1 banana	0.5 mg	Broccoli (100g or 3½oz)	1.0 mg
Total iron intake - 14.9 mg					

OMEGA 3 FATS

So how does current government advice that "we" should try to eat at least two servings of fish a week, including one serving of oily fish, as part of a healthy balanced diet translate into dietary advice for vegetarians? And what should you do if your GP suggests fish oils for creaking joints or to thin your blood? Well, the first thing to remember is that the vegetarian diet is widely recognised as being protective against heart disease, the main ailment that the advice is aimed at, so vegetarians have a head start already, and of course the general population don't exactly eat much oily fish, or indeed offal, the other "good" source of omega 3 fats.

To begin with we must distinguish between the two polyunsaturated fatty acids which are termed essential because they can not be made in the body and therefore must be present in the diet. They are linoleic acid (LA), an omega 6 fat, which is widely available in a vegetarian diet, being present in large quantities in most oils and other vegetable based fatty foods, and alpha-linolenic acid (ALA), an omega 3 fat, which is not so widely available in a vegetarian diet, and is generally considered to be the more beneficial of the two EFAs.

Alpha-linolenic acid is what is known as an omega 3 fat, and is a precursor of the longer chain omega 3 fats eicosapentaenoic acid (EPA) and docosahexaenoic acid (DHA)- i.e., EPA and to a lesser extent DHA can be made in the body from ALA. These two fatty acids are the ones available in significant amounts in oily fish, and fish oil supplements. All three omega 3 fats have been shown to offer numerous physiological benefits, notably their anti-inflamatory properties and their ability to offer cardioprotective effects especially in people with pre-existing cardiovascular problems, though EPA and DHA are more potent than simple ALA.

Generally, vegetarian, and especially vegan, diets are relatively low in ALA compared with LA, and provide little EPA and DHA directly (though a certain amount of DHA is found in eggs, especially from hens fed on flax seeds or algae), and tissue levels of long chain omega 3 fatty acids have been shown to be relatively low in vegetarians and vegans, even though ALA intake varies little across vegans, vegetarians and omnivores.

Taking an overview of the various fatty acids intake recommendations worldwide, and the confounding factors surrounding the common vegetarian diet, leads to a conclusion that an ALA intake of 1.5% of total energy is optimum for vegetarians-or roughly 4g a day. This should provide enough of the parent omega 3 fat to ensure significant amounts of EPA and DHA are formed by the body (conversion rates are around 5-10% for EPA and 2-5% for DHA). However it is also important for vegetarians to ensure that their intake of LA is not too high compared with ALA since a higher intake of LA interferes with the process in which the human body converts ALA into the even more beneficial EPA and DHA, so a LA to ALA ratio of around 4 to 1 or slightly lower is considered to be the optimum, but any steps to bring down an excessively high amount of omega 6 fats in the diet would be beneficial.

Sources of Omega 3 Fats		
Flaxseed oil	1 tablespoon (14g)	provides 8.0g of ALA and relatively insignificant levels of LA
Flaxseed, ground	1 tablespoon (24g)	provides 3.8g of ALA
Rape Seed oil	1 tablespoon (14g)	provides 1.6g of ALA and only twice as much LA
Walnuts	1 oz (28g)	provides 2.6g of ALA but also four times as much LA
Tofu	4.5oz (126g)	provides 0.7g of ALA but also seven times as much LA

Practical Steps

There are a number of steps to take to ensure that the optimum levels of all the omega 3 fats are present in the body.

1. Make sure you include a good source of ALA in your diet, the simplest source would be one teaspoon of flax seed oil a day, taken either on its own or mixed into dressings etc. Flax oil is also available in vegetable capsules. Alternately include 4 to 5 teaspoons of ground flax seeds, or rape seed oil in your diet-though do not heat any of the oils, and only add the flax seeds to any foods at a late stage since heating will destabilise the ALA. It is important that the flax seeds are ground or at least crushed, if left whole much of the fat will be unavailable.

2. Replace fats high in omega 6 oils, such as sunflower oil or corn oil, with fats higher in monounsaturated fats, such as olive oil or rape seed oil which do not disrupt the formation of EPA and DHA.
3. Other foods can add to your intake of ALA. Most of the little fat in leafy green vegetables is ALA-broccoli has 0.13g per 100g, cabbage 0.11g per 100g, so simply eating your greens is making a positive addition to your intake. Walnuts and tofu are also good sources but are comparably high in LA.

Pregnant or nursing mothers who are uncertain whether their diet is providing enough omega 3 fats may wish to consider supplementing their diet with a direct source of DHA since this appears to play an important part in the development of immature brains. DHA supplements derived from algae and encased in non gelatine capsules are now available. It has also been suggested that DHA supplements may be of help to children with certain behavioral or learning difficulties.

Protein

Being vegetarian does not mean your diet will be lacking in protein. Most plant foods contain protein and in fact it would be very difficult to design a vegetarian diet that is short on protein. Excess dietary protein may lead to health problems. It is now thought that one of the benefits of a vegetarian diet is that it contains adequate but not excessive protein.

Proteins are made up of smaller units called amino acids. There are about 20 different amino acids, eight of which must be present in the diet. These are the essential amino acids. Unlike animal proteins, plant proteins may not contain all the essential amino acids in the necessary proportions. However, a varied vegetarian diet means a mixture of proteins are consumed, the amino acids in one protein compensating for the deficiencies of another.

Structure and Functions

Proteins are highly complex molecules comprised of linked amino acids. Amino acids are simple compounds containing carbon, hydrogen, oxygen, nitrogen and occasionally sulphur.

There are about 20 different amino acids commonly found in plant and animal proteins. Amino acids link together to form chains called peptides. A typical protein may contain 500 or more amino acids. Each protein has it's own unique number and sequence of amino acids which determines it's particular structure and function.

Proteins are broken down into their constituent amino acids during digestion which are then absorbed and used to make new proteins in the body. Certain amino acids can be made by the human body. However, the essential amino acids cannot be made and so they must be supplied in the diet. The eight essential amino acids required by humans are: leucine, isoleucine, valine, threonine, methionine, phenylalanine, tryptophan, and lysine. For children, histidine is also considered to be an essential amino acid.

Proteins are essential for growth and repair. They play a crucial role in virtually all biological processes in the body. All enzymes are proteins and are vital for the body's metabolism. Muscle contraction, immune protection, and the transmission of nerve impulses are all dependent on proteins. Proteins in skin and bone provide structural support. Many hormones are proteins. Protein can also provide a source of energy. Generally the body uses carbohydrate and fat for energy but when there is excess dietary protein or inadequate dietary fat and carbohydrate, protein is used. Excess protein may also be converted to fat and stored.

Dietary Sources

Most foods contain at least some protein. Good sources of protein for vegetarians include nuts and seeds, pulses, soya products (tofu, soya milk and textured soya protein such as soya mince), cereals (wheat, oats, and rice), free-range eggs and some dairy products (milk, cheese and yoghurt).

Different foods contain different proteins, each with their own unique amino acid composition. The proportions of essential amino acids in foods may differ from the proportions needed by the body to make proteins. The proportion of each of the essential amino acids in foods containing protein determines the quality of that protein. Dietary proteins with all the essential amino acids in the proportions required by the body are said to be a high quality protein. If the protein is low in one or more of the essential amino acids the protein is of a lower quality. The amino acid that is in shortest supply is called the limiting amino acid.

Protein quality is usually defined according to the amino acid pattern of egg protein, which is regarded as the ideal. As such, it is not surprising that animal proteins, such as meat, milk and cheese tend to be of a higher protein quality than plant proteins. This is why plant proteins are sometimes referred to as low quality proteins. Many plant proteins are low in one of the essential amino acids. For instance, grains tend to be short of lysine whilst pulses are short of methionine. This does not mean that vegetarians or vegans go short on essential amino acids. Combining plant proteins, such as a grain with a pulse, leads to a high quality protein which is just as good, and in some cases better, than protein from animal foods. Soya is a high quality protein on its own which can be regarded as equal to meat protein.

Sources of protein (single servings)					
Good sources		**Fair Sources**		**Poor sources**	
Chick peas (200g or 7oz)	16.0g	Brown rice (200g or 7oz)	4.4g	1 Carrot	0.4g
Baked beans (225g or 8oz)	11.5g	Broccoli (100g or 3½oz)	3.1g	1 Apple	0.3g
Tofu (140g or 5oz)	10.3g	Potatoes (200g or 7oz)	2.8g	Cream, double (20g or 2/3oz)	0.3g
Cow's milk (½ pint)	9.2g	Porridge [water] (160g or 6oz)	2.4g	Butter/margarine	None
Lentils (120g or 4¼oz)	9.1g	-	-	Vegetable oil	None
Soya milk (½ pint)	8.2g	-	-	Sugar or syrup	None
Muesli (60g or 2¼oz)	7.7g	-	-	-	-
Egg, boiled	7.5g	-	-	-	-
Peanuts (30g or 1oz)	7.3g	-	-	-	-
Bread, (2 slices)	7.0g	-	-	-	-
Hard cheese (30g or 1oz)	6.8g	-	-	-	-

The limiting amino acid tends to be different in different proteins. This means when two different foods are combined, the amino acids in one protein can compensate for the one lacking in the other. This is known as protein complementing. Vegetarians and vegans eating a well-balanced diet based on grains, pulses, seeds, nuts and vegetables will be consuming a mixture of proteins that complement one another naturally without requiring any planning. Beans on toast, cheese or peanut butter sandwich, muesli with milk (soya or cow's), and rice with peas or beans are all common examples of protein complementing. Previously, it has been thought that protein complementing needed to occur within a single meal. However, it is now known that this is not necessary as the body keeps a short-term store of the essential amino acids. A well-balanced vegetarian or vegan will easily supply all the protein and essential amino acids needed by the body.

Vegan Nutrition

A vegan is a strict vegetarian who does not eat any dairy products or eggs. Most vegans do not eat honey. A well balanced vegan diet can provide all the essential nutrients you require and shares the same health advantages as a vegetarian diet. Nutritional guidelines for vegans are essentially similar to those for vegetarians. However, vegetarians gain certain nutrients from dairy products and eggs. Vegans need to ensure their diets contain plant food sources of these nutrients.

Protein

Obtaining adequate protein on a vegan diet is not a problem. Nuts & seeds, pulses, wholegrain and grain products and soya products all supply protein. Previously, it has been thought that plant proteins are of a lower quality than animal proteins in terms of their essential amino acid content. However, this is no longer regarded as a problem and eating a balanced diet of plant foods will provide all the essential amino acids in adequate amounts.

Essential Fatty Acids

There are two essential fatty acids which must be supplied by the diet. These are linoleic acid and a-linolenic acid. Essential fatty acids are important for cell membrane function, cholesterol metabolism and the synthesis of various metabolites. Good sources of essential fatty acids are vegetable oils. It is important to have the correct balance between linoleic acid and a-linolenic acid. It has been suggested that vegans should use soyabean or rapeseed oils rather than sunflower or corn oils as these help give a better dietary balance.

Vitamin B2 (Riboflavin): Certain studies have found vegans to have a low intake of the vitamin, riboflavin. Riboflavin is important in converting protein, fats and carbohydrates into energy, and the synthesis and repair of body tissues. Good sources of riboflavin include whole grains, mushrooms, almonds, leafy green vegetables and yeast extracts.

Vitamin B12: Vitamin B12 is found primarily in meat, dairy products and eggs and is absent from plant foods. Considerable research has been carried out into possible plant sources of B12. Fermented soya products, seaweeds and algae such as spirulina have all been proposed as containing significant amounts of B12. However, the present consensus is that any B12 present in plant foods is likely to be in a form unavailable to humans and so these foods should not be relied upon as safe sources.

Vitamin B12 is important in the formation of red blood cells and the maintenance of a healthy nervous system. When deficiency does occur it is more likely to be due to a failure to absorb B12 from the intestine than a dietary deficiency.

Vegans can obtain B12 from a wide range of foods which have been fortified with the vitamin. These include certain yeast extracts, veggieburger mixes, breakfast cereals, vegetable margarines and soya milks. You should check the packaging to see which individual products are fortified with B12.

Vitamin D: Vitamin D is present in oily fish, eggs and dairy products in variable amounts. It is not found in plant foods. However, vegans can obtain vitamin D from vegetable margarines, some soya milks and certain other foods which are fortified with the vitamin.

Vitamin D is also synthesised by the skin when exposed to sunlight. Synthesis of vitamin D in this way is usually adequate to supply all the body's requirements. Most vegans will obtain sufficient vitamin D providing they spend time outdoors on bright days. Fortified foods further ensure adequate amounts.

Vegans who may be confined indoors may be recommended a vitamin D supplement. Also, infants who are seldom outdoors or who are dark-skinned may require supplements. Asian vegans may also be at risk of deficiency, particularly Asian women who may be required to keep their skin covered for cultural reasons.

Calcium: The major source of calcium in British diets is generally milk and dairy products. Vegans can obtain adequate calcium from plant foods. Good sources include tofu, leafy green vegetables, watercress, dried fruit, seeds and nuts. Also, white bread is fortified with calcium, as are some soya milks. Hard water can also provide significant amounts of calcium.

Iodine: Milk is the primary source of iodine in the British diet and studies have indicated some vegans may have a low iodine intake. Seaweeds are a good source of iodine, and vegetables and grains can contain iodine depending on the amounts in the soil.

Infants: It is perfectly possible to bring up a child on a vegan diet. Vegan children should be given plenty of nutrient rich foods and need good sources of protein, calcium, vitamin B12 and vitamin D. High fibre foods can fill up a child without filling their nutritional needs as well as interfering with mineral absorption from the intestine. For these reasons, foods high in fibre shouldn't be overused.

Vegan Storecupboard: Dairy products can largely be replaced with various soya products. There are several brands of soya milk. It can be purchased either sweetened or unsweetened, plain or flavoured. Different brands may be fortified with vitamin B12, vitamin D and calcium. Soya cheeses, yoghurts and cream are all available from health food stores. Eggs can be replaced in recipes by commercial egg replacer products, also available from health food stores.

Vitamin B12

Vitamin B12 is a member of the vitamin B complex. It contains cobalt, and so is also known as cobalamin. It is exclusively synthesised by bacteria and is found primarily in meat, eggs and dairy products.

There has been considerable research into proposed plant sources of vitamin B12. Fermented soya products, seaweeds, and algae such as spirulina have all been suggested as containing significant B12. However, the present consensus is that any B12 present in plant foods is likely to be unavailable to humans and so these foods should not be relied upon as safe sources. Many vegan foods are supplemented with B12.

Vitamin B12 is necessary for the synthesis of red blood cells, the maintenance of the nervous system, and growth and development in children. Deficiency can cause anaemia. Vitamin B12 neuropathy, involving the degeneration of nerve fibres and irreversible neurological damage, can also occur.

Functions

Vitamin B12's primary functions are in the formation of red blood cells and the maintenance of a healthy nervous system. B12 is necessary for the rapid synthesis of DNA during cell division. This is especially important in tissues where cells are dividing rapidly, particularly the bone marrow tissues responsible for red blood cell formation.

If B12 deficiency occurs, DNA production is disrupted and abnormal cells called megaloblasts occur. This results in anaemia. Symptoms include excessive tiredness, breathlessness, listlessness, pallor, and poor resistance to infection. Other symptoms can include a smooth, sore tongue and menstrual disorders. Anaemia may also be due to folic acid deficiency, folic acid also being necessary for DNA synthesis.

B12 is also important in maintaining the nervous system. Nerves are surrounded by an insulating fatty sheath comprised of a complex protein called myelin. B12 plays a vital role in the metabolism of fatty acids essential for the maintenance of myelin. Prolonged B12 deficiency can lead to nerve degeneration and irreversible neurological damage.

When deficiency occurs, it is more commonly linked to a failure to effectively absorb B12 from the intestine rather than a dietary deficiency. Absorption of B12 requires the secretion from the cells lining the stomach of a glycoprotein, known as intrinsic factor. The B12-intrinsic factor complex is then absorbed in the ileum (part of the small intestine) in the presence of calcium. Certain people are unable to produce intrinsic factor and the subsequent pernicious anaemia is treated with injections of B12.

Vitamin B12 can be stored in small amounts by the body. Total body store is 2-5mg in adults. Around 80% of this is stored in the liver.

Vitamin B12 is excreted in the bile and is effectively reabsorbed. This is known as enterohepatic circulation. The amount of B12 excreted in the bile can vary from 1 to 10ug (micrograms) a day.

People on diets low in B12, including vegans and some vegetarians, may be obtaining more B12 from reabsorption than from dietary sources. Reabsorption is the reason it can take over 20 years for deficiency disease to develop in people changing to diets absent in B12. In comparison, if B12 deficiency is due to a failure in absorption it can take only 3 years for deficiency disease to occur.

Dietary Sources

The only reliable unfortified sources of vitamin B12 are meat, dairy products and eggs. There has been considerable research into possible plant food sources of B12. Fermented soya products, seaweeds and algae have all been proposed as possible sources of B12. However, analysis of fermented soya products, including tempeh, miso, shoyu and tamari, found no significant B12.

Spirulina, an algae available as a dietary supplement in tablet form, and nori, a seaweed, have both appeared to contain significant amounts of B12 after analysis. However, it is thought that this is due to the presence of compounds structurally similar to B12, known as B12 analogues. These cannot be utilised to satisfy dietary needs. Assay methods used to detect B12 are unable to differentiate between B12 and it's analogues, Analysis of possible B12 sources may give false positive results due to the presence of these analogues.

Researchers have suggested that supposed B12 supplements such as spirulina may in fact increase the risk of B12 deficiency disease, as the B12 analogues can compete with B12 and inhibit metabolism.

The current nutritional consensus is that no plant foods can be relied on as a safe source of vitamin B12.

Bacteria present in the large intestine are able to synthesise B12. In the past, it has been thought that the B12 produced by these colonic bacteria could be absorbed and utilised by humans. However, the bacteria produce B12 too far down the intestine for absorption to occur, B12 not being absorbed through the colon lining.

Human faeces can contain significant B12. A study has shown that a group of Iranian vegans obtained adequate B12 from unwashed vegetables which had been fertilised with human manure. Faecal contamination of vegetables and other plant foods can make a significant contribution to dietary needs, particularly in areas where hygiene standards may be low. This may be responsible for the lack of aneamia due to B12 deficiency in vegan communities in developing countries.

Good sources of vitamin B12 for vegetarians are dairy products or free-range eggs. ½ pint of milk (full fat or semi skimmed) contains 1.2 µg. A slice of vegetarian cheddar cheese (40g) contains 0.5 µg. A boiled egg contains 0.7 µg. Fermentation in the manufacture of yoghurt destroys much of the B12 present. Boiling milk can also destroy much of the B12.

Vegans are recommended to ensure their diet includes foods fortified with vitamin B12. A range of B12 fortified foods are available. These include yeast extracts, Vecon vegetable stock, veggieburger mixes, textured vegetable protein, soya milks, vegetable and sunflower margarines, and breakfast cereals.

Required Intakes

The old Recommended Daily Amounts (RDA's) have now been replaced by the term Reference Nutrient intake (RNI). The RNI is the amount of nutrient which is enough for at least 97% of the population.

Reference Nutrient Intakes for Vitamin B12, μg/day. (1000 μg = 1mg)

Age	RNI
0 to 6 months	0.3 μg
7 to 12 months	0.4 μg
1 to 3 yrs	0.5 μg
4 to 6 yrs	0.8 μg
7 to 10 yrs	1.0 μg
11 to 14 yrs	1.2 μg
15 + yrs	1.5 μg
Breast feeding women	2.0 μg

Pregnant women are not thought to require any extra B12, though little is known about this. Lactating women need extra B12 to ensure an adequate supply in breast milk.

B12 has very low toxicity and high intakes are not thought to be dangerous.

4

VITAMINS, MINERALS AND OTHER NUTRIENTS

Vitamins

Vitamins are organic substances that are required in small amounts in the diet. They are necessary for numerous special functions in the body and are essential for good health. They can be affected by environmental conditions such as light, heat and air. Food storage, processing and cooking can all act to reduce the level of vitamins in food.

Vegetarians can obtain all the vitamins they need from a balanced diet. Vitamins may be either fat-soluble or water-soluble. The fat-soluble vitamins are vitamins A, D, E and K. Fat-soluble vitamins can be stored in the body and so dietary sources are not needed every day.

The water-soluble vitamins are vitamin C and the B group of vitamins. The B group of vitamins includes B1, B2, B3, B6, B12, folic acid, biotin and pantothenic acid. The body is less able to store water-soluble vitamins (with the exception of vitamin B12 which is stored in the liver) and so they are needed daily. Water-soluble vitamins are more likely to be lost during cooking.

Vitamin A (retinol): For healthy skin, growth of bones, resistance to infection and night vision. Found in carrots, spinach, peppers, butter, margarine, watercress, dried apricots, full-fat dairy products. In plant foods it is present as its precursor, beta-carotene.

Vitamin B1 (thiamin): For breaking down carbohydrates for energy. Found in yeast extract, brazil nuts, peanuts, rice, bran, oatmeal, flour, wholemeal bread, sunflower seeds.

Vitamin B2 (riboflavin): Helps convert proteins, fats and carbohydrates into energy and for the growth and repair of tissues and healthy skin. Found in almonds, cheese, wholemeal bread, dried prunes, mushrooms, cashews, millet, avocados.

Vitamin B3 (niacin): For energy production, healthy skin, and the nervous system. Found in most foods including yeast extract, peanuts, wholemeal bread, mushrooms, sesame seeds.

Vitamin B6 (pyridoxine): For red blood cell formation and protein metabolism. Found in bran, wholemeal flour, yeast extract, hazelnuts, bananas, peanuts, currants.

Vitamin B12: For red blood cell formation, growth, and a healthy nervous system. Found in eggs, dairy products and fortified plant foods including soya milks, breakfast cereals, veggieburger mixes, yeast extracts and herbal soft drinks.

Folic Acid or Folate: For red blood cell formation, protein synthesis and DNA metabolism. Some functions are linked with vitamin B12. Found in yeast extract, spinach, broccoli, peanuts, almonds, hazelnuts.

Biotin: For energy production and healthy skin. Found in yeast extract, pulses, nuts, most vegetables.

Pantothenic Acid: For energy production and antibody formation. Widely found in most foods.

Vitamin C (Ascorbic acid): For healthy skin, bones, teeth and gums, resistance to infection and wound healing, energy production and growth. Found in citrus fruits, broccoli, spinach, berries, peppers.

Vitamin D: For the absorption of calcium and phosphate and healthy bones and teeth. Found in dairy products and margarine. Also produced by the action of sunlight on the skin. The elderly, young children and anyone confined indoors may need to consider a vitamin D supplement especially if vegan.

Vitamin E: Acts as an antioxidant protecting vitamins A and C and other important substances in the body. Found in vegetable oils, wheatgerm, hazelnuts, avocados.

Vitamin K: For effective blood clotting. Found in spinach, cabbage, cauliflower. Vitamin K is also obtained from bacterial synthesis in the intestine. Deficiency is rare.

Minerals

The main minerals required in the diet are calcium, magnesium, sodium, potassium, chlorine, phosphorus and sulphur. Other minerals which are required in only tiny quantities (less than 100mg/day) are called trace elements.

Sodium and Potassium: Both are important in maintaining the body's water balance controlling the composition of blood and other body fluids. Sodium chloride (salt) is present in processed foods and in small amounts in vegetables, fruits and grains. Most people consume too much sodium which can lead to high blood pressure. Potassium is widely found in plant foods, especially root vegetables and wholegrain cereals.

Calcium: For building and maintaining strong bones and teeth, muscle contraction and blood clotting. Found in dairy products, leafy green vegetables, almonds, sesame seeds, dried fruit, pulses, fortified soya milks.

Magnesium: For strong bones and enzymes involved in energy production. Widely found in plant foods and deficiency is very rare.

Phosphorus: Required with calcium for strong bones and teeth, muscle function and a vital component of all body cells. Found in nearly all foods and dietary deficiency is unknown.

Sulphur: Plays a role in some enzyme systems. Most dietary sulphur is in the sulphur-containing amino acids. There is no indication of sulphur deficiency except in association with protein deficiency.

Iron: An essential component of haemoglobin which transports oxygen in the blood through the body. Iron deficiency is one of the most common nutritional problems in a typical British diet. Research shows vegetarians are no more prone to iron deficiency than meat-eaters. Found in leafy green vegetables, pulses, wholemeal bread, dried fruit, pumpkin seeds, molasses. Vitamin C helps to absorb iron. Tea can reduce the amount of iron absorbed.

Zinc: Plays a role in a wide range of enzyme systems and is essential for DNA metabolism and growth. Vegetarian diets tend to contain less zinc than meat-based diets. Found in sesame and pumpkin seeds, green vegetables, cheese, lentils, wholegrain cereals.

Copper: For red blood cell formation and many enzyme functions. Found in green vegetables, yeast, nuts, wheatgerm.

Iodine: For the production of thyroid hormones important in body metabolism. Found in milk (used as a disinfectant in milk production), seafoods. Amount in plant foods depends upon the amount in soil in which plants were grown.

Selenium: For red blood cell function and acts as an antioxidant. Selenium in plant foods depends on selenium in the soil and can vary considerably.

Chromium: Necessary to maintain blood glucose level. Exact nutritional role is uncertain. Good sources include black pepper, yeast and wholemeal bread.

Fluorine: For strong bones and teeth. Main dietary source is fluoridated water also tea.

Manganese: For the function of many enzymes and also muscle function. Deficiency has never been observed. Found in tea, green vegetables, wholegrain cereals, nuts, spices.

Molybdenum: Essential part of some enzyme systems though deficiency has never been observed. Amount in plant foods depends on the amount in the soil.

Other Elements: Vanadium, boron, nickel, silicon and other elements are present in very small amounts in the body. There is some debate on whether they have any nutritional role. All the elements can be toxic if taken in excess. Some elements such as aluminium, cadmium, mercury and arsenic have no known nutritional role and are toxic at very low levels. These toxic Elements are often environmental pollutants.

ZINC

The mineral zinc is present in every part of the body and has a wide range of functions. It helps with the healing of wounds and is a vital component of many enzyme reactions. Zinc is vital for the healthy working of many of the body's systems. It is particularly important for healthy skin and is essential for a healthy immune system and resistance to infection.

Functions

Zinc has a range of functions. It plays a crucial role in growth and cell division where it is required for protein and DNA synthesis, in insulin activity, in the metabolism of the ovaries and testes, and in liver function. As a component of many enzymes, zinc is involved in the metabolism of proteins, carbohydrates, lipids and energy.

Our body contains about 2-3g of zinc. There are no specific storage sites known for zinc and so a regular supply in the diet is required. Zinc is found in all parts of our body, 60% is found in muscle, 30% in bone and about 5% in our skin. Particularly high concentrations are in the prostate gland and semen. Men need more zinc than women because male semen contains 100 times more zinc than is found in the blood. The more sexually active a man the more zinc he will require. The recommended amounts of zinc for adult men are 1/3 higher than those for women.

The first signs of zinc deficiency are impairment of taste, a poor immune response and skin problems. Other symptoms of zinc deficiency can include hair loss, diarrhoea, fatigue, delayed wound healing, and decreased growth rate and mental development in infants. It is thought that zinc supplementation can help skin conditions such as acne and eczema, prostate problems, anorexia nervosa, alcoholics and those suffering from trauma or post-surgery. It is always better to seek the advice of an expert before dosing yourself with supplements. If you choose to take a zinc supplement you should not need more than the daily recommended amount unless medical advice says otherwise.

Dietary Sources

Zinc is present in a wide variety of foods, particularly in association with protein foods. A vegetarian diet often contains less zinc than a meat based diet and so it is important for vegetarians to eat plenty of foods that are rich in this vital mineral.

Good sources for vegetarians include dairy products, beans and lentils, yeast, nuts, seeds and wholegrain cereals. Pumpkin seeds provide one of the most concentrated vegetarian food sources of zinc.

Only 20% of the zinc present in the diet is actually absorbed by the body. Dietary fibre and phytic acid, found in bran, wholegrain cereals, pulses and nuts, inhibit zinc absorption. Phytic acid forms a highly insoluble complex with zinc which the body cannot absorb. Cooking processes can reduce the adverse effects of both phytic acid and dietary fibre on zinc absorption. Baking can destroy over half the phytic acid in wholemeal bread. Zinc deficiency occurs where a large part of the diet consists of unleavened bread, such as Iran and other Middle East countries. High levels of the toxic mineral cadmium can also prevent zinc absorption because these two minerals compete for absorption. Conversely high levels of zinc in the diet can prevent the absorption of cadmium. Various chemicals added to many processed foods can also reduce zinc absorption eg phosphates, EDTA. A deficiency of zinc in the diet means zinc absorption is improved. Zinc is lost via the faeces, urine, hair, skin, sweat, semen and also menstruation.

Sources of zinc (single servings)					
Good sources		Fair sources		Poor sources	
Chickpeas (200g or 7oz)	2.8mg	Peanut butter (20g or 2/3oz)	0.6mg	Dried dates (15g or 1/2oz)	0.04mg
Baked beans (225g or 8oz)	1.6mg	Peas, frozen/canned (80g or 2.5oz)	0.6mg	Butter (7g or 1/4oz)	0.01mg
1 Vegeburger (100g or 3.5oz)	1.6mg	3 Dried figs (60g or 2oz)	0.5mg	Raisins & Sultanas (15g or 1/2oz)	0.01mg
Pumpkin seeds (20g or 2/3oz)	1.3mg	3 Brazil nuts (10g or 1/3oz)	0.4mg	.	.
Muesli (60g or 2.25oz)	1.3mg	Potatoes, boiled (200g or 7oz)	0.4mg	.	.
Cheddar cheese (30g or 1oz)	1.2mg	1 Orange (140g or 5oz)	0.3mg	.	.
Tahini paste (20g or 2/3oz)	1.1mg	6 Almonds (10g or 1/3oz)	0.3mg	.	.
1 Fruit yoghurt (150g or 5.25oz)	0.9mg	.	.	.	.
Dried yeast (10g or 1/3oz)	0.8mg	.	.	.	.
Wholemeal bread (40g or 1.5oz)	0.8mg	.	.	.	.

Required Intakes

The old Recommended Daily Amounts (RDAs) have now been replaced by the term Reference Nutrient Intake (RNI). The RNI is the amount of nutrient which is enough for at least 97% of the population.

Nutrient Intakes for Zinc, mg/day.

Age	RNI	Age	RNI
0 to 6 months	4.0mg	Adult men	9.5mg
7 months to 3 yrs	5.0mg	Adult women	7.0mg
4 to 6 yrs	6.5mg		
7 to 10 yrs	7.0mg	Pregnant women	7..0mg
11 to 14 yrs	9.0mg	Breast feeding women	9.5 to 13mg

Pregnant women do need extra zinc, but it is thought that demands are met by increased absorption from the gut. Breast feeding mothers need extra zinc in their diet. Breast milk contains over 2mg of zinc in the first four months and women need an extra 6mg a day to cover these demands. Breast feeding women must include a generous serving of at least one good source of zinc in their diet each day. The iron supplements routinely prescribed for pregnant women when there is no sign of anaemia may compromise zinc status. This is because the interactions between essential minerals are complex and too much of one may cause an imbalance of another. Excess zinc is toxic. Too much zinc will interfere with the metabolism of other minerals in the body, particularly iron and copper. Symptoms of zinc toxicity occur after ingestion of 2g of or more and include nausea, vomiting and fever.

Meal Plan

Sample one day's meal plan to meet the RNI of 9.5mg for an adult man.					
Breakfast		**Lunch**		**Evening meal**	
Bowl of muesli with milk	1.32mg	Baked beans (225g or 8oz)	1.57mg	Potatoes, boiled (200g or 7oz)	0.4mg
1 slice of toast	0.8mg	2 slices of toast	1.6mg	Peas (80g or 2.5oz)	0.56mg
		Cheese (30g or 1oz) (or Pumpkin seeds, 20g or 2/3oz)	1.2mg	1 Vegeburger (100g or 3.5oz)	1.3mg
				1 Fruit yoghurt	0.94mg
Total zinc intake 9.69mg					

ALCOHOL

The use of animal derived products in the production of alcoholic beverages is fairly widespread not because no alternatives exist, but because they always have been used and there is little demand from the consumer for an alternative.

The main obstacle when trying to judge the acceptability to vegetarians of any given product is a clause in the 1984 Food Labelling Regulations (UK) which exclude from the 1984 Food Act all drinks with an alcohol content exceeding 1.2% by volume (ABV), leaving only very low or non-alcoholic beers, wines and ciders being required to list all ingredients.

The main appearance of animal derived products is in the fining or clearing process, though others may be used as colorants or anti-foaming agents.

It must be pointed out that alcohol is routinely tested on thousands of animals each year (though this is not usually done directly by any individual company).

Beer

Cask-conditioned ales need fining to clear the material (especially the yeast) held in suspension in the liquid. This is invariably done by adding isinglass, derived from the swim bladders of certain tropical fish especially the Chinese sturgeon, which acts as a falling suspension. If you were to hold a pint of real ale up to the light and see cloudy lumps swirling around that would suggest that the cask had been recently disturbed and the isinglass shaken up from the bottom. Bottled naturally conditioned beers will not always have been treated with isinglass. Keg Beers and Lagers are pasteurised and usually passed through Chill Filters, as are canned beers and some bottled beers, however a considerable number of breweries still use isinglass to clear their pasturised beers, though sometimes only to rescue selected batches which are considered too hazey. Also occasionally the sometimes animal derived additive Glyceryl Monostearate is used in place of 900 Dimethylpolysiloxane as a foam-control agent in the production of keg beers.

It is sometimes possible to buy barrels of cask-conditioned beer from a brewery before it has been fined. The beer would then have to be left for a considerable time to stand before consumption. To our knowledge, only one pub in England sells unfined real ale on draught: The Cumberland Arms in Byker, Newcastle on Tyne.

Cider

Most of the main brands of cider will have been fined using gelatine. Scrumpy type ciders are less likely to have been fined.

Wine

With wine, it is again in the fining process that animal derived ingredients make an appearance. Finings can be isinglass, gelatin, egg albumen, modified casein (from milk), chitin (derived from the shells of crabs or lobsters) or ox blood (rarely used today). But alternatives do exist in the form of bentonite, kieselguhr, kaolin and silica gel or solution. Also newer methods such as centrefuging and filtering are becoming more popular.

The majority of organic wines do not use animal derived finings-but some do, Thorson's Organic Wine Guide by Jerry Lockspeiser and Jackie Gear, lists those wines which are suitable. You might like to note that the Wine Development Board claim that the fining agents are removed at the end of the process with the possible exception of very minute quantities.

Spirits

Most spirits appear to be acceptable to vegetarians, with the possible exception of Malt Whisky, some blended whiskies and Spanish Brandies which have been conditioned in casks which had previously held sherry which may have been treated with animal derived finings. (Brandy itself is not produced from wine which has undergone any fining processes). Also some imported Vodkas may have been passed through a bone charcoal filter.

Fortified Wines

All ports except crusted port are fined using gelatin. Sherry should be treated in a similar way to wine.

Colorants

E120 cochineal produced by extracting the red body material from pregnant scale insects of the species Dactilopius Coccus is used as a colorant in a small number of red wines, soft drinks and Campari.

CHEESE AND RENNET

Cheese is made by coagulating milk to give curds which are then separated from the liquid, whey, after which they can be processed and matured to produce a wide variety of cheeses. Milk is coagulated by the addition of rennet. The active ingredient of rennet is the enzyme, chymosin (also known as rennin). The usual source of rennet is the stomach of slaughtered newly-born calves. Vegetarian cheeses are manufactured using rennet from either fungal or bacterial sources. Advances in genetic engineering processes means they may now also be made using chymosin produced by genetically altered micro-organisms.

Manufacture

The exact processes in the making of cheese varies between different varieties. However, all cheeses are made by essentially the same method. Initially, the milk is usually pasteurised by heating at 72°C for 15 seconds to destroy potentially harmful bacteria. The milk is then cooled to around 30°C and a starter culture of lactic acid bacteria is added to help souring. These convert lactose into lactic acid and help in the coagulation process. In addition, they also have a beneficial effect on the eventual quality, taste and consistency of the cheese. Some cheeses are coagulated entirely by lactic acid bacteria and are known as lactic-curd or acid-curd cheeses. However, some cheeses sold as lactic-curd cheese may have had rennet added.

The next stage is the addition of rennet, containing the enzyme chymosin. Rennet is usually sourced from the abomasum (fourth stomach) of newly-born calves. Here, chymosin aids the digestion and absorption of milk. Adult cows do not have this enzyme. Chymosin is extracted by washing and drying the stomach lining, which is then cut into small pieces and macerated in a solution of boric acid or brine at 30°C for 4-5 days. Pepsin may sometimes be used instead of chymosin. This is usually derived from the abomasum of grown calves or heifers, or less commonly pigs. Pepsin may be mixed with calf rennin. Rennet coagulates the milk, separating it into curds and whey. This is called curdling.

Chymosin breaks down the milk protein casein to paracasein which combines with calcium to form calcium paracaseinate, which separates out. Milk fat and some water also becomes incorporated into this mass, forming curds. The remaining liquid is the whey. The strength of different rennets can vary, though usual strength varies between 1:10,000 and 1:15,000 i.e. one part rennin can coagulate 10-15,000 parts milk.

Other substances may also be added during the cheese making process. Calcium chloride is added to improve the curdling process, and potassium nitrate is added to inhibit contaminating bacteria. Dyes (e.g. annatto, beta-carotene), Penicillium roquefortii mould spores to promote blue veining, or propionic acid bacteria to encourage hole formation may be added.

Following curdling, the curds are cut and drained. The size of the cut and the methods used vary for different cheese varieties. For soft cheeses, the curds are sparingly cut and allowed to drain naturally. For hard cheeses, the curds are heated and more whey is drained off. The curds are then cut into small pieces, placed in vats and pressed.

After pressing, the curds may be treated in a number of ways. They may be moulded into different shapes, soaked in a saltwater solution, be sprayed with mould forming spores or bacteria, washed in alcohol, or covered in herbs.

The final stage is ripening, or maturation. This can vary in length from 4 weeks to 2-3 years, depending on the type of cheese. During ripening flavours develop, the cheese becomes firmer and drier, and special characteristics such as holes, blue veining and crust formation occurs.

Vegetarian Cheeses

Vegetarian cheeses are made with rennets of non-animal origin. In the past, fig leaves, melon, wild thistle and safflower have all supplied plant rennets for cheese making. However, most widely available vegetarian cheeses are made using rennet produced by fermentation of the fungus Mucor miehei. Vegetarian cheese may also be made using a rennet from the bacteria Bacillus subtilis or Bacillus prodigiosum.

Advances in genetic engineering techniques mean that some vegetarian cheeses may now be made using chymosin produced by genetically engineered micro-organisms. The genetic material (DNA) which encodes for chymosin is introduced into a micro-organism which can then be cultured to produce commercial quantities of chymosin.

This is done by extracting genetic material from calf stomach cells which acts as a template for producing the chymosin encoding DNA. This can then be introduced into the micro-organism. Once the genetic material is introduced there is no further need for calf cells. Alternatively, the chymosin encoding DNA can be bio-synthesised in the laboratory without the use of calf cells.

The chymosin produced is identical to that produced by calf stomach cells. The development of genetically engineered chymosin has been encouraged by shortages and fluctuations in cost of rennet from calves. It's manufacturers claim that genetically engineered chymosin will end the cheese making industry's reliance on the slaughter of calves.

Chymosin encoding DNA has been introduced into three different micro-organisms. These are the yeast Kluyveromyces lactis, the fungus Aspergillus niger var awamori, and a strain of the bacteria Escherichia coli. All of these have now been approved and cleared for use by the Ministry of Agriculture, Fisheries & Food. There is no legal requirement for manufacturers to state whether a genetically engineered rennet has been used in the cheese making process.

Vegetarian cheeses are widely available in supermarkets and health food stores. A wide variety of cheeses are now made with non-animal rennet and labelled as suitable for vegetarians. No particular type of cheese is exclusively vegetarian. Soft cheeses are as likely to be non-vegetarian as hard cheese

Types of Cheese

The type of cheese produced depends on the milk used and the cheese making process. The milk used may be full fat, semi-skimmed or fully skimmed, this affecting the fat content of the cheese. It may be pasteurised or unpasteurised. Milk from different animals and different breeds is important in determining the final flavour. As well as cow's milk, cheese may be made from sheep or goat's milk.

Soft cheeses may be fresh or ripened. Fresh cheeses include quark, cottage cheese and cream cheese. Ripened soft cheeses include Brie and Camembert. Semi-soft cheeses include Stilton, Wensleydale and Gorgonzola. Hard cheeses include Cheddar, Cheshire, and Gruyere. Parmesan is a strongly pressed, very hard, dry cheese ripened for 2-3 years and then grated. Whey cheeses such as Ricotta are made as a by-product of other cheeses from the whey removed during pressing. Processed cheeses are either made with trimmings that are left over from the manufacture of other cheeses, or from dried milk powder. Flavourings, colourings and other additives are used.

Nutritional Aspects

Cheese is a good source of protein, calcium, zinc, and vitamin B12. However, full fat cheese is a major source of saturated fat which can lead to raised serum cholesterol levels. Also, it contains no carbohydrate or fibre, and is a very poor source of iron. Vegetarians, particularly new vegetarians, should be wary of too high a consumption of cheese.

E Numbers

Always non-vegetarian

E120 Cochineal

Can be produced from both vegetarian and non-vegetarian sources

E104** Quinoline Yellow

E160a(ii)** Alpha-, beta-, gamma carotene (may be held in gelatine matrix)

E161(g) Canthaxanthin

E252 Potassium Nitrate

E270* Lactic Acid

E304(i) Ascorbyl Palmitate

E304(ii) Ascorbyl Stearate

E322* Lecithin (may be made from battery eggs)

E325* Sodium Lactate

E326* Potassium Lactate

E327* Calcium Lactate

E422 Glycerol/Glycerin

E431 Polyoxyethylene (40) stearate

E432 Polyoxyethylene (20) sorbitan monolaurate

E433 Polyoxyethylene (20) sorbitan mono-oleate

E434 Polyoxyethylene (20) sorbitan monopalmitate

E435 Polyoxyethylene (20) sorbitan monostearate

E436 Polyoxyethylene (20) sorbitan tristearate

E442 Ammonium Phosphatides

E445 Glyceryl esters of wood rosin

E470(a) Sodium, potassium and calcium salts of fatty acids

E470(b) Magnesium salts of fatty acids

E471 Mono-and di-glycerides of fatty acids

E472(a) Acetic acid esters of mono-and di-glycerides of fatty acids

E472(b) Lactic acid esters of mono-and di-glycerides of fatty acids

E472(c) Citric acid esters of mono-and di-glycerides of fatty acids

E472(d) Tartaric acid esters of mono-and di-glycerides of fatty acids

E472(e) Mono-and di-acetyl tartaric acid esters of mono- and di-glycerides of fatty acids

E472(f) Mixed acetic and tartaric acid esters of mono-and di-glycerides of fatty acids

E473 Sucrose esters of fatty acids

E474 Sucroglycerides

E475 Polyglycerol esters of fatty acids

E476 Polyglycerol esters of polycondensed fatty acids of caster oil

E477 Propane-1,2-diol esters of fatty acids

E479(b) Thermally oxidised soya bean oil interacted with mono-and di-glycerides of fatty acids

E481 Sodium stearoyl-2-lactylate

E482 Calcium stearoyl-2-lactylate

E483 Stearyl tartrate

E491 Sorbitan monostearate

E492 Sorbitan tristearate

E493 Sorbitan monolaurate

E494 Sorbitan mono-oleate

E495 Sorbitan monopalmitate

E570 Stearic acid

E585 Ferrous Lactate

E631 Sodium 5'-inositate

E635 Sodium 5'-ribonucleotides

E640 Glycine and its sodium salt

E920 L-cysteine and L-cysteine hydrochloride

E966 Lactitol

E1105 Lysozyme (made from eggs)

E1518 Glycerol mono-, di-and tri-acetate

All other E Numbers are to the best of our knowledge always vegetarian

*E numbers marked * may theoretically be made in a non vegetarian version, but are practically always suitable*

*E numbers marked ** are not themselves non vegetarian but may be carried in a gelatine carrier especially when used in liquids*

NUTS AND SEEDS

Nuts are seeds that are covered with a hard shell. Most are the seeds of trees, but the seeds of a few other plants that are not strictly nuts will also be considered here as they can be conveniently classified with nuts for culinary purposes.

Nuts can be used in many ways. Whole, flaked and ground nuts and nut butters are widely available. A classic vegetarian savoury is nut roast and many vegetarian cook books give a recipe for one, which can be endlessly varied with different herbs and flavourings and different combinations of nuts and cereals. Nuts can be added to sweet dishes, cakes and biscuits, and nut butters can be added to soups and stews to thicken them.

Nutrition

Nuts in general are very nutritious, providing protein and many essential vitamins, such as A and E, minerals, such as phosphorous and potassium, and fibre. Nuts are also high in carbohydrate and oils, so shouldn't be eaten in excess.

Whereas pulses all belong to the legume group of plants, nuts come from a variety of different plant groups, so the nutritional content is more varied too. A brief description of individual varieties is given below, together with the main nutrients they contain.

Storage

Nuts should be stored in cool, dry conditions in airtight containers away from the light. Because of their high fat content, many of them benefit from storage in the fridge or freezer to deter rancidity.

NUTS

Almonds

Probably originated in the Near East but now grows in Southern Europe, Western Asia, California, South Australia and South Africa. Almond oil is used for flavouring and for skin care preparations and is extracted from the kernel of the Bitter Almond. The Sweet Almond is grown for nuts for eating and have the largest share of the nut trade world-wide. Almond flour is available and it is possible to make a nutritious nut milk from almonds. Almonds are particularly nutritious, 100g contain 16.9g protein, 4.2mg iron, 250mg calcium, 20mg vitamin E, 3.1mg zinc and 0.92mg vitamin B2.

Brazils

A native of South America. The nuts grow inside a hard, woody fruit rather like a coconut shell which has to be broken open to expose the 12-24 nuts inside. Brazils are high in fat, which causes them to go rancid very quickly, and protein. 100g of brazils contain 12g protein, 61g fat, 2.8mg iron, 180mg calcium, 4.2mg zinc.

Cashews

Native to America but now grown extensively in India and East Africa. It will withstand rather drier conditions than most other nuts. The nut grows in a curious way on the tree, hanging below a fleshy, apple-like fruit It is related to the mango, pistachio and poison ivy. High in protein and carbohydrate, 100g cashews contain 17.2g protein, 60 micrograms vitamin A, 3.8mg iron.

Chestnuts

The sweet chestnut is a native of South Europe but is planted elsewhere extensively for both nuts and timber. The nuts can be used in soups, fritters, porridges, stuffings and stews, as well as being roasted or boiled whole. Available fresh (in autumn), dried, canned-whole or pureed, or ground into flour. Dried chestnuts need soaking for at least 1-2 hours and boiling for 45-60 minutes, fresh need boiling for 40 minutes before being peeled. Preserved in syrup they become the famous delicacy, Marron-glace. High in starch, but low in protein and fat, 100g chestnuts contain 36.6g carbohydrate, only 2g protein (the lowest of all nuts) and 2.7g fat.

Coconuts

The coconut palm is common in tropical regions all over the world. The nut is covered in a fibrous outer coating on the tree and all parts of the tree are useful, the trunks for timber, the leaves for thatch, the fibrous husk produces coir-the starting material for ropes and coconut matting-and the nuts are used for food. Unripe nuts contain coconut milk. The nutmeat can be eaten fresh or dried (desiccated or flaked coconut) and is also available in blocks of creamed coconut. A valuable oil is also extracted from the nut meat and used for cooking (although it is very high in saturated fat), margarines, soaps and detergents. 100g fresh coconut contain 3.2g protein and 36g fat, dessicated contain 5.6g protein and 62g fat.

Hazels

Hazel, also called Cob, is a common wild tree in Europe and Asia and its nuts have been eaten by humans since earliest times. The cultivated varieties are bigger and the filbert is a similar but bigger species from SE Europe. Used in sweet and savoury dishes, they are available whole, ground and flaked, or made into oil and nut butter. 100g hazel nuts contain 7.6g protein, and they are lower in fat than most other nuts.

Macadamia Nuts

A native of NE Australia now also grown commercially in Hawaii. Notoriously difficult to extract from their shells, they are expensive but have a delicious creamy flavour and crunchy texture. Low in carbohydrate, but quite high in fat, 100g Macadamia nuts contain 7g protein and 40mg calcium.

Peanuts

Also known as groundnuts or monkey nuts, peanuts are actually legumes. Of South American origin, it's now an important crop all over the tropics and southern USA. It gets its name groundnut because as the pods ripen, they are actually forced underground. Peanuts are high in protein and contain 40-50% oil. The oil is used in cooking, as salad oil, in margarines and the residue is fed to animals. Whole peanuts can be eaten raw or roasted or made into peanut butter (look out for brands which do not contain hydrogenated oils, which are highly saturated). As they are usually inexpensive, they can be mixed with other kinds of nuts to bring down the cost, while still maintaining flavour and good nutrition. 100g peanuts contain 24.3g protein, 2mg iron and 3mg zinc.

Pecans

A native of N America where it is used extensively in ice cream, cakes, nut bread and confectionery. The flavour is rather like a mild, sweet walnut. 100g pecans contain 9.2g protein, a very high fat content of 71.2g, 130 micrograms vitamin A (also very high), 2.4mg iron and 73mg calcium.

Pine Nuts

These are the seeds of the Stone Pine, a native of the Mediterranean region, but the seeds of various other pines are eaten in various parts of the world including the seeds of the Korean Pine or North American pinon tree. They are very difficult to harvest, hence their cost. They are vital for pesto sauce, and are delicious lightly toasted. They become rancid very easily and should be stored in the fridge or freezer. 100g pine nuts contain 31g protein, the highest of the nuts and seeds.

Pistachios

Native to the Near East and Central Asia but has long been cultivated in the Mediterranean region and more recently in the Southern US. The kernels are green and are prized as much for their ornamental colour as for their flavour. Also sold roasted and salted in their shells. They are more expensive than most other nuts. 100g pistachios contain 19.3g protein, 14mg iron, 140mg calcium.

Walnuts

The walnut is native to SE Europe and West & Central Asia but is now grown in the UK, California and China as well. It is grown for timber as well as its nuts. Walnut oil has been used for centuries in the preparation of artists paints. The black walnut is a native of North America, introduced into Britain in the 17th century. The butternut is also from North America. These two have much thicker shells than European walnuts. High in fat, they go rancid very quickly and should be stored in the fridge or freezer. 100g walnuts contain 10.6g protein and 2.4mg iron.

SEEDS

Pumpkin

Can be eaten raw or cooked in both sweet or savoury dishes. Delicious toasted and sprinkled, while hot, with soya sauce and served on salads. They are rich in protein, iron, zinc and phosphorous. 100g pumpkin seeds contain 29g protein, 11.2mg iron and 1144mg phosphorous.

Sesame

Of African origin but now common in tropical and sub-tropical Asia. An oil is extracted from the seed and used for cooking, salad oil and margarines. It is also available as toasted sesame oil for oriental cooking. The whole seeds can also be eaten and are most often seen as a decoration on cakes, confectionery etc. Sesame seed paste, tahini, is used in many dishes e.g. hummus. Halva, a sweet made from sesame seeds is often found in health food shops. A good source of protein and calcium, 100g sesame seeds contain 26.4g protein, 12.6mg vitamin B3, 7.8mg iron, 131mg calcium and 10.3mg zinc.

Sunflower

An annual plant belonging to the daisy family, it probably originated in North America or Mexico. North American Indians cultivated sunflowers as long as 2,000 years ago. The oil extracted from its seeds is used in margarine, varnishes and soaps but the seeds can be eaten whole, raw or cooked. They can be added to breads and cakes or sprinkled over salad or breakfast cereals. A good source of potassium and phosphorous, 100g sunflower seeds also contain 24g protein and 7.1mg iron and 120mg calcium.

PULSES

Peas, beans and lentils are known as pulses. They are the seeds of plants belonging to the family Leguminosae, which gets its name from the characteristic pod or legume that protects the seeds while they are forming and ripening. With approximately 13,000 species, the family Leguminosae is the second largest in the plant kingdom and it is very important economically.

Different kinds of legumes provide us with food, medicines, oils, chemicals, timber, dyes and ornamental garden plants. Legume products include carob, senna, gum arabic, balsam, indigo and licorice. Pulses are valuable because they contain a higher percentage of protein than most other plant foods.

Origins

Pulses have been used as food for thousands of years. The lentil was probably one of the first plants ever to be domesticated by humans. Most pulses prefer warm climates but there are varieties which grow in temperate regions. They can be eaten fresh or dried and come in a great number of varieties with a range of colours, flavours, and textures. In spite of its common name, the peanut or groundnut is also a legume rather than a nut.

Nutrition

All pulses, except for soya beans, are very similar in nutritional content. They are rich in protein, carbohydrate and fibre, and low in fat which is mostly of the unsaturated kind. They are also important sources of some B vitamins. Fresh pulses contain vitamin C, but this declines after harvesting and virtually all is lost from dried pulses. Canned pulses however, retain about half their vitamin C except for canned, processed peas which have been dried before canning. Canning doesn't affect the protein content, eliminates the need for soaking and considerably reduces the cooking time compared with dried pulses. Frozen peas will have also lost about a quarter of their vitamin C content. Pulses are usually eaten for their high protein content. A typical nutritional breakdown is that for haricot beans which are used to make baked beans, contain, per 100g dried beans: 21.4g protein, 1.6g fat, 45.5g carbohydrate, 25.4g fibre, 6.7mg iron and 180mg calcium.

The nutritional quality of the soya bean is superior to that of other pulses. It contains more protein and is also a good source of iron and calcium. The nutritional breakdown of soya is per 100g of dried beans: 34.1g protein, 17.7g fat, 28.6g carbohydrate, 8.4mg iron and 226mg calcium. Dried soya beans are lengthy to prepare because they need at least 12 hours soaking and 4 hours cooking time, boiling for the first hour, but nowadays a large number of soya based foods including tofu, tempeh and textured vegetable protein (soya mince or chunks) are available.

Storage and Cooking

One advantage of dried pulses is that they will store very well for long periods if kept in a dry, airtight container away from the light. However it is best to eat them as fresh as possible. Pulses toughen on storage and older ones will take longer to cook. Allow about 55g dried weight per person, once soaked and cooked they will at least double in weight. Most dried pulses need soaking for several hours before they can be cooked, exceptions are all lentils, green and yellow split peas, blackeye and mung beans. Soaking times vary from 4-12 hours, it is usually most convenient to soak pulses overnight. Always discard the soaking water, rinse and cook in fresh water without any salt, which toughens the skins and makes for longer cooking. Changing the water will help to reduce the flatulence some people suffer when eating pulses, also reputed to help is the addition of a pinch of aniseeds, caraway, dill or fennel seeds.

Toxins in Pulses

Consumers should be aware that it is not safe to eat raw or undercooked kidney and soya beans. There is no need to avoid them as long as they are thoroughly cooked.

Red kidney beans: Incidents of food poisoning have been reported associated with the consumption of raw or undercooked red kidney beans. Symptoms may develop after eating only four raw beans and include nausea, vomiting and abdominal pain followed by diarrhoea. A naturally occurring haemaglutin is responsible for the illness, but can be destroyed by high temperature cooking, making the beans completely safe to eat. For this reason, kidney beans must not be sprouted. Kidney beans should be soaked for at least 8 hours in enough cold water to keep them covered. After soaking, drain and rinse the beans, discarding the soaking water. Put them into a pan with cold water to cover and bring to the boil. The beans must now boil for 10 minutes to destroy the toxin. After this the beans should be simmered until cooked (approximately 45-60 minutes) and they should have an even creamy texture throughout-if the centre is still hard and white, they require longer cooking.

Soya Beans: Contain an anti-trypsin factor (or trypsin inhibitor) which prevents the assimilation of the amino acid methionine. Soya beans also require careful cooking to ensure destruction of this factor. They should be soaked for at least 12 hours, drained and rinsed then covered with fresh water and brought to the boil. Soya beans should be boiled for the first hour of cooking. They can then be simmered for the remaining 2-3 hours that it takes to cook them. Soya flour should state heat treated on its packaging. Other soya products (e.g. tofu, tempeh, soya milk, soya sauces and miso) are quite safe to use. Soya beans can be sprouted, but the sprouts should be quickly blanched in boiling water to inactivate the trypsin inhibitor.

Pressure Cooking: The temperatures achieved in pressure cooking are adequate to destroy both haemaglutins and the trypsin inhibitor. Pressure cooking also considerably reduces cooking times-kidney beans 10-20 minutes, soya beans 1 hour.

Canning: The temperature achieved in the canning process also renders pulses quite safe.

Slow Cookers: Pulses must be soaked and boiled for 10 minutes before being added to a slow cooker, as they do not reach sufficiently high temperatures to destroy the toxins. As beans and peas are all very similar nutritionally, with the exception of soya, they can be interchanged in most recipes if you want to experiment or have run out of one kind, as long as you take into account the different cooking times. If the beans are likely to need a lot longer to cook than the other ingredients, try pre-cooking them in a separate pan before adding to the other ingredients or using canned beans.

Sprouting

Many whole pulses (e.g. aduki, chickpeas, whole lentils, marrowfat peas, mung and soya beans) can be sprouted which increases their nutritional value.

SOYA AND MYCOPROTEIN

Soya

The soya bean is the seed of the leguminous soya bean plant. Soya foods have been a staple part of the Chinese diet for over 4000 years but have only been widely consumed in Western countries since the 1960's. Soya foods include tofu, tempeh, textured vegetable protein (chunks, mince etc), miso, soya sauces, soya oil and margarine, and soya dairy alternatives.

Soya is an excellent source of high quality protein, is low in saturated fats and is cholesterol free. Recent research has indicated soya has several beneficial effects on health in addition to its nutritional benefits. Soya beans contain high concentrations of several compounds which have demonstrated anti-carcinogenic activity. These include isoflavonoids, protease inhibitors and phytic acid. The low incidence of breast and colon cancer in China and Japan has been partially attributed to the high consumption of soya products. The low incidence of menopausal symptoms in Japanese women has also been attributed to high consumption of soya. Soya diets have also been shown to reduce levels of serum cholesterol.

Textured Vegetable Protein

Textured vegetable protein is basically defatted soya flour which has been processed and dried to give a substance with a sponge-like texture which may be flavoured to resemble meat. Soya beans are dehulled and their oil extracted before being ground into flour. This flour is then mixed with water to remove soluble carbohydrate and the residue is textured by either spinning or extrusion. Extrusion involves passing heated soya residue from a high pressure area to a reduced pressure area through a nozzle resulting in the soya protein expanding. The soya protein is then dehydrated and may be either cut into small chunks or ground into granules. Textured vegetable protein may be purchased either unflavoured or flavoured to resemble meat. It is prepared simply by mixing with water or stock and leaving to stand for a few minutes, after which it may be incorporated into recipes as a meat substitute. Soya protein is also available incorporated into various vegetarian burgers, sausages, canned foods etc. As well as being a good source of fibre and high quality protein, Textured vegetable protein is fortified with vitamin-B12.

Tofu

Tofu is soya bean curd made from coagulated soya milk. Soya beans are soaked, crushed and heated to produce soya milk to which a coagulating agent such as calcium sulphate or calcium chloride is added. The resulting soya curd is then pressed to give tofu. Tofu is sometimes known as soya cheese, and is sold as blocks packaged in water. It can be bought as silken tofu, which is soft and creamy in texture, or as a denser, firmer version. The firmer kind may also be purchased smoked or marinated. Tofu tends be fairly bland tasting and is best used in recipes where flavour is imparted by other ingredients. Firm tofu may be marinated, fried, stir-fried, deep-fried, sauteed, diced and added to salads or casseroles. Silken tofu can be used for dips, spreads, sauces and sweet dishes. As well as having a high protein content, tofu also contains calcium, iron, and vitamins B1, B2 and B3.

Tempeh

Tempeh is a fermented soya bean paste made by inoculating cooked soya beans with the mould Rhizopus oligosporous. This mould forms a mycelium holding the soya beans together and is responsible for the black specks in tempeh. Tempeh has a chewy texture and distinctive flavour and can be used as a meat substitute in recipes. It may be deep-fried, shallow-fried, baked or steamed.

Miso

Miso is a fermented condiment made from soya beans, grain (rice or barley), salt and water. Miso production involves steaming polished rice which is then inoculated with the fungus Aspergillus oryzae and left to ferment to give an end product called koji. Koji is then mixed with soya beans which have been heated and extruded to form strands, together with salt and water. This is then left to ferment in large vats. Miso varies widely in flavour, colour, texture and aroma. It is used to give flavour to soups, stews, casseroles, and sauces.

Soya Sauces

True soya sauce, called shoyu, is made by fermenting soya beans with cracked roasted wheat, salt and water. Tamari is similar but slightly stronger and made without wheat (and so is gluten-free). Fermentation for shoyu and tamari takes about one year. Much of the soya sauce available in supermarkets is not true soya sauce but is made by chemical hydrolysis from defatted soya flour, caramel colouring, and corn syrup without any fermentation process.

Soya Dairy Alternatives

Soya milk is an alternative to dairy milk and is widely available in supermarkets and health food stores. It is most commonly made by soaking soya beans in water which are then strained to remove the fibre. It can also be made from soya protein isolate or soya flour. Compared to full fat cow's milk, soya milk has a lower fat content, a lower proportion of saturated fat, and no cholesterol. It is low in carbohydrate and provides a good source of protein. Some brands may be fortified with calcium, vitamin-D2, vitamin-B12 and vitamin-B2. Soya milk provides an alternative to cow's milk for people with cow's milk protein and lactose intolerance. Cow's milk allergy is most common in infants, and specially formulated soya milks are available for babies. Other soya milks are not suitable as sole foods for young infants.

Previously, the media has linked soya milk with having a high aluminium content. However, the aluminium content of soya milks is generally lower than cow's milk, and falls well within acceptable limits dictated by the World Health Organisation. Aluminium in soya milks can be regarded as negligible. Certain infant formulas (both cow's milk and soya milk based) produced from concentrates have been reported as having high levels of aluminium and their suitability for infants has been questioned. A number of different brands of soya milk may be purchased. These may be sweetened or unsweetened and vary in flavour. Market leaders are Provamel, Granose and Plamil. Some supermarkets also sell own-brand soya milk. In addition to soya milk, a range of flavoured soya desert and soya yoghurt products are available.

Other Soya Products

Soya oil and margarine are widely used and are high in polyunsaturated fats and low in saturated fats. Other less easily available soya foods include soya sprouts, soya nuts (roasted and seasoned soya beans), natto (fermented soya beans made with a bacteria, Bacillus subtilis), yuba (the skin formed on heated soya milk), soya flakes, soya flour, and high protein soya isolates and concentrates.

Mycoprotein

Mycoprotein is a food made by continuous fermentation of the fungus, Fusarium gramineurum. The fungus is grown in a large fermentation tower to which oxygen, nitrogen, glucose, minerals, and vitamins are continually added. After harvesting, the fungus is heat treated to reduce its RNA content to World Health Organisation recommended levels before being filtered and drained. The resulting sheet of fungal mycelia is mixed with free range egg egg albumen which acts a binder. Flavouring and colouring may also be added. The mycoprotein is then textured to resemble meat, before being sliced, diced or shredded. Mycoprotein is a source of protein, fibre, biotin, iron and zinc, and is low in saturated fat. Mycoprotein was developed by Rank Hovis McDougall, and is marketed under the name of Quorn by Marlow Foods Ltd (now owned by Premier Foods). A wide range of Quorn ready meals are available including curries, pies, and casseroles, and it may also be purchased as chunks, mince, sausages, burgers, fillets etc. Since January 2005 the entire Quorn range have been approved by the Vegetarian Society (previously the manufacturers had not been able to source enough free range eggs to use accross whole product range).

Wheat Protein

Wheat protein is derived from wheat gluten. It is sometimes called Seitan. Gluten is extracted from wheat and then processed to resemble meat. Wheat protein is marketed under the name of Wheatpro by Lucas Ingredients of Bristol. It has a greater similarity to meat than textured vegetable protein or mycoprotein and is used as a meat substitute in a range of foods. It is available in some health food stores.

Stumbling Blocks

- *Additives.*
- *Albumen:* Derived from eggs, probably battery.
- *Alcohol:* Many alcoholic drinks are fined (ie clarified) using animal ingredients, see beer and wine. Spirits are suitable for vegetarians except for some Russian and Eastern European Vodkas which may have used bone charcoal in their production. Watch out for cochineal in Campari.
- *Alpaca:* Animal derived clothing material.
- *Anchovies:* Small fish, found on pizzas and in some brands of worcester sauce.
- *Angora:* Animal derived clothing material.
- *Animal:* Fat Carcass fat not milk fat.
- *Aspic:* Savoury jelly derived from meat or fish.
- *Beer:* All cask conditioned "real" ales will have been fined with isinglass, and some keg, bottled and canned bitters, milds and stouts also. Lagers are generally chill filtered, but some brands may use isinglass on occasion.
- *Biscuits:* Quite likely to contain animal fats.
- *Bone:* Used in bone china and cutlery handles.
- *Bread:* Most large producers use vegetable based emulsifiers (E471, E472 etc), but local bakers may not. Some bakers may grease the tins with animal fat.
- *Breakfast Cereals:* Often fortified with vitamin D3.
- *Brushes:* Animal hair is commonly used for paint and shaving brushes.
- *Butter:* Pure butter is suitable for vegetarians.
- *Capsules:* Usually made from gelatine, vegetarian alternatives are coming onto the market.
- *Cashmere:* Animal derived clothing material.
- *Catering/Cookery:* Training may require the handling of meat.

- *Caviar Fish Eggs:* The fish must be killed to obtain the eggs.
- *Cheese:* Likely to have been produced using animal rennet.
- *Chewing Gum:* Often contain glycerine. Wrigleys use a vegetable glycerine.
- *Chips:* May have been fried in animal fat.
- *Chitin:* Produced from crab & shrimp shells.
- *Chocolate:* Watch out for whey and emulsifiers.
- *Clothing:* Many materials derived from animals, others causing environmental problems.
- *Cochineal E120*, made from crushed insects.
- *Crisps:* Often use whey as a flavour carrier, ready salted are the only clearly vegetarian flavour, though some beef crisps are flavoured with yeast extract and are therefore suitable.
- *Down:* Usually from slaughtered ducks or geese, though some live plucking does occur, used in bedding.
- *E Numbers:* European food additives numbering system, not all vegetarian.
- *Edible Fats:* Can mean animal fats.
- *Eggs:* Some vegetarians may wish to avoid battery eggs and/or barn eggs. The Vegetarian Society does not award its seedling symbol to any products containing eggs other than free range.
- *Emulsifiers:* May not be vegetarian.
- *Fast Food:* Watch out for Bean/Vegetable burgers being cooked with fish/chicken/meat products.
- *Fatty Acids:* May be of animal or vegetable origin.
- *Feathers:* Clothing material
- *Felt:* Made from wool or fur.
- *Fur:* Clothing material

- *Gelatin/Gelatine:* A gelling agent derived from animal ligaments, skins, tendons, bones etc. Alternatives such as Agar Agar, Carrageen and Gelozone exist.
- *Glycerine/Glycerol:* May be produced from animal fats, synthesised from propylene or from fermentation of sugars.
- *Gravy:* Vegetarian gravy mixes are available. Be careful in restaurants.
- *Honey:* Avoided by most vegans.
- *Ice Cream:* Look out for non dairy fats, E numbers, eggs.
- *Isinglass:* A fining agent derived from the swim bladders of certain tropical fish, especially the Chinese sturgeon.
- *Jelly:* Usually contains gelatine though Alternatives are available.
- *Lactose:* Produced from milk, sometimes as a by product of the cheese making process.
- *Lanolin:* Produced from sheep's wool. Used to make vitamin D3.
- *Leather:* Around 10% of the value of an animal at slaughter is in its skin.
- *Lecithin:* Nearly always produced from soya beans, though can be produced from eggs.
- *Margarines:* May contain animal fats, fish oils, vitamin D3, E numbers, whey, gelatine.
- *Mohair:* Animal derived clothing material.
- *Olive Oil:* No problems! Just worth knowing about.
- *Pasta:* May contain egg.
- *Pastry:* May contain animal fat.
- *Pepsin:* Enzyme from a pig's stomach, used like rennet.
- *Pet Foods:* Dogs are omnivorous and can be fed on an exclusively vegetarian diet. Canned and dried dog foods are available.
- *Photography:* All Photographic film uses gelatine.

- *Postage Stamps:* The backing glue is free from animal products.
- *Rennet:* An enzyme taken from the stomach of a newly killed calf used in the cheese making process. Vegetarian cheese is produced using microbial or fungal enzymes.
- *Restaurants:* Watch out for non-vegetarian cheese, battery eggs, stock.
- *Roe Fish:* Eggs.
- *Shellac:* Secreted under tree bark by insects. To be treated in a similar way to Honey.
- *Shoes:* Quality synthetic shoes are becoming more widely available.
- *Silk:* Harvesting silk used in invariably causes the death of the silk worm.
- *Soap:* Many soaps are not vegetarian since they use animal fats and/or glycerine. Vegetable oil based soaps are quite widely available.
- *Soft Drinks:* Some canned Orange drinks use gelatine as a carrier for added Beta Caratine. (This would not appear on the ingredients panel).
- *Soup:* Watch out for the stock.
- *Spirits:* (alcoholic that is!) possible problems with fining and filtering.
- *Stearic:* Acid May be vegetarian or not.
- *Stock:* May contain animal fat.
- *Suet:* Usually made from animal fat, vegetable versions are available.
- *Sweets:* Look out for gelatine in boiled sweets and mints, and cochineal in boiled sweets and Smarties. (some vegetarian sweets are listed by chocolate manufacturers.)
- *Toothpaste:* Many brands contain glycerine.
- *Vegan:* The Vegan Society produces The Animal Free Shopper which lists branded products suitable for vegans (available from The Vegetarian Society).

- *Vitamins:* Vitamin D2 is produced by sunlight acting on bacteria, however D3 is derived from lanolin from sheeps' wool therefore only D3 which is guaranteed sourced from wool sheared from live sheep is considered acceptable.
- *Seedling Symbol:* You can be sure that any products carrying the Vegetarian Society's V symbol have been thoroughly checked to ensure they are suitable for vegetarians.
- *Washing Powder:* Soap based powders may contain animal fats.
- *Whey:* Whey and whey powder are usually by-products of the cheese making process which mainly uses animal rennet.
- *Wine:* May have been fined using isinglass, dried blood, egg albumen, gelatine, chitin. Vegetarian alternatives include bentonite, kieselguhr, kaolin and silica gel. Non vintage port is fined with gelatine.
- *Wool* may not be so sheep friendly.
- *Worcester:* Sauce Most brands contain anchovies.
- *Yoghurts:* Some low fat yoghurts contain gelatine.

5

VEGETARIAN VITALITY

INTRODUCTION

One development in Britain's eating habits has dwarfed all others during the course of the last twenty years. Unprecedented in both speed and scale, vegetarianism has transformed the way we look at food, and the way we look at ourselves. The figures speak for themselves, we are discussing a change of diet which:

- had 100,000 adherents in 1945 but which today has over 3 million
- has doubled in size over the last ten years, with 2,000 people swelling its ranks every week.
- has convinced 40 per cent of the British population to cut down on or eliminate the red meat in their diet

Vegetarianism is nothing new, and various forms of meat-free eating have been practiced for thousands of years, but in the USA, many parts of Europe, and particularly here in the United Kingdom, this new diet has taken our dinner plates, our menus and our supermarket shelves by storm. Awareness of vegetarian health and vegetarian issues will play an increasingly important part in the work of anyone involved in food, catering, nutrition and health.

So what is a vegetarian? This may seem a superfluous question given the fact that we have all met vegetarians and have probably all eaten vegetarian food, but with so important a phenomenon, common definitions and terms of reference are invaluable. The Vegetarian Society, the acknowledged expert in this area, defines a vegetarian as: One who eats no fish, flesh or fowl and avoids all by-products of slaughter.

Within vegetarianism there are one or two other definitions which may be helpful, they represent the degrees to which vegetarian eating patterns are adhered to by individuals:

A lacto-ovo-vegetarian eats no fish, flesh or fowl but does consume both dairy products and eggs. Lacto ovo-vegetarians are undoubtedly the majority group amongst vegetarians.

A lacto-vegetarian follows the diet of a lacto-ovo-vegetarian, but he or she will not eat eggs.

A vegan is one who avoids all animal products, i.e. fish, flesh, fowl, eggs and dairy products.

Those who are new to vegetarianism may be curious as to why so many people are making so dramatic a change to their diet. Studies show vegetarians to be motivated by three key factors:

Respect for Animals

As our concern over animal welfare grows, particularly over factory farming systems, many individuals have chosen vegetarianism as a way to avoid inflicting unnecessary suffering upon animals.

Environmental Awareness

The Earth's natural resources and habitats are precious indeed.. Pollution, global warming and deforestation can all be linked to livestock farming. Many vegetarians see their diet changes as an immediate and effective way to halt environmental damage.

Human Health

As this report shows, the health benefits of a vegetarian diet are better documented now than ever. Heart disease, for example, unheard of before this century kills more people than any other single cause. Many are moving away from meat for the sake of their health. Every vegetarian is different and so may have other reasons than those above for excluding meat, but each vegetarian has one thing in common: a thought out and forward thinking attitude to the food on their plate.

VEGETARIAN HEALTH

A vegetarian diet confers a wide range of health benefits. Research has proven that vegetarians suffer less from many of the dieases linked to a modern Western diet: obesity, coronary heart disease, hypertension, type II diabetes, diet-related cancers, diverticular disease, constipation and gall stones (British Medical Association,1986; Dwyer, 1988).

Mortality

Epidemiological studies provide clear evidence that vegetarians have a reduced general and cause-specific mortality (McMichael, 1992).

In an 11-year study of 1,900 vegetarians in Germany, Chang-Claude (1992) found mortality from all causes was reduced by one-half compared with the general population. This was mainly attributable to reduced cardiovascular disease in both men and women. A longer duration of vegetarianism was associated with a lower risk, pointing to a real protective effect of the lifestyle (Chang-Claude, 1993).

A 12-year follow-up study of 6,115 British vegetarians and 5,015 meat-eaters found all cause premature mortality to be 20 per cent lower among the vegetarians after adjusting for the confounding effects of smoking, body mass index and socioeconomic status (Thorogood, 1994). Cancer mortality was 39 per cent lower and ischaemic heart disease 28 per cent lower among the vegetarians.

A 21-year study of Californian Seventh-Day Adventists also revealed a significant association between meat consumption and all causes of mortality (Kahn, 1984).

While other factors influencing health such as socioeconomic differences, smoking and physical activity may play a confounding rôle in these studies, there is sufficient evidence to suggest that a reduced risk of mortality is directly linked to a vegetarian diet.

Cardiovascular Disease

Cardiovascular disease is the main cause of premature mortality in Britain, with most deaths being caused by coronary heart disease.

Vegetarians have a significantly lower incidence of coronary heart disease than meat-eaters. Burr and Butland (1988) found mortality from heart disease was 29 per cent lower in a study of more than 6,000 British vegetarians compared with a control group of health-conscious meat-eaters.

A study of more than 25,000 Seventh-Day Adventists noted a definite dose-related link between meat consumption and heart disease (Snowdon, 1984). Among men aged 45 to 64, those who ate meat daily were three times more likely to die from heart disease than those who did not eat meat.

The degenerative processes leading to heart disease can begin at an early age. Atherosclerosis, the forming of fibrous plaques on arterial walls and one of the first stages in the development of cardiovascular disease, has been observed in young children and adolescents. The Coronary Artery Risk Development in Young Adults (CARDIA) study examined the relationship between diet and health in more than 5,000 young adults aged 18 to 30 (Slattery 1991). Vegetarians were found to have a greatly improved cardiovascular fitness and a lower risk of heart disease.

One way that a vegetarian diet is thought to protect against heart disease is the lower cholesterol levels seen in vegetarians. Raised cholesterol is widely recognised as a primary risk factor for heart disease and studies have consistently demonstrated serum cholesterol levels in vegetarians as being around 10 per cent lower than in non-vegetarians (Burr, 1981; Knuiman and West, 1982; Thorogood, 1990). This figure may result in a 20 to 50 per cent reduction in the incidence of heart disease (Law, 1994). The lower serum cholesterol levels in vegetarians is largely due to lowered low-density-lipoprotein (LDL) cholesterol. This is the cholesterol fraction associated with heart disease.

Healthy eating advice aimed at reducing the risk of heart disease often encourages the use of lean meat cuts. However, in a comparison between a vegetarian diet and a lean meat diet (Kestin, 1989), the vegetarian diet was shown to lower cholesterol more effectively and so lessen the risk of cardiovascular disease.

The California Lifestyle Heart Trial indicated that a low-fat vegetarian diet together with other lifestyle changes such as increased exercise and stress management can actually reverse the progress of heart disease by reducing cholesterol plaques in arteries (Ornish, 1990). Barnard (1992) has shown a low-fat vegetarian diet can achieve high levels of compliance and acceptability among patients with heart disease.

Obesity

Obesity is a major health problem in the UK and its incidence is increasing in both adults and children. Around 12 per cent of women and 8 per cent of men are clinically obese (Gregory, 1990) and many more are overweight.

Obesity predisposes sufferers to a range of conditions including cardiovascular disease, type II diabetes, and hormone-dependent cancers such as breast cancer. Vegetarians are typically leaner than meat-eaters and obesity is less common in vegetarian populations. Body mass index (BMI) for vegetarians is lower than in meat-eaters and closer to desirable levels (Thorogood, 1989). Levin (1986a) found the prevalence of obesity to be 5.4 per cent in a vegetarian group compared with 19.5 per cent in non-vegetarians. This may be due to vegetarians' lower energy intake overall, with a lower proportion of energy being supplied by fat.The established measure for obesity is the Body Mass Index (BMI). This is obtained by dividing a persons weight (kg) by the square of their height (m). Normal weight is defined as a BMI of 20-25. A BMI of 25 to 30 is overweight, over 30 is obese.

Obesity is caused by an individual taking in more energy from food than they are using up in physical activity. Dieting is generally ineffective and repeated weight loss and gain can play a part in osteoporosis and heart disease. A healthy diet based on starchy foods such as bread, potatoes, rice and pasta together with fruits and vegetables and combined with increased physical activity is far more effective in bringing about successful weight loss.

Hypertension

Hypertension, or high blood pressure, can contribute to heart disease, strokes and kidney failure. Both cross sectional populaton studies (Armstrong, 1977; Rouse, 1983) and controlled trials in hypertensive subjects (Margetts, 1986) provide evidence that vegetarians have lower blood pressure than non-vegetarians.

The reason for this is unclear. Studies suggest that the effect is not due to changes in any specific nutrient intake but the overall effect of combined nutrient change (Beilin, 1990).

Diabetes

Around one million people in the India suffer from diabetes. Of these, about 75 per cent have type II diabetes (non-insulin dependent).

A study found vegetarians had a substantially lower risk of type II diabetes than non-vegetarians. The link between meat consumption and incidence of diabetes remained after contributory factors such as weight, physical activity and other dietary factors were accounted for.

Dietary recommendations for diabetics encourage a high intake of complex carbohydrates and fibre and low consumption of total and saturated fat. Vegetarian diets tend to match these recommendations more closely.

The relative leanness of vegetarians also protects against diabetes, obesity being a major risk factor.

Gall Stones

Gall stones are composed af cholesterol, bile pigments and calcium salts. They form in the gall bladder and can cause severe pain.

A study of more than 750 women found that non-vegetarians were almost twice as likely to develop gall stones as vegetarians.

Diverticular Disease and Bowel Function

Diverticular disease is widespread in the UK. Symptoms include abdominal pain and a disturbed bowel habit, usually constipation but sometimes diarrhoea. Gear (1979) found it to be significantly less frequent among vegetarians, probably due to the higher fibre content of vegetarian diets.

The high fibre content of vegetarian diets has also been linked with decreased incidence of constipation, appendicitis, irritable bowel syndrome, haemorrhoids and varicose veins (Dickerson, 1985).

Cancer

Cancer is second only to coronary heart disease as a cause of death in Britain. Accounting for around 25 per cent of all premature deaths with lung, breast and colo-rectal cancers being the most common.

It is estimated that at least one third all cancers are directly related to diet. Research has indicated that vegetarian diets may offer protection against diet-related cancer.

Plant Foods and Cancer

Plant foods contain a number of substances which are believed to protect against cancer. Indoles, lignans, isoflavones, protease inhibitors and others have all been shown to be potent anti-carcinogens and may play an important role in the lower cancer incidence among vegetarians.

In contrast, cooked meat and fish contains carcinogens known as heterocyclic amines (HA's). These are present at high levels in the urine of people consuming cooked meats and have been shown to be metabolically active in humans. Evidence suggests meat-derived HA's may play a role in breast, colon and pancreatic cancer (Snyderwine 1994).

HEALTHY EATING

Vegetarian diets vary greatly between individuals, as do eating patterns. However, a typical vegetarian diet can closely match current dietary recommendations for healthy eating.

There is a high level of consensus concerning healthy eating recommendations. Cannon (1992) analysed one hundred reports on food, nutrition and public health published between 1961 and 1991 and found that experts worldwide agreed that diets high in fat and saturated fat and with insufficient fruit, vegetables, cereals and other starchy foods were a major cause of coronary heart disease, some cancers, obesity, diabetes and constipation.

Current healthy eating advice focuses on reducing total and saturated fat intake while increasing the consumption of complex carbohydrates and dietary fibre. The major sources of total fat and saturated fat in the diet are meat and dairy products. Complex carbohydrates and fibre are provided by plant foods.

By far the easiest method of successfully implementing dietary advice is to limit the intake of foods of animal origin and increase the consumption of fruit, vegetables, cereals and pulses.

As a basic guide, it is recommended that a vegetarian diet should include the following each day:

- 3 or 4 servings of cereals/grains-provides energy, fibre, B vitamins, calcium and iron.
- 2 or 3 servings of pulses, nuts or seeds-provides protein, energy, fibre, calcium, iron and zinc
- 4 or 5 servings of fruit or vegetables, including: dark green leafy vegetables-for folate, calcium and iron; red, orange and yellow vegetables-for beta-carotene; fresh fruit-for vitamin C; dried fruit-for fibre and iron.
- 2 servings of dairy or soya products-provides protein, energy, calcium and other minerals, vitamin B12, vitamin D.
- A small amount of plant oils, margarine or butter-provides energy, essential fatty acids, vitamin E (plant oils) and vitamins A and D (margarine or butter).

VEGETARIAN NUTRITION

Energy

Energy intakes of vegetarians and vegans meet UK recommended levels (Thorogood, 1990; Draper, 1993) and are in line with World Health Organisation recommendations for adults engaged in light to moderate activities (WHO, 1985). They are also similar to recorded energy intakes for meat-eaters (Gregory, 1990).

Fats

Accepted dietary recommendations are that most adults in the UK should reduce their total dietary fat intake.

The 1991 UK Dietary Reference Values; (DRV's) recommend that total fat intake for the population should be no more than 33 per cent of dietary energy (including alcohol) or 35 per cent of energy derived from food. Saturated fatty acids should provide no more than 11 per cent of food energy. The Government policy document The Health of the Nation (Department of Health, 1992) endorsed these targets.

The 1992 National Food Survey (MAFF, 1993) found that fat supplied over 41 per cent of food energy, with over 16 per cent coming from saturated fatty acids.

In general, vegetarians have a lower intake of fat than non-vegetarians (Taber and Cook, 1980). However, the percentage of food energy supplied by fats may still be higher than is desirable. Draper (1993) found 37 per cent of food energy came from fat among vegetarians. This was not significantly different from the 38 per cent among meat-eaters (Gregory, 1990). Vegan diets came closer to the ideal, with 34 per cent of food energy coming from fat. Vegetarians must ensure that they do not simply substitute high-fat dairy products or convenience vegetarian foods for meat and meat products.

While total fat intake may not always differ significantly between vegetarians and non-vegetarians, vegetarians have consistently been shown to have a lower intake of saturated fat, a higher intake of polyunsaturated fat, and a higher polyunsaturated to saturated fat (P:S) ratio. This may play a part in vegetarians' lower incidence of cardiovascular disease.

Essential Fatty Acids

Two polyunsaturated fatty acids must be present in the diet as the body is unable to synthesise them. These essential fatty acids are linoleic acid and alpha-linolenic acid. Linoleic acid is present at high levels in many vegetables, fruits, nuts, cereals and plant oils; alpha-linolenic acid is less abundant but is present in linseed, soyabean and rapeseed oils at high levels, as well as in pulses, walnuts, broccoli and leafy green vegetables.

Alpha-linolenic acid is converted to eicosapentaenoic acid (EPA) in the body, which is in turn converted to docosahexanoic acid (DHA). DHA is required for retinal and brain function and is important for foetal and infant development.

Fish Oils: Habitual consumption of fish oils have been shown to be associated with reduced mortality from heart disease. This is believed to be due to the high levels of eicosapentaenoic acid (EPA), an omega-3 fatty acid, present in fish oils.

EPA intake is low or lacking altogether on vegetarian or vegan diets. However, plant foods contain alpha-linolenic acid (ALA) which can be converted in the body to EPA. Research has shown that increasing ALA intake can lead to similar cardiovascular benefits as seen with increased EPA intake. These include reduced platelet aggregation and so a reduced risk of thrombosis (Renaud, 1986).

Vegan diets are devoid of EPA and DHA while vegetarian diets provide small amounts in dairy products. Vegetarian and vegan women should ensure their diets include sources of alpha-linolenic acid during pregnancy and breast feeding. Sanders (1992) has suggested vegans should use plant oils with a low ratio of linoleic acid to alpha-linolenic acid, eg soya bean or rapeseed oil, as a high ratio may inhibit conversion of alpha-linolenic acid to DHA. It is important that the diet has the correct balance of linoleic acid to alpha-linolenic acid and this can be achieved on a vegetarian diet.

Carbohydrates and Dietary Fibre

Dietary advice is to increase consumption of complex carbohydrates and dietary fibre (non-starch polysaccharides, or NSP) by increasing the consumption of plant foods. Compared with non-vegetarians, vegetarians typically have diets higher in both complex carbohydrate and fibre. Fibre consumption by vegetarians invariably exceed the DRV of 1.8g/day for adults, tending to range from 33g/day upwards. There has been some concern over the possibility that diets excessively high in fibre may reduce the bioavailability of certain minerals, including calcium, iron and zinc. However, populations habitually consuming high fibre diets are not characterised by mineral deficiencies.

Protein

Protein intakes of vegetarians are generally lower than those of non-vegetarians but still meet UK dietary recommendations. Jackson (1993) calculated the average intake of protein by vegetarians in the UK to be 57g/day, compared with 75g/day for non-vegetarians. Draper (1993) found protein intake in vegetarians to be 66g/day for men and 56g/day for women. UK recommendations are 55g/day for men and 45g/day for women. Vegetarians eating a balanced diet obtain protein from a variety of food sources. This means essential amino acid requirements can be met by plant foods. The idea of combining proteins from different plant sources to provide all of the necessary essential amino acids is known as protein complementing. Previous emphasis on protein complementing has been overstated and it is now widely accepted that it is not something vegetarians eating a balanced diet need consider.

In fact, the lower protein intake of vegetarians may be beneficial as there is concern that high protein intake may be associated with health risks. Poor or failing kidney function may be aggravated and the loss of calcium from bones increased by excessive dietary protein.

In both instances, animal protein appears to be more harmful than plant protein. A high intake of animal protein may also play a contributory role in raised blood pressure. A lower animal protein intake almost inevitably results in a lower fat intake, especially saturated fat, as foods high in animal protein also tend to be high in fat. Dietary advice is to increase the proportion of protein from plant sources (NACNE, 1983).

Vitamins

A balanced vegetarian diet supplies all the vitamins the body requires. Surveys have shown the vitamin status of vegetarian populations to be satisfactory (Shultz, 1983; Helman, 1987). Draper (1993) found intakes of most vitamins for adult vegetarians in the UK to be adequate and in many cases higher than the national average. Certain vitamins, such as vitamin B12 and vitamin D, are primarily found in animal foods and so concerns over the vitamin status of vegetarians and vegans tend to focus on these. The only reliable unfortified sources of vitamin B12 are animal foods. Research into possible plant food sources of B12 have found that either no significant amount of B12 is present or that any B12 present is a structurally similar analogue that cannot be utilised by the body. Vegetarians generally obtain adequate B12 from dairy products. Draper (1993) found mean intake of vitamin B12 in vegetarians to be 181 per cent of the RNI in men and 121 per cent in women.

Vegans tend to have lower vitamin B12 intakes which may or may not reach recommended levels. Vegans should be advised to ensure their diet includes foods that are fortified with vitamin B12. A range of vitamin B12 fortified foods is available, including yeast extracts, vegetable stocks, vegetable burger mixes, soya milks, margarines, breakfast cereals and herbal soft drinks.

Vitamin D is present in vegetarian diets in dairy products. Vegans tend to have low vitamin D intakes, fortified margarines being the main dietary source. However, it is assumed that sufficient amounts of the vitamin can be obtained by dermal synthesis due to the action of sunlight on exposed skin.

Vegans or vegetarians consuming limited dairy products and who are not exposed to sunlight may be advised to take supplementary vitamin D. Groups at risk of insufficient vitamin D include infants and elderly persons confined indoors.

Riboflavin (vitamin B2) may also be low on vegan diets, the main dietary source being milk and milk products. Vegans should ensure their diet includes other sources of riboflavin. such as fortified breakfast cereals, yeast extract and mushrooms.

Minerals

Vegetarians have adequate mineral intakes and a balanced vegetarian diet does not lead to mineral deficiencies (Abdulla, 1984; Freeland-Graves, 1988).

Studies of the mineral status of vegetarians have concentrated on iron and zinc, meat and meat products being a major source for both of these minerals. Vegetarians appear to be at no greater risk of iron deficiency than non-vegetarians and have an adequate intake of iron from plant food sources (Anderson, 1981; Levin, 1986b). Praper (1993) showed mean iron intakes of both vegetarians and vegans met the UK DRVs and indeed exceeded the mean intake of comparative non-vegetarian adults from a nationwide survey.

IRON AND DISEASE

Recent studies have suggested that high levels of iron in the body may be linked to both heart disease and cancer. Satonen (1992) studied nearly 2,000 men aged between 42 and 60 and found that both high blood ferritin levels and high dietary iron intake were linked to heart attack risk. Similarly, Stevens (1994) found that people with elevated levels of iron in the body developed cancer at nearly twice the rate of those with normal iron levels.

It is suggested iron can cause cell and tissue damage in the body by generating free radicals. As haem iron in meat is more readily absorbed than non-haem iron on plants then excess meat consumption may be linked with chronic disease.

Non-haem iron from plant foods is less readily absorbed by the body than haem iron from meat and meat products. However, vitamin C greatly improves non-haem iron absorption and vegetarian diets are generally rich in vitamin C. It is recommended that plant food sources of iron are consumed at the same time as vitamin C rich foods or drinks to facilitate absorption. Good sources of iron for vegetarians include leafy green vegetables, pulses (including baked beans), dried fruit, wholemeal bread and fortified breakfast cereals. There is some suggestion that vegetarians may adapt to their diet by an increased ability to absorb iron (Anderson, 1981). For this reason, new vegetarians may be at a greater risk of iron deficiency than long-term vegetarians (Helman, 1987).

Zinc status among vegetarians also appears to be adequate (Levin, 1986b; Draper, 1993). Freeland-Graves (1980) found no significant differences in mean zinc intakes between vegetarians and non-vegetarians. However, some vegetarian women had low zinc intakes and this was attributed to limited consumption of zinc-rich foods such as pulses and wholegrains. Low zinc intake reflects poor food choices rather than inadequate food sources.

The bioavailability of both iron and zinc is reduced by fibre, phytates and other dietary factors present in plant foods. However, Anderson (1981) found the iron and zinc status of vegetarian women was normal despite high fibre and phytate intake while other studies have confirmed that a high fibre intake does not appear to affect mineral utilisation by vegetarians (Rattan, 1986; Kelsay 1988).

Due to their avoidance of dairy products it has been suggested that vegans may be at risk of calcium deficiency. However, studies have indicated that vegan populations receive adequate calcium from plant foods (Abdulla, 1981, Draper, 1993). Vegetarians have calcium intakes similar to or exceeding those of non-vegetarians.

There is also evidence to suggest vegans may be at risk of iodine deficiency, milk and milk products being the main dietary source (Key, 1992; Draper, 1993). However, many vegans consume edible seaweeds which are good sources. Cereals and vegetables can also contain available amounts, depending on iodine levels in the soil in which they are grown.

SPECIAL DIETARY GROUPS

Some groups may have special dietary needs. These include pregnant and lactating women, infants and children, and those following a therapeutic diet for medical reasons. The needs of all these groups can be adequately met by a vegetarian diet.

Pregnancy and Lactation

During pregnancy, women have increased nutritional requirements for energy, protein, folate, vitamin A, vitamin C, and vitamin D.

The increased energy and protein requirements are small and can be met without any obvious changes in food intake. If energy intake is reduced due to appetite changes or morning sickness then a reduction in high fibre foods and increased energy and nutrient dense foods may be appropriate. The extra vitamins needed are generally present at higher levels in vegetarian than non-vegetarian diets, with the exception of vitamin D. Both vegetarian and non-vegetarian pregnant women may be advised to take supplementary vitamin D.

There are no official dietary recommendations for increased mineral requirements during pregnancy. However, it is important that adequate intakes are ensured in order to maintain body stores.

Ideally, all women should have sufficient body iron stores to cope with the demands of pregnancy. However, many women may have low levels of stored iron and mild anaemia is not uncommon during pregnancy. Vegetarian women need to ensure that they are obtaining adequate iron from their diets.

Vegan women need to ensure that their dietary needs for vitamin B12, vitamin D and calcium are met during pregnancy.

During lactation, increased protein and vitamin needs can be met by a varied vegetarian diet. Recommended intakes for calcium and zinc are also increased and so extra food sources of these may be appropriate.

Infants and Children

A vegetarian diet is suitable for children of all ages and can provide all the nutrients needed for normal growth and development.

Studies have found that vegetarian children show similar patterns of growth and development as non-vegetarian children. Anthropometric measurements indicate vegetarian children are similar in height, weight and skinfold measurements. Vegetarian children are often leaner and less likely to be obese. Sabate (1991) studied 895 non-vegetarian children and 870 vegetarian children aged 7 to 18 years and found that for both boys and girls the vegetarian children were taller. This did not change after adjustment for parental height and socioeconomic class. The vegetarian children consumed less convenience foods and dairy products and more starchy foods, pulses, fruit and vegetables which may play a part in their being taller.

No differences in maturation or timing of growth spurts has been observed between vegetarian and non-vegetarian boys. Vegetarian girls may have a delayed maturation onset, though heights finally attained are similar to non-vegetarian counterparts (Sabate, 1992). This maturation delay is linked with a later age of menarche which may be protective against breast and other hormone dependant cancers in later life.

Children raised on vegan diets also display growth and development within acceptable limits though they are more likely to be lighter and leaner and may also be shorter in stature than other children.

Where concern has been expressed over the growth of infants and children on vegetarian-type diets it has involved communities where diets followed are very restrictive and not typical vegetarian or vegan diets. These have included Dutch children on macrobiotic diets and Israeli Black Hebrews.

Infants, children and adolescents can meet all of their nutritional requirements on a vegetarian diet. Nutrient intakes for vegetarian children compare favourably with dietary recommendations providing that total fat intakes are not excessive and iron intakes are adequate.

Nutritional deficiencies are no more commonly reported among vegetarian children than among omnivore children. Vegan children may need more carefully planned diets to ensure nutrient needs are met, especially for vitamin B12, vitamin D and calcium.

As well as meeting dietary needs, vegetarian diets for children may be beneficial in promoting health and protecting against a variety of health problems including constipation, other bowel disorders and obesity The typical diet of school children in the UK is high in fat and low in fibre and complex carbohydrates and it is recommended children eat more starchy foods, fruit and vegetables.

A vegetarian diet can also protect against risk factors for chronic degenerative diseases in later life (Jacobs, 1988). Risk factors for diet-related diseases, including cardiovascular disease, can be identified in children and dietary habits which influence these risks are learnt in childhood. A vegetarian diet for children can help establish healthy dietary patterns which may be carried on into adult life and help protect against chronic disease.

A healthy adult diet is not necessarily appropriate for infants and young children under the age of five years. Diets low in fat and high in fibre are unsuitable for infants as their limited stomach capacity may be filled-up before they are able to meet their energy or nutrient needs. Infant diets need to include energy and nutrient dense foods such as cereal products, mashed lentils, vegetable oils, bananas and avocados. Excessive intake of high fibre or watery foods should be avoided.

Therapeutic Diets

As well as being protective against many chronic degenerative diseases, vegetarian diets have been effectively used in the treatment of various conditions including rheumatoid arthritis (Kjeldsen-Kragh, 1991) and nephrotic syndrome (D'Amico, 1992). A vegetarian diet is also appropriate for most people following a therapeutic diet for medical conditions, such as diabetes or coeliac disease. Professional dietetic assistance should be sought for all therapeutic diets.

Conclusion

1. A vegetarian diet can confer a wide range of health benefits and may protect against chronic degenerative diseases including coronary heart disease and diet related cancer.
2. Blood cholesterol level is typically 10 per cent lower in vegetarian groups compared with non-vegetarian populations. A 10 per cent lowering of blood cholesterol may result in up to a 50 per cent reduction in the incidence of heart disease.
3. A vegetarian diet is more effective at lowering blood cholesterol and reducing the risk of cardiovascular disease than a diet in which lean meat is regularly consumed. A low-fat vegetarian diet has been shown to be acceptable to heart patients and high levels of dietary compliance have been demonstrated.

4. A balanced vegetarian diet tends to correspond closely with current dietary advice for healthy eating. Vegetarians tend to have lower intakes of total and saturated fat and higher intakes of complex carbohydrates and dietary fibre.
5. Despite vegetarian diets generally being lower in fat, the percentage of food energy from fat may still be higher than dietary recommendations. Vegetarians need to ensure that consumption of high-fat foods, especially dairy products, convenience foods and margarine and plant oils, is not excessive.
6. A balanced vegetarian diet can supply all the vitamins and minerals required. Vitamin and mineral status in vegetarian groups is satisfactory and intakes are often higher than in non-vegetarians. Vegetarian diets high in fibre do not appear to compromise mineral status.
7. Vegetarians generally have satisfactory iron levels. It is recommended that dietary sources of iron are consumed together with vitamin C rich foods or drinks to facilitate iron absorption.
8. Vegans should ensure their diets include foods which are fortified with vitamin B12. These include certain yeast extracts, vegetable burger mixes, soya milks, margarines and breakfast cereals.
9. A vegetarian diet is appropriate for infants and children and provides all the nutrients required for normal growth and development. Vegetarian children are similar in height and weight to non-vegetarian children and are less likely to be obese or overweight.
10. A healthy vegetarian diet for adults is not appropriate for infants or children below the age of 5 years. Diets low in fat and high in fibre can fill up infants before they have received adequate energy and nutrients. Infant diets need to include fewer fibre rich foods and more energy and nutrient dense foods.

6

Diet and Diseases

CANCER

Cancer is the second leading cause of death in Britain, accounting for 25% of all deaths. It has been estimated that diet may be linked to 30-70% of cancers (Doll, 1990). Certain cancers, such as colon, breast and prostate are clearly diet related (Cummings & Bingham, 1998).

Sir Kenneth Calman, Chief Medical Officer, has stated (1997) that "there is a relationship between eating red meat and cancer".

The Oxford Vegetarian Study found cancer mortality to be 39% lower among vegetarians compared with meat-eaters (Thorogood, 1994).

A study of 23,000 largely vegetarian Seventh Day Adventists found cancer mortality rates to be 50-70% of those of the general population for several cancer sites unrelated to smoking or alcohol (Phillips, 1975).

Professor Nick Day of the University of Cambridge and the European Prospective Study into Cancer has stated that vegetarians may suffer 40% fewer cancers than the general population.

The World Cancer Research Fund's dietary advice to minimise cancer risk involve reducing the intake of dietary fat and increasing the consumption of fruits, vegetables and wholegrains.

COLON CANCER

Vegetarians have lower rates of colon cancer than non-vegetarians (Phillips, 1980). Incidence of colon cancer has been strongly linked to the consumption of meat (Armstrong, 1975, Singh & fraser, 1998). Willett (1990) carried out a study of over 88 000 women aged 34 to 59 years. Women eating red meat daily ran over twice the risk of developing colon cancer than women eating red meat less than once a month.

Reduced incidence of colon cancer in vegetarians may be attributed to dietary differences which include increased fibre intake, increased consumption of fruit and vegetables, and decreased intake of total fat and saturated fat. The mechanism by which a vegetarian diet is protective against colon cancer is unclear and a great deal of research is being carried out in this area.

It has been suggested that secondary bile acids are carcinogens which may play an important role in colon cancer. These are derived by bacterial metabolism from primary bile acids made in the liver and secreted into the intestine. Vegetarians have lower levels of secondary bile acids than non-vegetarians (Turjiman, 1984). The differences in bacterial populations between the intestines of vegetarians and non-vegetarians may also be important. Bacterial flora in vegetarians has been shown to possess reduced ability to transform bile acids into potential carcinogens (Johansson, 1990).

The role of dietary fibre in prevention of colon cancer may also be important. This was first noted in 1971 when it was suggested the high incidence of colon cancer in Western countries was linked to low fibre diets. Other dietary components associated with high fibre foods, such as folate, have also been implicated as having protective effects.

Chen (2002) found that the risk of distal stomach adenocarcinoma was positively associated with red meat intake.

BREAST CANCER

Evidence also suggests a vegetarian diet is protective against breast cancer (Phillips, 1975). This may be due to the increased fibre and reduced fat intake of vegetarian diets. Vegetarian diets can alter the levels of circulating sex hormones which may have a beneficial effect. Fibre is thought to be protective by modifying circulating oestrogen levels.

Studies of adolescent girls have shown age of menarche to be delayed in vegetarians (Sabate, 1992). Later age of menarche is believed to lower the risk of breast cancer in adult life.

OTHER CANCERS

Studies have shown vegetarians to suffer less from various other cancers.

Mills (1989) studied the incidence of prostate cancer amongst 14,000 Seventh Day Adventists and found a relationship between increased risk and increasing animal product consumption.

Mills (1988) also found pancreatic cancer to be associated with consumption of animal products. Increasing consumption of fruit, vegetables and pulses was shown to have a protective effect.

Rao (1989) found a vegetarian diet to be protective against oesophageal cancer.

Studies have also shown vegetarians to have lower incidence of lung cancer. This can be largely attributed to vegetarians tending to be non-smokers. High consumption of fruit has also shown to be protective against lung cancer (Fraser, 1991).

DIVERTICULAR DISEASE

Diverticular disease affects the colon and symptoms include lower abdominal pain and disturbed bowel habit. It occurs frequently in western countries where intake of dietary fibre is low. Gear (1979) found diverticular disease to be less frequent in vegetarians, 12% of vegetarians studied having diverticular disease compared with 33% of non-vegetarians. This is thought to be due to the increased fibre of vegetarian diets.

Gall Stones

Gall stones are composed of cholesterol, bile pigments and calcium salts. They form in the gall bladder and can cause severe pain. A study of over 750 women found the incidence of gall stones to be less frequent in vegetarians. 25% of non-vegetarians compared with 12% of vegetarians had gall stones. After controlling for age and body weight, non-vegetarians were found to have a relative risk of gall stones almost twice that of the vegetarians. Vegetarians are leaner, and consume more dietary fibre and less dietary cholesterol, all of which is believed to protect against gall stone formation.

Kidney Stones

Kidney stones form in the kidney and can cause considerable pain when passing down the urinary tract. Prevalence of kidney stones is lower in vegetarians.

A high intake of animal protein increases the urinary loss of calcium and oxalate, known risk factors in kidney stone formation. Meat is also high in purines which leads to increased uric acid in the urine. Urinary uric acid is also a risk factor for kidney stones.

Osteoporosis

Osteoporosis is the loss of calcium from bone tissue, leading to bones that are brittle and liable to fracture. It is most commonly seen in postmenopausal women.

Some studies have suggested that vegetarians may be at lower risk of osteoporosis than non-vegetarians. Sellmeyer's study (2001) found that elderly women with a high dietary ratio of animal to vegetable protein intake had more rapid femoral neck bone loss and a greater risk of hip fracture than those with a low ratio.

Marsh (1988) found bone loss to be considerably less in postmenopausal women who were vegetarian than those who were non-vegetarian. The non-vegetarian diet contained higher amounts of sulphur, which derived from animal protein. Dietary sulphur increases the acidity of urine, which results in increased urinary calcium loss. Increased urinary calcium loss is related to increased calcium loss from bone tissue.

Hip fractures associated with osteoporosis has been shown to be higher in countries consuming a diet high in animal protein.

Appendicitis

The Oxford Vegetarian Study found that people who do not eat meat have a 50% lower risk of requiring an emergency appendicectomy that those who do.

OTHER DISEASES

A vegetarian diet has been claimed to reduce the risk of gout, hiatus hernia, constipation, haemorrhoids, and varicose veins. These diseases are linked to diets low in fibre and high in saturated fat.

Food Poisoning and Pesticide Residues

Over 50,000 cases of food poisoning are reported every year and the actual incidence of food poisoning is estimated to be ten times this figure. Meat, eggs and dairy products are the primary sources of food poisoning. Professor Richard Lacey of the University of Leeds has stated that "More than 95% of food poisoning is derived from meat and poultry products".

Pesticide residues in foods include PCB's and dioxins. These are found in highest concentrations in meat, fish and dairy products. Studies have shown these toxic chemicals can be passed on from pregnant women to infants during both pregnancy and lactation and may damage the developing nervous systems. Hall (1992) has stated a vegetarian diet minimises the risk of contamination.

Rheumatoid Arthritis

Studies have shown that vegetarian diets can be successfully used to treat the symptoms of rheumatoid arthritis and other rheumatic diseases. Kjeldsen-Kragh (1991) found that rheumatoid arthritis patients following a vegetarian diet suffered considerably fewer swollen and tender joints and less stiffness or pain.

Nephrotic Syndrome

Nephrotic syndrome is a kidney condition involving high levels of protein in the urine which may lead to progressive kidney damage as well as promoting atherosclerosis and heart disease. Studies have shown a low protein vegan diet can be used to reduce the symptoms of nephrotic syndrome (D'Amico, 1992).

The China Health Project

The China Project on Nutrition, Health & Environment is a massive study involving researchers from China, Cornell University in Ithaca, New York, and the University of Oxford, into the relationships between diet, lifestyles and disease-related mortality in 6500 Chinese subjects from 65 mostly rural or semi-rural counties.

The rural Chinese diet is largely vegetarian or vegan, and involves less total protein, less animal protein, less total fat and animal fat, and more carbohydrate and fibre than the average Western diet. Blood cholesterol levels are significantly lower. Heart disease, cancer, obesity, diabetes, and osteoporosis are all uncommon. Areas in which they are becoming more frequent are areas where the population has moved towards a more Western diet with increasing consumption of animal products.

The China Health Project has clearly demonstrated the health benefits of a diet based on plant foods. One of the Project's co-ordinators, Dr Colin Campbell of Cornell University, has stated that "We're basically a vegetarian species and should be eating a wide variety of plant foods and minimising our intake of animal foods."

7

Increase Food Intake

INTRODUCTION

If you have lost a lot of weight due to illness, your doctor or dietitian may advise you to increase your intake of energy and protein. They may try to persuade you that your vegetarian diet is unsuitable. Do stick to your principles. This Information Sheet is to enable you to choose vegetarian foods which will help you to gain weight and recover from illness.

The energy density of foods is important when trying to gain weight. Energy density refers to the amount of energy or calories compared to the weight of the food. Vegetable foods tend to be less energy dense and so it is particularly important for vegetarians to be aware of suitable foods.

When you are poorly, modern healthy eating advice to reduce fat, reduce sugar and increase fibre, is peripheral to your immediate needs. If you know you must increase your energy and protein intake, you can do so by increasing your fat and sugar intake, and also try to avoid large amounts of fibre.

If You are Underweight but Healthy

If you are not ill but feel you are underweight and need to gain then not all the advice on this sheet is suitable for you. You should try and increase your food intake without consuming too much fat and sugar although a little with the right type of food is fine. For example, you can use olive oil on baked or boiled potatoes and sugar in a nutritious wholemeal fruit cake.

Regular meals, especially breakfast, are important if you find it difficult to gain weight. Taking your time with meals and making sure you are relaxed is also important to ensure that your digestive system functions properly. A glass of wine with an evening meal is beneficial to relax you as well as stimulating your digestive juices.

Some people are just naturally thin no matter how much they eat and the envy of those who gain weight easily. As long as you are in good health and do not drop below the recommended range of weights for your height you should not worry. Exercise can help build up your muscles and make you feel better about your body shape.

Lack of Appetite

If your appetite is poor, you must not forget to eat. Try to have small but frequent meals, and if you can manage, snacks in between. You may like to try nutritious drinks between meals.

If you feel nauseous, try to avoid strong cooking smells and have a short walk or perhaps just sit in the fresh air before a meal.

PROTEIN

Protein is essential to the body, for repair, to enable the immune system to function and for recovery from illness. If you are recovering from illness, it is important to include adequate protein in your diet. Good vegetarian sources of protein include: cereals, nuts & seeds, soya products (soya milk, tofu, tempeh etc) and pulses. Milk, yoghurt, cheese, and free range eggs are also excellent protein sources for the non-vegan.

You must ensure that you include a protein source at each meal. Try to choose the energy dense sources of protein that are relatively soft and which do not contain to much fibre, for example, the soya or dairy sources of protein.

Try nut butters. There are many more available other than peanut butter, try others such as hazel nut or cashew nut butter.

Soya products are excellent and easily digested sources of protein. Choose the nutritional supplemented soya milks with added calcium and sugar.

If you use dairy products, make good use of soft milky puddings, such as custard and rice pudding. Vegans can also get a variety of soya pudding, including soya rice pudding. If you like, add jam, honey, ground nuts or cream to your pudding. Porridge with a couple of tablespoons of added vegetable oil, perhaps with some nuts and/or dried fruit, can be very nutritious.

If you prefer to have white bread, white pasta and refined rice, then do so. But remember that the wholemeal varieties are very good sources of the B vitamins.

Make good use of cereal products (wheat, barley, rye, oats etc.), although avoid too much fibre. Complement cereals with other sources of proteins, such as nuts, seeds, pulses, milk and cheese.

Seeds, such as sesame seeds (tahini) or sunflower seeds, when ground as a paste, can also provide an energy dense source of protein in the diet. Tahini is particularly good when combined with a mashed pulse, such as chick peas to make hummus.

Pulses are more easily digested, if well cooked and mashed. Try mashed lentils or pureed black eye beans.

ENERGY

In order to gain weight it is essential to increase the energy content of your diet. Also, in order for your body to make proper use of protein, you must ensure sufficient energy. The most concentrated form of energy in the diet is from fat. If you can tolerate fat then try and increase the fat content of your diet.

Alcohol is also a concentrated form of energy and can be taken in moderation, perhaps before meals, as it may help improve your appetite. Only take alcohol with your doctors permission.

If you can tolerate oils, try adding some vegetable oil or vegetable margarine to your food, particularly to mashed pulses, salads and potatoes. If you like fried foods, then have fried foods. Use cream if you can tolerate fats. A good vegan alternative to cream is cashew nut cream, made from ground cashew nuts and water.

Do not restrict your sugar intake, although always have sweet foods after the savoury part of your meal. Glucose is a less sweet and more concentrated form of sugar. Glucose can be added to foods and drinks, such as porridge and cocoa drinks to increase your energy intake. Check with your dietitian about using glucose. She may suggest that your doctor prescribes you a special type of non-sweet, high calorie supplement, which can be added to foods and drinks.

If you like to have soup, make sure the soup is as nutritious as possible. Add pureed lentils, vegetable oil, butter, whole milk, cream or cheese.

Make good use of the wide range of vegetable pates and spreads available.

GENERAL ADVICE

- You may prefer to take puddings half an hour to one hour after your first course, this will enable time for the first course to settle.
- You may find ice-cream, soya or dairy, refreshing after meals.
- Make good use of a food blender, if you have one, to blend fruit, vegetable and pulses.
- Have meals with a good sauce, made with pureed fried onions, perhaps with tomatoes or mushrooms. To increase the energy density of sauces use butter or vegan margarine and add soya milk, silken tofu, cow's milk or cream.
- Do make sure you include a source of vitamin C in your diet, perhaps fresh fruit juice, black-currant cordial or rosehip syrup.
- Try and eat some fresh fruit and vegetables or salad each day, especially green vegetables, to ensure you get your full compliment of vitamins and minerals. If you cannot tolerate whole fruit or crunchy vegetables, take

them as fruit juice or a pureed soup made with fresh vegetables.

- High energy drinks, can be made using whole cow's milk, sweetened soya milk or silken tofu, with glucose, honey or sugar and a flavouring of your choice such as chocolate or vanilla.
- You can buy products from the chemists, to have as meal replacements, when your appetite is particularly poor. Do check on their suitability for vegetarians.
- Ask your doctor or dietitian about including a vitamin or mineral supplement in your diet. If you choose to take a supplement, inform your doctor and dietitian. Multi-vitamin and mineral tablets should not do you any harm, as long as you stick to the recommended dose.

If You Still Need Extra Protein & Energy

Your doctor can prescribe for you special supplements which can help you to gain weight. You would usually be referred to a dietitian, who can nutritional assess you and recommend the correct type of supplement.

If you are concerned about the suitability of a any product, for vegetarians or vegans, which have been prescribed for you, contact your doctor. Also contact us if you are having problems with health professionals who may be sceptical about your vegetarian or vegan diet.

BALANCE OF GOOD HEALTH

A "portion" is, for example, a slice of bread, an apple, a glass of milk or two tablespoons of baked beans, but remember-it's the balance that matters so if you have a big appetite, increase the amount you eat in all categories, not just the fatty and sugary foods.

Fruit and Vegetables

5 portions a day: Fresh, frozen, juiced, tinned or dried fruit and vegetables are particularly good sources of vitamins, minerals and fibre.

Bread, other Cereals and Potatoes

5 portions a day: Base most of your meals on these starchy foods. Use wholemeal or wholegrain versions as much as possible and avoid adding lots of fat. These foods give us carbohydrates for energy, fibre, protein and some vitamins and minerals.

High Protein Foods

2-3 portions a day: Include a variety of pulses (for example beans, lentils, peas and chick peas), nuts, seeds, eggs, soya, mycoprotein (Quorn) or wheat proteins to give you plenty of protein, minerals and vitamins.

Milk and Dairy Products

2-3 portions a day: Good sources of calcium, protein and some vitamins. If you are avoiding dairy foods, choose fortified soya, rice or oat drinks or make sure that you eat other foods that are high in calcium.

Fatty and Sugary Foods

0-3 portions a day: Although we need to eat some fat, we all need to eat these foods sparingly and try low fat alternatives.

33% of the UK population only eat meat occasionally.

Gallup Poll for Realeat, August 2001

5% of the UK population is vegetarian

National Diet and Nutrition Survey 2001

"The British Dietetic Association considers that a well-planned vegetarian diet can be nutritionally adequate and health promoting for both adults and children."

Particular Nutrients

Although a balanced vegetarian diet is lower in fat and higher in fibre and anti-oxidants than a meat-based diet, many people still believe that vegetarians can't possibly be healthy because they think certain nutrients are only found in meat. This is simply not true.

Iron

Iron deficiency is one of the most common nutritional problems in a typical British diet. Research shows that vegetarians are no more prone to iron deficiency than meat-eaters and even those who do eat meat get 86% of their iron from vegetarian sources. Iron is found in leafy green vegetables, pulses, wholemeal bread, dried fruit and pumpkin seeds. If you are worried about getting enough iron, try eating something high in Vitamin C (or drinking a glass of orange juice) with a meal containing iron-rich foods because this can triple the amount of iron your body is able to absorb.

Protein

We need to eat eight different types of amino acid-the building blocks for protein. Most vegetarian sources don't include all eight, so are sometimes thought of as 'incomplete' protein, but a varied vegetarian diet does include them all-just from different sources. Your body keeps a pool of the amino acids it needs, so all you have to do is eat a variety of different high-protein foods through the week. Good vegetarian sources of protein include pulses (such as beans, lentils, peas or chick peas), nuts, seeds, grains, soya (eg tofu, soya mince), dairy products and eggs.

Vitamin B12

B12 is not naturally found in plant foods, so vegans need to eat fortified foods such as breakfast cereals and soya drinks, but anyone eating dairy products and eggs will get plenty of B12 from those foods.

Fatty Acids

The omega 3 essential fatty acids found in oily fish are also found in vegetarian foods such as rapeseed oil, flax seeds and walnuts.

So, what do you eat?

Eating vegetarian is a real culinary adventure. Once you've broken out of the conventional meat-and-two-veg, you can break all the rules, or stick with more familiar tastes if you prefer.

Many of your favourite dishes, such as spaghetti bolognaise, chilli, stir-fry and curries can be made with soya mince, pulses or just vegetables. Bean burgers, pizzas, veggie sausages, ratatouille, baked beans, scrambled eggs, jacket potatoes, many cheeses and all sorts of ready meals, pasta sauces and soups are all suitable for vegetarians already. A few recipe ideas are shown on the following pages, but before you start cooking, fill your cupboards with the right basic ingredients and you'll find the transition much easier, and tastier.

THE VEGETARIAN STORE CUPBOARD

Most people keep a few stock items in their kitchen cupboard or freezer. Many of the basics-bread, flour, vegetable oil, dairy products, free-range eggs, frozen chips etc-will be suitable for vegetarians, but you may find it helpful to use the following as a guide for your first big shop as a new veggie.

- Lots of fresh fruit and vegetables
- Vegetable oil
- Olive oil
- Vegetable stock cubes
- Vegetarian gravy granules (check the label, many meat-flavoured varieties are actually vegetarian)
- Yeast extract (eg marmite)
- White wine vinegar (or balsamic for a treat)
- Peanut butter
- Tinned beans and pulses
- Tinned tomatoes
- Tinned soup
- Dried pasta
- Rice
- Quick-cook noodles
- Cous-cous
- Dried soya chunks
- Tinned soups

- o Ready made pasta/curry sauces
- o Dried herbs and spices
- o Seeds (try sesame, pumpkin, sunflower and many others)

To Keep in the Fridge

- o Free range eggs
- o Milk
- o Vegetarian cheese
- o Butter or margarine
- o Natural yoghurt
- o Houmous
- o Vegetarian pesto
- o Tofu (look out for marinated or smoked varieties)
- o Tomato puree
- o Mustard
- o Quorn products (look for the Vegetarian Society approved products)
- o Jars of sun-dried tomatoes or other antipasto (mushrooms, olives, artichokes or peppers in seasoned oil)
- o Fresh soups, pies and ready-meals

To Keep in the Freezer

- o Soya and Quorn mince or chunks
- o Vegetarian sausages and burgers
- o Ready rolled pastry
- o Pizza bases
- o Tortilla wraps
- o A variety of frozen vegetables
- o Ready-made pies and meals (many supermarket freezers have a special vegetarian section)
- o Shelled nuts (try brazils, cashews, almonds and walnuts)- buy in bulk to save on the price and store in the freezer to keep them tasting fresh

RECIPES AND MEAL IDEAS

Roast Mushroom and Aubergine Wrap

Place mushrooms, pieces of aubergine, courgette and tomato in a baking tray and drizzle with olive oil. Bake until tender, at 200 C/400 F/Gas Mark 6. Once cooked, leave to cool, add a few pitted olives and wrap with a flour tortilla or use to fill a pitta.

The Hallelujah Baguette!

Fry a few slices of halloumi on a high heat until golden brown. Pop into a baguette, along with some chopped sun-dried tomatoes, fresh salad leaves and a few springs of fresh mint.

Mushroom Coronation Ciabatta

Gently fry a punnet of oyster mushrooms in olive oil with 4 or 5 spring onions (sliced) and 1tbsp of curry powder. Stir in1 tsp of sweet chutney or apricot jam, cool then add 2 tbsp of mayonnaise. Chill the mixture and use to fill a ciabatta or soft white rolls.

The RLT

Veggies don't have to miss out on old favourites-grill or fry some vegetarian rashers (or make your own by frying thinly sliced tempeh with soy sauce), sandwich between sliced bread on a bed of crisp lettuce and sliced tomato, add veggie mayo or relish to taste. Grated Carrot and Sultana Sandwich with Peanut Butter. Lightly toast 2 slices of granary bread and allow to cool. Spread one slice with margarine and one with peanut butter. Grate a carrot, mix with a handful of sultanas and pile onto the peanut butter. Add some shredded iceberg lettuce and finely sliced onion if you wish. Sandwich and scoff!

Avocado and Houmous Bagel

Fill your bagel with lashings of houmous and a layer of mashed or sliced avocado. Top with slices of tomato and cucumber and a good dose of coarse ground black pepper.

Pitfalls

Once you get used to cutting meat out of your diet you can start checking labels for non-vegetarian ingredients, which include lots of by-products of the slaughter house as well as obvious things like meat, poultry and fish. Most vegetarians also choose to avoid battery eggs. Luckily many vegetarian products are clearly marked as being suitable, including thousands of products which have our 'Vegetarian Society Approved' seedling symbol, guaranteeing that the product is 100% suitable to our own strict standards (including only free-range eggs). If you come across products that aren't clearly marked, it is best to take a look at the label. Common ingredients to steer clear of are gelatine (made from the bones and skin of slaughtered cows and pigs), animal fat (which always means carcass fat), fish oils and cochineal (E120-crushed insects), which are never suitable for vegetarians. Lots of ready-meals and other products also contain battery eggs-even if they are marked as 'suitable for vegetarians'.

Unfortunately there are also quite a lot of ingredients that can be made from both vegetarian and non vegetarian sources, so if you see them listed and the product is not marked as being vegetarian, you have to assume the worst. Ingredients that fit into this category include glycerine, lactose, magnesium stearate, stearic acid and whey, together with these E numbers opposite.

E numbers marked * may be theoretically made in a non-vegetarian version, but are practically always suitable.

Don't worry-the list looks long but there are an awful lot of e-numbers in the world, so they don't turn up on as many foods as you might think!

Products To Watch Out For

- *Beer & Wine:* Some will have been fined (or made clear) with isinglass, a fish gelatine, or other animal products.
- *Cheese:* A lot of cheese produced today is entirely vegetarian, and is often marked as such, but be careful-especially with continental cheeses-because traditional rennet (used to make the cheese set) is taken from the stomachs of young calves.
- *Chocolate Bars and Sweets:* Watch out for gelatine, non-vegetarian whey (made with traditional rennet) and cochineal in some brands.

- o *Worcestershire Sauce:* Some brands contain anchovies.
- o *Thai Curry Sauce and Paste:* May contain fish or fish sauce.

Beyond What You Eat: Many vegetarians prefer to avoid wearing leather and there is now a bigger choice of non-leather shoes and other goods available than ever before. As well as high-street stores, you may want to try specialist shops and mail order outlets. Toiletries and cosmetics are not all free from animal ingredients. For example, sodium tallowate-a common ingredient in soap-is an animal fat and toothpastes often contain glycerine, which may be derived from animal sources. Our website is a great resource for seeking out vegetarian-friendly clothing, toiletries, cosmetics and all sorts of other goods, either through our online shop or links to manufacturers and retailers. Vegetarian Society Approved products don't include any animal ingredients and have not been tested on animals either.

HEALTHY EATING FOR VEGETARIANS

A varied vegetarian diet will supply all the essential nutrients you need to help you keep fit and healthy. In fact, a vegetarian diet can offer a wide range of health benefits. Research has shown that vegetarians suffer less from obesity, coronary heart disease, high blood pressure, type II diabetes, certain diet related cancers, diverticular disease, appendicitis, constipation and gallstones. A healthy diet includes plenty of fruit and vegetables and starchy foods, moderate amounts of high protein foods (which you may think of as alternatives to meat and fish), dairy produce or alternatives, and small amounts of fatty and sugary foods. You don't need to obey strict rules every day, but the following advice gives you a general idea of how to balance different types of food. If you eat broadly the proportions described, with plenty of variety, you shouldn't have any problems achieving a healthy, balanced diet.

A BALANCED DIET

A balanced diet must contain carbohydrate, protein, fat, vitamins, mineral salts and fibre. It must contain these things in the correct proportions.

1. *Carbohydrates*: these provide a source of energy.
2. *Proteins*: these provide a source of materials for growth and repair.
3. Fats: these provide a source of energy and contain fat soluble vitamins.
4. *Vitamins*: these are required in very small quantities to keep you healthy.
5. *Mineral Salts*: these are required for healthy teeth, bones, muscles etc..
6. *Fibre*: this is required to help your intestines function correctly; it is not digested.
7. *Balanced Diets*: we must have the above items in the correct proportions.

Carbohydrates

Carbohydrates are the most important source of energy. They contain the elements Carbon, Hydrogen and Oxygen. The first part of the name "carbo-" means that they contain Carbon. The second part of the name "-hydr-" means that they contain Hydrogen. The third part of the name "-ate-" means that they contain Oxygen. In all carbohydrates the ratio of Hydrogen atoms to Oxygen atoms is 2:1 just like water.

We obtain most of our carbohydrate in the form of starch. This is found in potato, rice, spaghetti, yams, bread and cereals. Our digestive system turns all this starch into another carbohydrate called glucose. Glucose is carried around the body in the blood and is used by our tissues as a source of energy. Any glucose in our food is absorbed without the need for digestion. We also get some of our carbohydrate in the form of sucrose; this is the sugar which we put in our tea and coffee (three heaped spoonfuls for me!). Both sucrose and glucose are sugars, but sucrose molecules are too big to get into the blood, so the digestive system turns it into glucose.

When we use glucose in tissue respiration we need Oxygen. This process produces Carbon Dioxide and water and releases energy for other processes. Now try my starch test in the Virtual Laboratory

Proteins

Proteins are required for growth and repair. Proteins contain Carbon, Hydrogen, Oxygen, Nitrogen and sometimes Sulphur. Proteins are very large molecules, so they cannot get directly into our blood; they must be turned into amino-acids by the digestive system. There are over 20 different amino-acids. Our bodies can turn the amino-acids back into protein. When our cells do this they have to put the amino-acids together in the correct order. There are many millions of possible combinations or sequences of amino-acids; it is our DNA which contains the information about how to make proteins. Our cells get their amino-acids from the blood. Now try my Biuret test in the Virtual Laboratory

Proteins can also be used as a source of energy. When excess amino-acids are removed from the body the Nitrogen is excreted as a chemical called urea. The liver makes urea and the kidney puts the urea into our urine.

Fats

Like carbohydrates, fats contain the elements Carbon, Hydrogen and Oxygen. Fats are used as a source of energy: they are also stored beneath the skin helping to insulate us against the cold. Do not think that by avoiding fat in your diet you will stay thin and elegant! If you eat too much carbohydrate and protein, you will convert some of it into fat, so you will put on weight. You must balance the amount of energy containing foods with the amount of energy that you use when you take exercise.

You must have some fat in your diet because it contains fat soluble vitamins.

Vitamins

Vitamins are only required in very small quantities. There is no chemical similarity between these chemicals; the similarity between them is entirely biological.

Vitamin A: good for your eyes.

Vitamin B: about 12 different chemicals.

Vitamin C: needed for your body to repair itself.

Vitamin D: can be made in your skin, needed for absorption of Calcium.

Vitamin E: the nice one-reproduction?

Mineral Salts

These are also needed in small quantities, but we need more of these than we need of vitamins.

Iron: required to make haemoglobin.

Calcium: required for healthy teeth, bones and muscles.

Sodium: all cells need this, especially nerve cells.

Iodine: used to make a hormone called thyroxin.

Fibre

We do not/can not digest cellulose. This is a carbohydrate used by plants to make their cell walls. It is also called roughage. If you do not eat foods materials which contain fibre you might end up with problems of the colon and rectum. The muscles of you digestive system mix food with the digestive juices and push food along the intestines by peristalsis; if there is no fibre in your diet these movements cannot work properly.

A Balanced Diet

You must have carbohydrate, protein, fat, vitamins, minerals salts and fibre in the correct proportions. If there is not enough protein, you will not be able to grow properly and you will not be able to repair yourself i.e. wounds will not heal properly. If you do not have enough energy containing foods you will feel very tired, you will not have enough energy. If you have too much energy containing foods you will become overweight. If you think that you are overweight you might try taking more exercise to "burn off" some of the excess food which you ate at you last meal.

8

THE PHYSIOLOGY OF NUTRITION

ASPECTS OF HUMAN NUTRITION

Human Nutrition comprises a wide variety of disciplines and requires the integration of a number of different conceptual models for research and clinical purposes. Nutrition begins with food choices, which are determined by availability as well as individual and social factors. These whole foods are the expression of eating behaviors, but they can also be analyzed in terms of their provision of macronutrients, micronutrients, and fiber. Nutrition can be further reduced to considerations of carbohydrate metabolism, individual amino acids and protein quality, and lipid composition and fatty acid metabolism.

Vitamin, mineral and nutrient deficiencies are rare in the U.S. today due to food fortification, but the challenge for the future will be to combat the problems of overnutrition with fat and calories. In order to understand the problems of obesity and overnutritior it is important to realize that all food components can be interconverted and stored as fat when there are excess calories. In addition, the efficiency with which extra calories are converted to fat is genetically determined. Therefore. there is a gene-nutrient interaction of importance with every nutritional disorder.

The basic processes of oxidant stress have influenced both plant and human evolution. Plants contain a number of natural antioxidants and humans have developed endogenous enzyme systems, as well as endogenously produced antioxidants which are relevant to the nutritional environment. For example, humans do not manufacture vitamin C as do most other animal species due to its abundance in a plant-based human diet. Scurvy only occurred once man moved to the food supplies of the last few hundred years that are significantly less diverse when compared to the ancient biodiverse diet of 50,000 to 100,000 years ago.

Plants also contain a number of unique phytochemicals not available as supplements. These phytochemicals stimulate the cells of our bodies to develop enzymes to metabolize these substances. For example, someone taking 500 mg per day of vitamin C has a different panel of metabolizing enzymes in their liver than someone taking only 20 mg per day of vitamin C. The interaction of the nutritional environment and the human body occurs at the molecular genetic, cellular, organ and whole body levels. Modern dietary recommendations need to consider the basic science of nutrition and the current problems of overnutrition, obesity, and chronic disease. Recommendations for dietary intake among populations often take the form of pyramids with the base of the basis of the diet.

The base of the USDA pyramid developed in the late 1980's consists of cereals and grains without an emphasis on the fiber content of those grains. The fruits and vegetables appear on the second level and are two separate groups. In a new pyramid developed in 1997 by the UCLA Center for Human Nutrition, a modified plant-based diet is recommended. The base consists of fruits and vegetables to provide unique phytonutrients for chronic disease prevention. The second level emphasizes high fiber cereals and grains to provide the benefits of fiber from these foods as well as from fruits and vegetables. The protein level is made up of low fat protein choices from both the plant and animal kingdoms. The top tier of the USDA pyramid has only dots representing fats and sweets with the mixed message "use sparingly". The top tier of the new California Pyramid emphasizes taste enhancers including olives, avocados, garlic, onion, nuts, cheese, chili peppers, and small amounts of monounsaturate or omega-3-rich oils needed to enhance taste. The overall fat recommendation of the USDA pyramid is 30% or less of calories from fat, while the California pyramid reflects the decreased fat intake in the population recommending 20% or less of calories from fat.

Physiology

Research and intensive supervision of food has widened the knowledge about the physiology of nutrition. The activity of newspaper, broadcasting and television searching for sensational news have mobilized the food industry in order to optimize their products.

The interest of the industry on nutrition physiology developed a great know how in the sector of laboratory analysing methods, in processing technologies, in packaging material and in storage.

All these efforts resulted in better quality and safety.

The consumer, however needs more information. Many basic rules for healthy nutrition are not known and misleading information are spread by commercials seeking sales increase resulting sometimes in extreme reactions of certain groups of consumers.

Failure of nutrition is responsible for most of our diseases and rotten health. Diets are a wide field of incomprehensible efforts to correct mislead nutrition.

The classic function of diets are to reduce body weight.

A great number of women try diets to reduce their weight. They are looking for better health or want to improve aesthetics. Body culture is getting important in actual society.

Weight reduction should only be considered if there are clinical reasons. Body weight is genetically controlled. If one feels good with a certain weight everything no diet should be considered. Much outdoor exercise keeps you healthy. There are some ways to determine normal weight:

- Broca normal-weight
- Table of the American life insurance companies
- Bodymass Index BMI

The Broca Normal-weight

The Broca normal weight is given in kg and is defined as body size in cm minus 100 for man.

For women the body size minus 100 minus 5 to 10% is used. Over-and underweight in relation to broca normal weight is given in percent. The Broca-Indexis the quotient of the actual weight and the Broca normal-weight.

Table of the American life insurance companies

With this table the actual weight is put in relation to the normal weight for the corresponding age and body size.

The Bodymass Index BMI

The Bodymass index is the quotient of the body weight and the square of the body size (kg/m). This index gives best informations about the mass of the body fat. It is less used as Broca because it is less informative for the patient.

Age	Bodymass index (kg/m)
19-24 years	19-24
25-34 years	20-25
35-44 years	21-26
45-54 years	22-27
55-64 years	23-28
over 65 years	24-29

(National Research Council 1989)

	Grade of overweight	BMI(kg/m^2)	Broca-overweight(%)
Normal weight	0	20 up to 24,9	-
Moderate overweight	I	25 up to 29,9	0 up to 20 (-40)
Strong overweight	II	30-40	20-70 (-80)
Extreme overweight	III	> 40	> 70 (> 80)

Dubious Pharmaceutical industry and flat magazines recommend all kind of diets. There are made increasing turnovers in this field, not always without damage of health of the consumer. Advertising uses terms like"slim", "calorie reduced", "light", "Du darfst"(You may), "fat reduced" and others to promote selling of their products.

With great publicity campaigns in magazines, TV and radio appetite of the group of overeaters is stimulated rather then reduced. The result of these products are therefore negative.

Examples of diets lacking any scientific background:

- The apple diet
- The mayo diet
- The Max-Plank-diet
- The Book "Fit for live"H. and M. Diamond, USA
- The separation diet of DR. Howard Hay in USA and Dr. Walb in Germany
- the Atkins diet
- The point diet

Lowcarb Diets

Lowcarb diets are low in carbohydrates and rich in protein and fat. The most prominent lowcarb diets are the Atkins diet, the Southbeach diet, the Ketogen diet the Anabole diet and the LOGI diet (Low Glycemic Index) from Dr. Nicolai Worm.

Vegetarian Food with Animal Ingredients

Many vegetarian labelled foods of industrial origin do contain animal ingredients such as bovine suet, lard, restaurants prepare their meals labelled as vegetarian with meat broth and marine oil.

Psychology of Diet Plans

Diet plans and diet systems to be successful must observe some basic psychological rules:

1. At the beginning of a diet plan the dangers of overweight are enumerated. This is the most dangerous part of the plan as those who do not succeed with the diet will later on create a deeper psychological conflict. Their real problems which took them to overeat will then be boosted. Such an introduction should always be banned from a diet plan as it frightens the reader, it increases the inferiority complexes. Instead of telling the reader how

bad its life is, a diet plan should make its introduction enumerating the benefits.

2. The promise that overweight can be reduced to normal values using a specific diet is not honest. As weight reduction is coupled to intake and output of calories over the whole life, the necessary modification of life style cannot be achieved in one or two weeks of sometimes strange procedures which lack any explanation of how it should work. The explanations should be short and come to the point precisely. If the principles are unknown this part should be omitted completely.

3. Reference of people who were successful with the diet. Usually well known people of the public life and TV stars are cited. This increases the desire to participate of the life of these persons. Awaking from the fairy tales the monotony of the daily round will be more sad then before.

4. Certainty that everyone can succeed with the diet is a claim which is untrue.

   Many people are unsuccessful and have great psychological distress failing in what is told to be easy for everyone.

5. Explanation of the foundations of the diet should only be given based on well known statements. If there is no explanation available no comment suggesting miracles should be given.

The cause of failure of diet plans and how to do it better. Mislead diets are not caused by alteration of the basic metabolism. The real cause is the lack of learn effect to adapt the life Style to a healthy way of life and to correct the bad habits. Wolfgang Stabel, during a course to get rid of smoking habit said: "Mankind can live 170 seconds without air, 12 days without water and 46 days without food. Without tobacco it can live a whole life."

To this statement one can add: one can live without chocolate, without candies and hamburgers.

The essential message of diet plans should be to change the life habits: How to to it better:

1. Drink 2 litre of water per day, eat fibre rich food.
2. Do not bother about calories, but spare fat and alcohol.
3. Eat on regular hours, do not eat in between.
4. Eat enough vitamins, minerals and proteins
5. Noting is forbidden, you can eat everything, but always without excesses
6. Enjoy a small dish. Eat always with attention.
7. Act against stress with physical activity and relaxation exercise and not with eating junk food
8. Stay realistic. Set small scores. Distrust crash-diets and miracle-diets. Do it the safe way changing food habits.
9. Activate the fat break down with physical activity. The more muscles you activate more calories are burned.
10. Money back guarantee in case of failure of the diet is a bad trick. Less than 10% complain in case of failure. The majority does not dare to do it. Who wants tc admit to have failed when it is being told that all other do succeed ?

The National Weight Control Registry (NWCR): The National Weight Control Registry (NWCR), is a research study from the University of Colorado that seeks to gather information from people who have successfully lost weight and kept it off for long periods of time. The findings of this study are: A little over one-half of the sample lost weight through formal programs (such as Weight Watchers, or professional assistance, such as Overeaters Anonymous, a psychologist or a registered dietitian; the remainder lost weight on their own.

Both groups reported having used both diet and exercise to lose weight and nearly 77% of the sample reported that a triggering event had preceded their successful weight loss. Mean (+/-SD) current consumption reported by registry members was 5778 +/-2200 kJ/d, with 24 +/-9% of energy from fat, Members also appear to be highly active: they reported expending approximately 11830 kJ/wk through physical activity.

Surprisingly, 42% of the sample reported that maintaining their weight loss was less difficult than losing weight. Nearly all registry members indicated that weight loss led to improvements in their level of energy, physical mobility, general mood, self-confidence, and physical health.

Diet Pills and Powders

Many pills and powders are sold in super market in health stores and in pharmacies. They promise wonders for much money without success:

L-carnitin.

Bodybuilder were the first to use L-carnitin as fat-burner.

L-carnitin works only with long time persistent muscle training, together with fat reduced food. L.carnitin under these condition can act as a biocarrier in the energy system of the mitochondria of the muscle cells.

Without physical activity fat is not burned. Even carnitin cannot change that. Oxygen must burn the fatty acids and the resulting energy must be used.

L-carnitin can be obtained by the body through synthesis using methionine and lysin in liver and kidneys.

Carnitin is present in bovine and in sheep meat. That is the etymology of carnitin (Carne-latin=meat).

Vegetarians could get an undersupply of carnitin. However there are no signs of over weight because vegetarians eat less fat. The use of pills containing carnitin is therefore unnecessary.

Tyrosine

Tyrosine is an hormone of the thyroid gland. It is supposed to stimulate burning of food components. Tyrosine is sometimes prescribed by physician to compensate an insufficient function of the thyroid gland gland. In normal persons the use of tyrosine can lead to hyperfunctioning of the thyroid gland gland causing insomnia, restlessness, heart throbbing, tachycardia, trembling, fear and overexcitability as well as intensive sweat.

Instead of using tyrosine normal persons should have more activity.

Genistein

Genistein is a phytoestrogen (plant hormone) found in soybeans being of great importance in human and in animal nutrition. The fertility of sheep and birds were found to be reduced by high amount of genistein. It may be a natural defence of plants against natural enemies. Genistein has reduced affinity to estrogen receptors and thus a reduced activity compared with estrogen.

As the use of soy beans in nutrition is increasing high levels of genistein in blood stream is to be expected. Importance has the nutrition in Asia which has 50 times in normal nutrition and 400 times more genistein in baby food with soy bean diet than European baby food and normal nutrition respectively. It is however interesting that there have been no reports on negative activities with these nutrition. A certain protection against women Breast cancer is brought into combination with an interference of genistein in the hormone household of hormones which enlarges the menstrual cycle of Asiatic women.

Natural dietary approaches to menopause disorders: The natural hormone replacement therapy concepts came about as a result of population studies in Asia. The outcomes of these studies were that many menopausal disorders of Western civilisation (1 to 5 mg/day of soy isoflavones) were absent in the East due to large amount of soybean products (daily soy isoflavone intake of estimated 50 mg/day) associated with a low fat intake.

Entering menopause a diet is being recommended being moderate in protein and complex carbohydrates, with 15 to 20 % of the calories coming from fat. Saturated fat from animal products should be low, unsaturated fats should come from cold water fish (salmon, tuna, mackerel and herring). A good portion of the diet should come from soybean products, such as tofu. To keep bowel bacteria in balance Lactobacillus acidophilus should be included in the program.

Isoflavone intake amounts: The US National Guideline Clearinghouse (NGC) suggests the following isoflavone intake amounts: Optimal cholesterol reduction seems to require approximately 50 mg/day of isoflavones; this amount would be found in approximately 25 g/day of soy protein.

For effects of arterial compliance amounts of 40-80 mg/day isoflavones are needed.

For antioxidant effect on lipids 10 mg/day may be effective.

For bone health a minimum of 50 mg/day of isoflavones are needed.

For hot flashes and vasomotor symptoms 40-80 mg/day of isoflavones were used in studies.

Iodine and Algae

Algae (Fucus vesiculosus)are sometimes used to increase the supply of iodine. and are sometimes added to diet pills and diet powders.

Iodine is needed for the synthesis of thyroid gland hormones which regulate the energy household. Iodine can be obtained from marine fish, iodised kitchen salt, and food prepared with iodinated salt. The daily intake of 180 to 200 mcg is recommended. Increasing the intake over this value no further activity on the fat burning machine is takes place.

Appetite Depressant

Ephedrine, Norephedrine, Fenfluramine can cause heart throbbing, restlessness, insomnia, and hypertension. They can cause addiction.

Laxatives

Long time use of laxatives leads to an important loss of potassium ions which on its turn increases the intestinal inactivity.

Laxatives increase the problems. More physical activity and enough water during meals can solve it.

Cynarine

The bitter constituent and enzyme of chicory can promote the production of biliary acids which act on the digestion of fatty acids.

Cynarine does not destroy fat as often is being told. Physical training is better than cynarine.

Bromelain and Papain

These enzymes are found in tropical fruits such as pineapple, papaya and mango. They help the digestion of food increasing the absorption. In this way these enzymes do not reduce or destroy fat. As a matter of fact the assimilation of the food is optimized. This has nothing to do with weight reduction.

Herbal Metabolism Boosters: Some herbal metabolism boosters can temporarily cause weight drop, however, they do not eliminate excess of fat. Most of them contain stimulants which increase the central nervous system and decrease appetite. They are mild diuretics. They can cause unpleasant side effects such as dizziness, nausea, and frequent urination. As soon the administration of these drugs is ended the weight returns to its original height.

How to avoid diet pills:

- Instead of appetite depressant chew longer during meals. Eat slowly. Drink a glass of water before meals and eat a great portion of salad before the main dish.
- Instead of laxatives eat fibre rich food, drink enough water and make physical training
- Instead of dehydration pills use less salt in the kitchen. Eat more vegetables and fruit juices, rice containing much potassium
- Instead of enzymes eat protein and vitamins rich foods. The body can produce sufficient enzymes from proteins and vitamins which exist in nature.
- Instead of carnitin reduce the fat in your meals.

The separation diet of Dr. Howard Hay: Dr. Howard Hay was during his life attacked by a renal insufficiency. To help himself Dr. Hay studied the composition of the body noting that it was built of 80% of alkaline material and 20% of acid material. Starting from this hypothesis Dr. Hay divided food in alkaline generator and in acid generators. He introduced the following modification in his nutrition:

Acid Generators: Great part of the proteins and part of carbohydrates.

Alkaline Generators: Vegetables, fruits and salads. According to Dr. Hay the the alkaline generators may neutralize acid elements, helping their excretion.

Dr. Hay augmented the amount of vegetables being half cooked and the other half raw.

Dr. Hay says that the failure of balance between the acid generator food and the alkaline generator food is responsible for diseases like obesity, insomnia and depression.

Dr. Hay separated the protein rich food from the carbohydrate rich food, putting them in different meals. This gave the name to his diet.

Dr. Hay established the rules to his diet:

- Do not be hungry. The body should be supplied continuously with energy
- Distribute the food through 6 meals between 7:00 am and 10:00pm
- The portions should be small
- Between the meals there are only fruits permitted
- Chew long enough. The old saying "Chew every bit 36 time" is to be rejected. 20 times are enough.

If food is not sufficiently ground the enzymes cannot do its job and repleteness cannot be achieved.

- Beverages: Mineral water is permitted. Herb tea and fruit tea, but not black tea is permitted

Take the beverages before or after the meals in order not to disturb digestion. Most of the catabolists are excreted between 5:00 am and 12:00 am. It is that why Dr. Hay recommends to take great part of the liquid after wake up.

GOOD DIETS

Low Fat-30 Diet: It is a weight reduction program for all who want to reduce their weight together with a group. Participation is for the time being limited to Germany. The most important facts about low fat nutrition is given in small groups. Meals should not contain more than 30% of calories coming from fat. You should eat only when feeling hungry. At the first sign of satiation one should finish the meal. The diet is based on points. Minimum amounts of foods are given. Once a week brochures on special topics are given.

A long-lasting modification of the nutritional habits are essential in order to avoid overweigh.

Natural Weight Program: This program was developed by Dr. Doris Wolf She herself had been overweighted and tried to amend it using here knowledge as a psychologist and psychotherapist developing the Natural Weight Program.

Putting on weight because of emotional problems and stress are the main reasons for many people to skip all good intentions of an healthy nutrition. Frustration, anger and other negative emotions are compensated by eating. Alternatives to get emotionally balanced other than overeating are strategies of modern psychology. How to to handle one's emotions and how to accept one's own body not as an enemy, but as a fried, are important subjects of the Program. The negative attitude towards their body must be changed.

According to Dr.Doris Wolf all kind of diets are unsuitable for the majority of persons. There are biological and psychological reasons which are responsible for the fact that only 2 to 5 per cent of those who follow a diet register lasting weight reduction.

Dr. Wolf uses four principles as basis for her Program:

The four principles:

1. Eat only when you are physically hungry and not when mental hungry.
2. Eat what you like for the moment.
3. Eat consciously, being aware of what you eat and how your body reacts.
4. Stop eating when you feel satisfied

THE RISKS OF BAD DIETS

The Potential Risks of Low-carbohydrate Diets: The American Heart Association, the American Dietetic Association and the American Kidney Fund warn about the potential risks from the long-term use of low-carbohydrate, high-protein diets. Low-carbohydrate diets, like Atkins diet avoid carbohydrates (starches or sugar) reducing or even eliminating the intake of fruit, fruit juices, starchy vegetables, beans, bread, rice, cereals pasta and other grain products. This leads to a nutrition consisting mainly of fat and proteins. Permitted are meat, cheese, non-starchy vegetables. Everything else is limited to a minimum. Later on the carbohydrate restriction is reduced but high fat and proteins persists. Despite initial weight loss higher than rob obtained with other diets, low-carb diets however have a net weight loss after one year which is not significantly different from other diets in comparison.

Many nutritionists attack the Atkins weight loss regime for its high fat content, increasing the risk of clogged arteries heart attack, diabetes, stroke and several types of cancer in the long term.

Deleterious effects on cardiovascular disease risk factors were demonstrated by Larosa in a study of 24 obese individuals who followed the Atkins diet for 3 month. Caloric Intake declined, but LDL cholesterol levels rose despite the weight loss. Most of the weight loss occurred in the first few weeks, which suggests the combined effects of fluid loss and potential anorectic (reduction of desire to eat) effects of induced ketosis.

The American Heart Association does not recommend high-protein diets because they restrict foods that provide essential nutrients. An undersupply of vitamins and minerals, as well as potential cardiac, renal, bone and liver abnormalities may result.

A new study carried out at the University of Oxford demonstrates a direct affect on the heart caused by this diet. The results were presented at the American Heart Association conference in November 15, 2005, in Dalas.

According to this study, the energy stores in the heart were reduced by an average of 16 per cent as a result of the Atkins diet recommendations. One of the authors, Dr. Damien Tyler says that similar patterns in a more severe form in patients with heart failure, and type 2 diabetics also suffer from low energy stores.

Evaluation of High-Protein Diets

Evaluation of high-protein diets must be done ensuring that the American Heart Association Dietary Guidelines regarding eating patterns and the primary prevention for coronary Omega 6 from the National Cholesterol Education Programme are observed:

1. Total Protein intake should not be excessive (average 50 to 100 g/d) and should reasonably proportional (around 15% of kilocalories per day) to carbohydrate (around 55% of kilocalories per day) and fat (around 30% of kilocalories per day) intake.
2. Carbohydrates should not be omitted or severely restricted. A minimum of 100 g carbohydrate per day is recommended to ensure overall nutritional adequacy through the provision of a variety of healthful foods.
3. Selected protein foods should not contribute excess total fat, saturated fat, or cholesterol.
4. The diet should be safely implemented over the long term, i.e. it should provide adequate nutrients and support dietary compliance with a healthful eating plan to prevent increases in disease risk.

The AHA summarises: "Successful weight loss occurs most frequently when a nutritionally adequate diet that allows for caloric deficits (around 500 kcal/d for each 1 lb lost per week) is tailored according to individual food preferences.

A minimum of 1200 kcal/d for women and 1500 kcal/d for men should be provided.

Total energy deficit has the greatest overall impact on weight reduction, especially when coupled with increased physical activity and behaviour modification to maintain negative energy balance. Over the long term, diet composition should be consistent with a balanced eating plan that supports weight maintenance and lowers chronic disease risk.

Fit for Live

The book "Fit for Life " describes a separation diet like that of Dr. Atkins.

It gives an additional recommendation not to eat simultaneously products rich in proteins together with dietary fibres.

Arguments against the diet of Dr. Atkins and the book "Fit for Live"

Traditional physiology does not agree with the diet of separation of Dr. Atkins. Meat does not have dietary fibres. It is therefore necessary to eat meat together with vegetables and fruits. The fibres absorb rests of digestion.

Protein digestion starts in the stomach with chloridric acid, together with pepsin. In the intestines there are proteases such as produced by the pancreas and by the gall bladder.

Important Proteasesare: trypsin peptidase elastase ribonuclease and others.

As the external layer of the intestines is also composed by proteins the danger of proteases to digest his own meat. Nature protects against an own digestion secreting a protective layer of mucus made of mucopolysaccharides. This is the origin of the denomination"mucous membrane" which is not attacked by proteases.

Sometimes however particles of enzymes get through the mucus barrier. damaging mucous cells which can regenerate rapidly.With protein rich nutrition there are more proteolytic enzymes secreted as in case which should of a normal nutrition.

Fibres of vegetables, fruits and cereals absorb excesses of enzymes.Fibres also accelerates passage of not digestible material through the intestines.

The diet of Dr. Hay advises the ingestion of proteins at night when the body rests permitting the enzymes to stay longer in the intestines.

The danger of intestinal cancer and other gastric malfunctions are possible.

Other Low-carbohydrate Diets

Zone Diet: The Zone Diet was developed by Barry Sears, a former researcher in biotechnology at the Massachusetts

Institute of Technology. It is based on the control of insulin by balancing protein and carbohydrate at each meal (1-4). The American Heart Association notes that food must be eaten in required proportions of protein (40), fat (30), carbohydrates (30). Menues are not appealing. Vegetable portions are very large. Food is low in copper. Theories and long-term results are not validated. Couuld result in weight maintenance if carefully followed.

Protein Power: The Protein Power diet was developed by Michael R. Eades, M.D., and Mary Dan Eades, M.D. The principle of Protein Power is the restriction of carbohydrates-in particular refined ones.

The American Heart Association notes that this diet is not practical for long term. Rigid rules must be observed. The diet is low in calcium, fibre, pantothenic acid, copper, manganese. It has limited food choice and is not practical for long term. It is high in total fat and saturated fat. No long term, validated studies are published.

Sugar Busters: Sugar busters involves eating high fibre vegetables and whole grains. Fruits are encouraged and discourages saturated fats and transfats. It is important to eat three regular meals daily. Moderation in portions size is most important. Exercise is also on the program.

The American Heart Association notes that Sugar Buster eliminates many carbohydrate foods. Discourages eating fruit with meals. It is low in calcium, vitamin D, vitamin E, pantothenic acid, copper, potassium.

Stillman Diet: It is a severe form of ketogenic diet. Nothing is permitted if it is not mentioned in a list. The american Heart Association notes that Stillman diet is low in fibre, vitamin A, thiamine, vitamin C, vitamin D, folate, pantothenic acid, calcium, copper, magnesium, manganese, potassium. There are no long-term, valid studies published. There are extreme limitations in food choice, and very little variety.

Ketosis and the Ketogenic Diet: Elevated levels of ketones in the blood is called ketosis. It can occur during fasting, during a very high fat diet or during a long lasting deficiency in carbohydrate supply. This is the principle of the ketogenic diet. Atkins diet, which is used basically as low-glycemic index diet, may also cause ketosis. There are three ketones formed under hunger (also called " ketone bodies"): acetoacetate, acetone and beta-hydroxybutyrate (BHBA).

The fatty acids with participation of glucagon are digested in the liver to ketone compounds in order to liberate the needed energy. This is to see in opposition to the formation of D-glucose from carbohydrates to liberate energy. Ketones are burned in muscle and other tissues. High levels of ketones in tissue reduce the pH level. This is called ketoacidosis. One ketone is acetone which may cross the blood/brain barrier and, if in high concentration, causes central nervous disorders.

Deficiency of insulin in diabetics may lead to ketosis.

It seems that fasting or high fat diet known as ketogenic diet is appropriate to induce ketosis for medical treatment of a specific neurological disorder. It should not be used as a body weight reducing diet.

Triglycerides used in Ketogenic Diets

Medium-chain triglyceride ketogenic diet for adults is being suggested by Schiff and colleagues. The researchers recommend a therapeutic trial of the ketogenic diet in intractable epilepsy for all ages.

Foods used in the diet include high â□" triglyceride dairy products (e.g., butter, cream), mayonnaise and peanut butter. Carbohydrates, found in bread and starches, are eliminated in the diet, and liquid and calorie intake are often restricted as well in order to aid ketone accumulation.

Dr. Richard Veech at NIH in a study, concludes that ketone bodies increase metabolic efficiency, while decreasing production of free radicals, may treat neurological diseases such as Alzheimer's and Parkinson's disease, and the heart and brain operate 25% more efficiently using ketones as a source of energy.

Alternative sources of ketones to avoid high fat diet for Alzheimer's and Parkinson's patients:

Richard Veech and colleagues (2000) found that the elevation of ketones may offer neuroprotection in the treatment or prevention of both Alzheimer's disease, where therapy is lacking, and Parkinson's disease, where therapy with L-dopa is time limited. The researchers recommend alternative sources of ketones, produced biotechnologically to overcome the atherogenic potential of the high-fat ketogenic diet used in childhood epilepsy.

The Mayo Diet

The Mayo diet has no connection with the famous Mayo-Clinic of USA. It is a protein rich and fat reduced diet (1.000 to 1.500 kcal)

The diet includes 3 eggs every day, meat, fruits and vegetables.

The diet is not well balanced. It is very high in cholesterol, and even for short time not suitable.

Ovo-lacto-vegetarian Diets

Bircher-Benner Diet

It is the ovo-lacto-vegetarian diet from Dr. Max Bircher-Benner which according to Dr. Bircher-Benner

- Mobilizes the ability of self healing
- Stimulates the intestines
- Fresh vegetable food containing high energy of the sun
- contains only three meals.

The Diet Contains Minimal Amount of Food: The diet contains lacto-vegetable food, at least 70% food of vegetable origin as muesli, fresh fruits, vegetable, salads, only moderate heat is used to prepare food. All ingredients should be of ecological origin.

No Potatoes and no Fish is Allowed: The Birchner-Benner diet avoids meat and meat products being therefore low in animal fatty acids, cholesterol and purine. This is positive in case of gout, coronary diseases and disorder of the fatty acid metabolism. Like every lacto-vegetarian diet undersupply of iodine and iron can take place.

Evers Diet from the Physician Josev Evers: The Evers Diet was at first developed to be applied in case of Multiple sclerosis.

It is a moderate ovo-lacto-vegetarian diet with germinated cereals (containing high level of polyunsaturated fatty acids.) Ingredients should be of natural, unmodified origin. " Denaturated" food resulting from industrial processing was considered as being the reason for diseases of industrial era.

The diet has different levels to be applied on different diseases:

- In case of disease only unheated vegetarian food, no potatoes are given.
- For convalescents low-fat meat, ground unheated meat, fresh fish and raw ham are given.

Comment

The ban of potatoes is unreasonable. Potatoes are low in calories, and dietary fibres and vitamin rich.

Ground, unheated meat is a danger to weak patients because of possible bacterial hazard.

Waerland diet, Waerland, Sweden: This diet was established to clean intestines, to balance acid and base metabolism.

Regulate the intestinal flora. Useful bacteria from milk and plants are in confrontation with harmful bacteria from meat, eggs and fish. The diet has low amount of food. Raw vegetable meals are followed by cereals meals. Milk, fruits and vegetables are considered as alkaline food. Instructions about sleeping and working time are given. In the morning 1/2 litre of potato-vegetable soup is taken followed by warm bed rest lying on stomach. The Waerland diet cannot be explained. Meat, eggs and fish cannot be considered as harmful and many claims are not true.

Danger of Sudden Changes of Nutrition

Increasing Salads and other vegetables increase intake of certain vitamins like folate, vitamin A and K.

Decreasing high caloric foods like dairy products, red meat, salad oil or eggs reduces intake of minerals such as calcium zinc and selenium, vitamin D, E, B12 and essential fatty acids.

Anthroposophical Nutrition

It was established by Rudolf Steiner. It should develop consciousness, to live in reconciliation with nature, nutrition as part of the holistic doctrine.

Ovo-lacto-vegetable nutrition with low content of meat. Avoid potatoes as they destroy instinct and promote materialism. Ban of use of pressure cooking and frozen food as they are "enemies of life".

Comment

Many of the doctrines of anthroposophy cannot be followed. The ban of potatoes, pressure cooking and frozen food is not tenable.

Macrobiotic Nutrition According M. Kushi

Macrobiotic nutrition was founded by G.Ohsawa, Japan. His nutrition was dangerous and some people died using this diet. In USA macrobiotic nutrition according Ohsawa was prohibited.

M. Kushi modernized the content of macrobiotic nutrition. A short use of this nutrition is harmless. It is harmful and not indicated to be followed for a log period. Macrobiotic nutrition is a part of Zen-Buddhism a kind of philosophy of life.

Life energy comes from vegetable nutrition, cereals in the highest form.

Contrast from passive to active, from night to day, from feminine to masculine, is the principle of Yin and Yang which were transferred to food by Kushi. No milk, and milk products, no meat and tea are consumed.

The Jo-Jo Effect Reviewed

Two important studies recently reviewed the knowledge about the Jo-Jo effect, following a diet. These studies received much attention in 2007 following the effort to tackle the obesity problem in large parts of the population of developed countries.

Rena Wing and James Hill of the University of Colorado started in 1994 " The National Weight-Control Register".

In Germany Joachim Westenhöfer of the Hamburger Hochschule für Angewandte Wissenschaften started years ago the "Lean Habits Study".

The Strategy: Both studies agreed with foregoing studies in the strategy to counter overweight:

- Reduction of intake of energy.
- Increase of energy
- Overcome of the own psyche
- Only one of these three items may become a great help to reduce weight and keep it down, but using a bit of all three recommendations has the best chance to avoid Jo-Jo effect.

The Physiology of Overweight and Jo-Jo Effect

The authors stress the fact that a variety of reasons account for overweight and a jo-jo effect following a diet. The body reacts to weight loss due to famine or diet with defence mechanisms such as increased hunger and reduced energy consume.This makes weight-reduction and to keep it down so difficult

- *Thyroid Gland:* The thyroid glad reduces the production of hormones as soon as the body weight diminishes. Some parts of the nervous system are also less active reducing thus the metabolism.

  Less calories are transformed.
- *Adipous Tissue:* The adipous tissue elaborates leptin, a compound which signalises the brain to increase the feeling of hunger, and the body temperature is slightly reduced, reducing thus the basal metabolism.
- *Stomach:* The stomach produces ghrelin which is an hormone triggering hunger feeling in the brain.

- *Pancreases:* The pancreases produces insulin which is reduced when the body weight falls. Less insulin brings the brain to increase appetite and reduces energy consumption.
- *Muscle Mass:* Body weight reduction is related with loss of muscle mass, this means that the overall consumption of calories is also reduced resulting again in weight gain.

The studies clearly state that overweight is not bound to a genetic code, what is settled is the individual energy output. Seven strategies are recommended:

1. *Stay Mobile:* Sport and mobility during work reduces the risk of overweight. The main goal of sport and mobility is to keep, or build muscle mass. Walking, swimming or biking are recommended by the authors.
   - Make sport of 30 minutes three times a week
   - Don't use elevators. Use stairs instead of escalators. Use your bike or walk to your office.
2. *Never Say "Never":* Trying to avoid everything brings frustration the moment you make a small error. You may have a nice fatty dinner as long you compensate it the next day with vegetables or you insert an extra sport session.
3. *Don't Loose the Rhythm:* Eat always at the same time. Take your time for your meals.do not eat in a hurry. Do not miss your breakfast.
4. *Controll is Necessary:* Weigh yourself once a day or at least once a week, so you can take countermeasures as soon as your weight rises.
5. *Be Stingy with Fat:* You can do without butter, fatty cheese, heavy sauces and fatt pork. Instead of this you can eat vegetables and fruits instead.
6. *Fresh Vegetables:* You can eat as much vegetables and salad. as you wish. You get enough dietary fibre and have a low calorie intake. Eat small portions of fruits spare with banana, raisins, grapes and dates.

7. *Join a Weight Club:* You may feel strong in company of kindred spirit in a weight club. Avoid people who seduce you to eat the wrong foods.

SPECIAL NUTRITION

Adventists of 7 Days

Nutrition of Adventists is reduced in proteins and may chose between 3 types:

1. Rigid vegetable nutrition (veganism)
2. Ovo-lacto-vegetable nutrition (approximately 50% of adventists follow this nutrition)
3. Conventional nutrition low in meat, avoiding completely the intake of pork and his derivatives, molluscs and blood.

Every meal should have many grains of cereals, fruits and vegetables. Strong spices are avoided,

Old cheese and spicy cheese such as roquefort as well as alcoholic beverages or caffeine are not allowed.

There are only three meals each day without any coffee break.

It is interesting that there is a smaller number of cancer of adventists and Mormons as found in other groups. There is no doubt that the different nutrition of adventists and Mormons is one important factor of lower cancer rate.

Batiste

They have moderate meals and negation of alcohol.

Buddhists

Nutrition generally veganic, no bulb vegetables are eaten(onions, garlic etc). Ban of alcohol and caffeine.

Hare Krishnas

Vegetarian nutrition, raw meals. Veganic nutrition is seldom followed. Ban of alcohol and caffeine.

Hindus

1. *Lower Castes:* Mixed nutrition with little meat, sheep, lamb, goats, pork, chicken and fish. Bovine and buffalo meat are not eaten
2. *High Castes (Brahmans):* Lacto-vegetal nutrition with exclusion of any kind of meat and fish, often exclusion of eggs. The nutrition avoids bulb vegetables (onions, garlic and leek). Alcohol is forbidden.

Mormons

Mormons are moderate in nutrition. They eat fruits and vegetables and have a moderate consumption of meat.

Such moderate nutrition is reduced in fat, albumin, cholesterol and purines. Vitamins and dietary fibres are higher as found in normal nutrition.

Mormons and adventists have lower cancer rate as other groups. There way of life and their nutrition seems to be the reason for favorable statistics.

Jews

Jews try to avoid any kind of excesses. There are detailed rules concerning consume of meat. The animals are chosen and killed ritualistic by a butcher which is determined by the community. Bovine meat is permitted, as well as goats, lamb, poultry (excluding carnivorous birds) fish with scales and fins.

Forbidden is pork, meat of horses, camels, rodents, carrion eating animals, bird of prey, eel, octopus, Crustacea, milk and eggs of forbidden animals, blood and meat with rests of blood, fatty acids from organs such as kidneys, sciatic nerve.

Supply of meat and derivatives is made by communities.

Milk and meat are not consumed together. Milk has to be taken immediately before meals containing meat, or 5 to 6 hours after. Milk substitutes of vegetable origin have no restriction.

Milk and milk products in soups, margarine, ice cream and chocolate must always be taken in consideration.

Food containing milk are to be kept and handled separated from food containing meat and their derivatives. This refers also to utensils such as pots, knifes, forks and spoons, plates, napkin have to be used only for one type of food. Dish washing of both types of food must be separately.

Fish, eggs and vegetable food can be consumed together with meat. There is no restriction.

During Passah (the Jewish eastern) unleavened bread is eaten.

Kosher Foods

The food scares in Europe and in US shows a great need of further food quality control through official governmental ruled authorities.

Industry and retail service are engaged in a catastrophic price war in the struggle for might and power. That is why the level of assessment between good and evil in the practice of business world is being lowered and gives chances to outlaw practices in food industry.

In this struggle ethics are put aside, unfortunately also by governments such as the case of BSE meat being forced to be sold in the European Community by directives of the Commission of the European Community. It is that why US consumer starts to buy kosher foods in the hope to get food produced under strictly controlled environmental technologies.

In US the market of kosher food is growing by over 10% each year and even over 40% of all grocery items are kosher certified in the Northeast America. Religion is not the only motivation for these customers.

Over 60 % of kosher food buyers are not Jewish. Muslims, Seventh Day Adventists, vegetarians, people with specific allergies and consumer seeking extra quality look for food labelled as kosher.

What is Kosher Food ? Kosher means "fit" and is regarded as prepared in accordance with Jewish food laws.

The laws are biblical in origin coming from the five books of the Bible. Interpretation and extentions were made by rabbits in order to include new foods and new processes such as new technologies.

Slavery of Desires and Emancipation of Animal Inclinations

Rabbi Grunfeld wrote in 1972 an essay about why Jews follow kosher dietary laws: "Holiness or self sanctification is a moral term; it is identical with moral freedom or moral autonomy. Its aim is the complete self-mastery of man."

"To the superficial observer it seems that men who do not obey the law are freer than law-abiding men because they can follow their own inclinations. In reality however, such men are subject to the most cruel bondage; they are slaves of their own instincts, impulses and desires. The first step towards emancipation from the tyranny of animal inclination in man is, therefore, a voluntary submission to the moral law. The constraint of law is the beginning of human freedom...Thus the fundamental idea of Jewish ethics, holiness, is inseparably connected with the idea of law; and the dietary laws occupy a central position in that system of moral discipline which is the basis of all Jewish laws."

"The three strongest natural instincts in man are the impulses of food, sex, and acquisition. Judaism does not aim at the destruction of these impulses but at their control and indeed their sanctification. It is the law which spiritualises their instincts and transfigures them into legitimate joys of life."

Certification of Kosher Food

In USA an organization makes an audit on the production line of the food which is going to be certified as kosher. Ingredients and technology is examined in order to see if it is in accordance to the Jewish law. With a contract the producer signs an obligation to avoid any change.

European certification is done by a rabbi which visits the plant. He alone decides if the product is kosher. There is no contract being made and the company can therefore change its produce after the rabbi has gone. This is a matter of ethics. A good company will maintain the rules imposed by the rabbi. Bad ethics will follow the way which is the best to it.

In London the Beth Din companyis specialized in certification of kosher food plants all over Europe.

Kosher Laws

Jewish religion laws are the basis of kosher laws. It seems that the rules based on the Old Testament of the Holy Bible developed from experiences such as diseases coming from pork which was contaminated by Trichinella spiralis. Eating pork with trichinosis could cause disease thus proving that pigs were impure animals.

Kashrus

The Kashrus magazine lists foods and ingredients which are certified as kosher, as well all kosher certification agencies of the world down to single Rabbis

Kosher Laws

First Law: Allowed animals.

Allowed are mammals which chew their cud and have a split hoof. So cows are permitted. Pigs and horses are forbidden.

Birds: Chicken, ducks and goose are allowed. Ostrich and Emu are forbidden.

Fish: All fish with fins and easily removable scales (without tearing the skin) are allowed.

Molluscs and Crustaceans: This includes shrimps lobsters and oysters are forbidden, such as lard, chitin and porcine lipase.

Ingredients: All ingredients derived from not kosher foods are forbidden. Ingredients such as gelatin, tallow or lard, chemicals derived from animal fat such as glycerol or monoglycerides are prohibited.

Emulsifiers such as used in the production of margarine containing mono and diglycerides are of great concern as their plant or animal origin are often unknown.

Second Law: Animal bloodBlood is considered to be a special fluid inherent to life. Consumption is forbidden. Slaughter must be performed by a trained person in a way to eliminate the blood from the remaining meat. Slaughter must therefore follow a specific procedure.

Heat, hot water and various acids to prevent microbial contamination are forbidden at this stage of processing. Inspection of the meat must guarantee that there are no specific defects. After that the meat is soaked and salted to remove last remains of blood. The second law does not apply to fish.

Third Law: Separation of dairy products from meat products and equipment used.

The third law says that all kosher foods, ingredients and equipment are classified in three categories:

1. Dairy products
2. Meat products
3. *Pareve:* Here are included all vegetable foods fish, eggs and honey. Pareve food and their ingredients must be dairy free.

People with allergies to milk and their derivates, allergies to egg proteins and vegan vegetarians welcome the third law as they can find the separation of these three categories which are not being observed by any other food laws. Pareve may contain a certain amount of milk and their derivates as it is sometimes not to be avoided. This may be tolerated for religious purposes but should be kept in mind of those who are very sensitive.

Ingredients allowed for pareve foods: Agar-agar, Carrageen, dextrose, gum arabic (Acacia), lecithin Chocolate may also contain milk and milk derivates. The technical equipment used for milk chocolate must be cleaned carefully before producing pareve chocolate. European chocolate may have up to 5% of other fats than cocoa fat. These fats can be of vegetable and of animal origin.

Fourth Law: Ban of leavened products made from grains of wheat, oats, rye, barley and spelt during the Passover week.

Permitted is matzo which is a specifically prepared unleavened bread, matzo meal and matzo cake flour.

Many baked products are available completely grain free giving persons with grain allergies such as coeliac disease to get foods which are free of certain allergens.

Grain-like Materials

Rabbis in Europe have extended the prohibition of the grain rules to other grain-like materials such as legumes, corn, rice mustard and sesame seeds.

Sugar and corn syrup are avoided as ingredients of many products during Passover The third rule supports the theory that the deep roots of the Jewish religious laws regarding kosher foods were unconciously based on veterinary and epidemiological experiences which had summed over centuries under the classification " this is good and that is bad".

Kosher Technology

The production and marketing of kosher food require:

1. A reputable rabbinical supervision agency (or a single Rabbi in Europe) must be contacted.
2. All ingredients are checked are included in the Kashrus. The equipment and their material must be examined to be kosher. There are restrictions on account of parts made of rubber ceramics and some plastics.
3. All ingredients must be completely labelled on kosher food thus providing a complete information for sensitive people, whereas normal food regulation use class names and exceptions allowed to hide some of the ingredients.

Ingredients which require kosher supervision: Casein, emulsifiers fats, fatty acids, lipids and whey.

MOSLEMS

Halaal Food: Halaal food means permitted, allowed lawful or legal for Muslims. The opposite of Halaal is Haraam meaning prohibited, not allowed, unlawful, illegal. Halaal is a set of Islamic dietary laws guided by the Qur'an the Holy Book and the teachings of Allah's profet Muhammad, may peace and blessing be upon him. Nutrition of Muslims differs from one region to another. There is a strong negation of pork and his derivates, gelatine, meat of dogs, birds of prey, frogs and snails.

Killing of animals are ritually. Alcohol is forbidden. Consume of blood is not allowed. The use of animal fat in baking is forbidden. Gelatine is not allowed.

Exceptions are allowed only in emergencies.

The rules for Halaal are very similar to those of kosher foods.

The most important rules for Halaal are:

1. Meat must be slaughtered in a particular way.
2. Only certain animal products are allowed
3. Technological processing, like Processing aids, cleaning materials and equipment used in production must be free from prohibited food traces.

These Restrictions are based on the Quran (The Revealed Book) and Sunna: The Islamic dietary laws which rule the production of Halaal foods is a religious matter which can be handled only by a Muslim expert. The Quran is the holy book of Muslims, being the last testament and revealed from God (Allah) as the Holly bible.

The Quran says: Sura five (The table) (Al-Maida) verse 4 to 5. "(4) It is forbidden to eat: From which has died by himself, blood and meat of swine and of that by whose slaughter another name as Allah has been invoked, and of that which has been suffocated dead by beating or which has fallen to death or which has been killed by the horns of other animals or have been killed by other wild animals, (except the animal which has been wounded by wild animal came to your hands still alive and you have finally killed it by yourself), and this what has been slaughtered in honour to wrong idols."

Other quotations are:

The Hadith (sayings of the last Prophet, Muhammad

The figh (jurisprudence) of the Muslim Jurists Hanafi, Shafii, Maliki and Hanbali.

The Muslim Food Board (UK) is one company which investigates and certifies Halaal foods.Heat, hot water and various acids to prevent microbial contamination are permitted. Technology and science has deeply changed production, ingredients and packaging enhancing shelf life, food colour and texture. Global spread of exotic foods and rapid changing of nutritional habits make it important to verify the lawfulness of food in compliance with the commands of the Islam.

Muslims are allowed to eat food prepared by people who are of other beliefs (5:5) and Muslim food is permitted to be eaten by them, on condition that these foods are pure and permitted foods. (5:88). This permits an interchange and living together of Muslims with other groups all over the world. This is very important for the functioning of our global world.

However some precautions should be made: 'Do not eat unless Allah's name has been taken and this (not taking Allah's name) practice is transgression' (Qur`an 6:121)

The Ahlul-kitaab of today are recognized by name, less faith. There is no guarantee that they take the name of Allah/ God when slaughtering an animal. Furthermore, they cannot be anymore trusted in matters pertaining to Halaal/haram. Unless there is certainty that the Ahlul-kitaab read the 'Tasmiyah' i.e. take the name of God when slaughtering an animal, only then the meat will be permissible. It was suggested that the Muslims in the U.S.A. and U.K. slaughter the animals themselves. This will make them independent from Christian/ Jewish sources.

The meat sold on the market such as supermarkets should be packed, sealed and stamped by a Muslim organisation consisting of reliable scholars and Úlama who have proper Islamic knowledge of the principles pertaining to Halaal/haram.

Intoxicants, such as alcohol are forbidden because they are harmful substances.(2:219) (5:91) Consume of blood is not allowed. The use of animal fat in baking is forbidden.

Exceptions are allowed only in emergencies, such as being forced by hunger, without intention to practice sin (2:175, 5:5)

The classification of new foods and their ingredients in Halaal and haram, based on the commandments of the Qum`ran the Holy Book can only be done by an Muslim expert. The Islamic religion does not have a central religious head which dictates latest findings but some authorities are accepted in their leadership, such as the mufti of the Al Azhar University of Cairo. Due to different translations of the Koran the local interpretation of its content differs from country to country.

Haram Ingredients: Any product or by-product (including any product used temporarily as a substitute) which contains any one or more of haram products in however minute quantity, whether as an ingredient or sub-ingredient or as a processing aid or as a releasing agent or as a glazing agent or as an additive or as a colour or in any other form, is haram.

Acacia gum	**E414**	**Ammonium carrageenan**	**Antioxidants (BHA and BHT)**
Acetic acid		Ammonium chloride	Arachidonic acids
Adipic acid (acidulant)	E355	Ammonium sulfate	Artificial colour
Agar	E406	Amylase	Ascorbic acid E300
Algin/calcium alginat	E404	Amylose	Aspartame

Baking soda		**BHT Butylated hydroxytoluene**	**E321**	**Sparrow, emu**
Benzoate of soda	E211	Bird, exclude bird of prey		Ostrich
Benzoic acid	E210	Chicken, duck, turkey, goose		Butyric acid
BHA Butylated Hydroxyyanisole	E320	Pigeon, dove, partridge, quail		

Calciferol (Vitamin D³)		**Calcium sorbate**	**E203**	**casein**
Calcium acid phosphate		Carbohydrates (natural)		Cellulose E460
Calcium carrageenan		CMC Carboxymethylcellulose	E466	Cellulose gum
Calcium disodium EDTA		Carotenoid		Cholecalciferol
Calcium carbonate		Carrageenen	E407	Choline fron yeast, soy
Calcium propionate	E282	Carrot oil		corn meal,corn starch
Calcium saccharin	E954	Carragecnin	E407	Corn syrup
Calcium silicate	E552	Carotene	E160a	Cultures,living microbes

Dextrin	**E1499**	**Diglyceride (plant)**		**Disacharides**
Dextrose		Dipotassium phosphate		
Dicalcium phosphate		Disodium inosinate	E631	

Erythorbic acid	**E315**	**Ergosterol**		**Enzyme (plant)**
Ergocalciferol				

Farina		**Ferrous sulfate**		**Fructose**
Fatty acids (plant)		Fibre		Fumaric acid E297
Ferric orthophosphate		Ficin		Fungal protease enzyme
Ferrous gluconate	E579			

Shubhah (Mushbooh)

Shubhah or Mushbooh means "suspected" and is applied for foods or drinks from which it is not known to be Halaal or haram.

Shubhah or Mushbooh foods, being doubtful foods or drinks should not be consumed.

Acetic acid ester of Mono-	Alanine	Animal fat
diglycerides (animal) E272a		
Beta-carotene, apocarotenal	Bile salts	Broth (animal)
using animal based gelatine		
Brilliant blue E133	Carcium stearoyl lactylate E482	Charcoal (animal)
Chelate	Cholesterol	Chymotrypsin
Citric acid ester of Mono-	Cobalamine	Cochineal E120
Diglycerides (animal) E272c		
Coloring extract	Cures	Cystein
Cystine	Diglyceride (animal)	Disodium guanilate
Dissodium inosinate	Dripping (animal)	EDTA
Enzyme (animal)	Etoxylated mono-/diglyceride	Fatty acids(animal)
Folic acid	Glyceride (animal)	Glycerol/glycerin
Glycerol stearates	Glycogen	Gum traganth E413
Histamine	Hormones (animal)	Hydrolysed animal protein
Inositol	Insulin	Keratin
Lactic acid ester of Mono-	Lactose made from whey	Lipids
diglyceride (animal) E272	which is produced from animal rennet	
Monoglycerides (animal)	Monopotassium tartarate E336i	Niacin
	(tartar Cream) from wine	
Oleic acid	Oxysterin	Para amino benzoic acid
Pepsin (animal)	Phenyl alanine	Phospholipid (animal)
Phosphoric acid E338	Polysacharides-glycogen	Polysorbate 60 E435
Polysorbate 80 E433	Polyunsaturated (animal)	Propylene glycol
		alginate E405
Propylene glycol monostearate	Quinoline yellow E104	Renin/rennet (unless it is
	if animal glycerol is use	of plant/microbial/synthetic
		origin)
Riboflavin	Rum flavour	Saccharine E954
Shortening(animal)	Sodium lauryl sulfate	Sodium stearate(animal)
Sodium stearoyl-2-lactylate E481	Sorbitan monostearate E491	Sodium nitrate E251
Sweetener-Aspartame	Sweentener-Cyclamate	Sweetener-Saccharine
Stearate	Stearic acid	Sunset yellow E110
Sucroglycerides E474	Tartaric acid E 334	Tartaric acid ester of Mono-
	from wine	diglycerides (animal) E272d
Tartazine E102	Thiamin	Tonic
Trypsin		

Alcohol	Animal fat	Alcoholic beverages
Animal shortening	Bacon (pork)	Boar
Carmin E120	CochinealCollagen (pork)	
Carnivorous animal (Lion,tiger, cheetah, dog, cat)	Cider (alcohol)	Cocaine
Codeine	Fermented malt	Gelatin
Lipase(animal origin)	Kosher gelatin	l-cysteine (if from human hair)
Monkey	Pepsin (Hog)	Pork
Rennet	Sodium nitrite E250	Uric acid
Snakes	Tallow	Vanilla extract (alcohol)
Wine	Whey (unless the rennet used is plant/microbial/ synthetic	

Ritual Slaughter

The Sunna describes the ritual slaughter. All animals should be slaughtered according to this Islamic ritual with exception to animals shot during hunting. Ritual slaughter should be done invoking the name of Allah and cutting the throat, artery and gullet with one stroke of a sharp knife. The animalö must be alive at the moment of slaughter in order to allow total bleeding because consumption of blood is forbidden.

Blood is therefore used as meal for animal feeding or dried together with the content of stomach and intestines as agriculture fertilizer. According German veterinary rules animals have to be made unconscious before bleeding. The University Al Azhar of Cairo has accepted stunning with electro shocks. This however is not according to the opinion of the majority of Moslems which consider such slaughter as haraam.

ANIMAL SLAUGHTER RESEARCH

At the University of Hanover, Germany Professor Schultz and Dr. Hazim used Electroencephalograph (EEG) and electrocardiogram (ECG) to compare the pain caused by Islamic slaughter and western method using captive bolt stunning.

According to both scientists the Halaal method caused no change in the graph of the EEG the first 3 minutes after cutting the throat of the animal according to Islamic ritual.The next tree minutes showed a condition of deep sleep, followed by a zero level.The heart was still pumping and convulsion of the animal due to a reflex of the spinal cord driving maximum quantity of blood out of the body. Islamic slaughter was therefore classified as humane and hygienic method.

Western method by captive bolting stunning showed in the graph of the EEG signs of severe pain. The heart stopped beating retaining much blood in the body.

The western method was therefore classified by the authors as unhumane and unhygienic for the consumer because of increased amount of blood being retained in meat.

Ramadan, the Fast-month

Consumption of food and beverages during daytime. There is only one meal right after sunset and one meal before sunrise. This rule is very difficult to be followed by hard workers, persons exposed to high temperatures and travelers.

Halaal (Lawful) Food Product Definition

The Muslim Food Board (U.K.) gives the following definition of food for Moslems:

Halaal food is defined as any food product that is free from all of the following:

Any product or by-product derived from:

a) Pig

b) Blood

c) Carnivorous animals (except fish]

d) Reptiles and insects

e) Any marine animals except fish

f) The bodies of dead animals

g) The bodies of Halaal animals (i.e. Buffalo, Cow, Sheep, Lamb, Goat, Deer, Rabbit, Chicken etc.) which are not slaughtered according to the Islamic Law.

h) Wine,Ethyl Alcohol or Spirits, where these remain in their original chemical form.

Vinegar, Produced from Alcohol: Fermentation is only permitted when vinegar as final product is wanted. A rest of 0,5% alcohol in the vinegar is permitted. A natural content of alcohol in fruit juices is tolerated even by deep religious people.

Any product or by-product (including any product used temporarily as a substitute] which contains any one or more of the above products in however minute quantity, whether as an ingredient or sub-ingredient or as a processing aid or as a releasing agent or as a glazing agent or as an additive or as a color or in any other form, is Haraam (unlawful) for Muslims.

Some examples of Halaal food products are as follow:

1. Milk (Cow, Sheep and Goats)
2. Honey
3. Eggs
4. Fish
5. Edible plants (including sea plants), which are not intoxicant
6. Edible fresh or naturally frozen vegetables
7. Edible fresh or dried fruits
8. Edible nuts like peanuts,cashew nuts, hazel nuts, Walnuts etc.
9. Edible grains such as wheat, rice, rye, barley, oats etc.
10. Edible condiments such as cardamom, clove, sage leaves, turmeric, chilli, curcumin etc.

1. Some common examples of Haraam (unlawful,forbidden) food products are as follows:

   Bone stocks or animal fats (e.g.: Lard, suet, dripping, gelatine, aspic, glycerol, stearates, stearic acid, proteins, amino acids, bone, charcoal, pepsin, animal renet etc.)

At the beginning of 1998 the Al Azhar University of Cairo redefined gelatine as Halaal. According to the University of Cairo is gelatine a food ingredient which is so strongly hydrolysed that there is no connection left with the original pig. This new point of view is official granted but not everywhere accepted by all Moslems. The industrial use of gelatine should therefore be avoided.

The Islamic religion does not have a central religious head which dictates latest findings but some authorities are accepted in their leadership, such as the mufti of the Al Azhar University of Cairo.

Due to different translations of the Koran the local interpretation of its content differs from country to country.

2. Any additive or color derived from animals:

   E 120 Cochineal

   E 104 Quinoline yellow (if glycerol is used)

   E 153 Carbon black (if animal charcoal is used)

   E 471 Mono and diglycerides of fatty acids (if animal products is used)

   E 472 (a to e) Acetic,lactic, citric, tartaric acid esters of mono and diglycerides of fatty acids (if animal product is used)

   E 474 Sucroglycerides (if animal product is used)

   E 476 Polyglycerol esters of polycondensated fatty acids of castor oil (if animal product is used)

3. Production of whey powder or whey solids using animal based rennet.
4. Lactose made from whey which is produced using animal rennet.
5. Lining of containers with animals or alcohol products as used in baking of bread, cakes etc.
6. Production of beta-carotene and apocarotenal using animal based gelatine.

7. Use of animal based glycerine as a coating for raisins or as a flower improver.
8. Vitamins A, D and beta-carotene which is protected in a matrix that do not conform to the above Halaal Food Production definition. The above are some examples of Halaal and Haraam food products,the list is by no means complete.
9. Plants which can cause drug addiction and cause doping.

Not permitted foods are called Haraam. The hypothesis that certain kinds of food were forbidden because of hygienic reasons was made by Lück in 1966 and Saleh in 1972. This hypothesis is nowadays denied unanimously.It is believed that all rules have strict religious origin. A food does not lose his halaal character when it proves to be allergic to a small part of the population.

Toxic foods such as containing aflatoxins are haraam because they are harmful.

DEFINITION OF HALAAL FOOD ACCORDING TO THE CODEX ALIMENTARIUS

Muslim halal dietary laws are found in the Qumramand the books of Hadith (the Traditions). Interpretation of these laws are made by Muslim scholars over the years to make an update to modern nutritional knowledge including new processes which are being used in modern technology.The basic principles of the Islamic laws should however not be altered. Because of the growing global Moslem population the committee of the Codex Alimentarius has set up rules for a global definition of Halaal Foods. According to the Codex Alimentarius are Halaal Foods those which are conforming with the Islamic laws. They do not contain anything which is forbidden by the Islamic laws. They were handled stored and free of any forbidden materials.During their production they were kept away from other food which are not conforming with Islamic laws.

The processing or storage of halaal foods is allowed in the same room where not halaal food is being processed or stored when it is absolutely sure that any contact between both foods are avoided.

It is allowed to prepare Halaal foods which equipments which have been used to prepare not halaal foods when cleaning of the equipment according to Islamic laws have been performed. Basic foods which are Halaal according to the Codex Alimentarius All foods are considered as Halaal with exception of specific animal origin or containing products or derivates from not law conform origin.

Haraam Animal Food

- Pigs and boars
- Dogs, snakes and monkeys
- Carnivorous animals with claws and tusks such as lions, tigers, bears, and similar animals.
- Birds of prey with talons, such as eagle, vulture and similar animals
- Pests like rats,centipedes, scorpions and similar animals.
- Animals which according to Islamic laws should not be killed such as ants, bees and woodpecker
- Repulsive animals such as lice,flies worms and similar animals
- Animals which can live on land and in water such as frogs, crocodiles and similar animals
- Mules and similar animals
- All poisonous and dangerous animals of the sea
- All animals which have been slaughtered disregarding the Islamic laws.
- Blood

Haraam Vegetable Foods

All poisonous and dangerous plants are considered as Haraam, unless the poison or the danger is being discarded during processing.

Haraam Beverages

All alcoholic beverages are haraam as well all forms of poisoning and dangerous beverages.

Haraam Additives

All additives which originate from the foods cited before are considered as Haraam.

Halaal Slaughter

- All animals living on land according to Islamic laws should be slaughtered in accordance to the Islamic hygienic rules.
- The person who slaughters the animal should be of Islamic religion and should know the Islamic slaughter procedure.
- The animals which are to be slaughtered should be in conformity with the Islamic laws
- ``The sentence "Bismillah" (in the name of Allah) should be uttered immediately before the slaughter of every animal.
- The slaughter instruments should be sharp and not withdrawn from the animal during slaughter
- Slaughter should happen cutting the windpipe,the gullet and the most important veins and arteries in the neck.

Labeling of Halaal Food According to the Codex Alimentarius

If Halaal characteristics are mentioned in relation to food the term "Halaal" should be declared on the label. Claims suggesting that Halaal foods are more nourishing or healthier than other foods should be avoided.

What is behind a Brand

Halaal Chocolate Confectioneries: Confectionery is commonly forbidden as ingredients as gelatin, enzymes and emulsifiers are considered Mashbooh because he origin of the ingredients is not known. Tesco, however wants to introduce the Ummah Foods chocolate range, being free of animal fat. "Ummah" means "the Muslim community" Ummah Foods already supplies the Halaal orange and caramel chocolate bars to Islamic bookshops, newsagents and universities in UK in 2006.

Launching his products among the Muslim population of East-London, Mr.Kahlid Sharif, director of Ummah Foods, believes that winning over the Muslim customer base, rather than targeting a broader ``ethical" market, is the key to success. Mr. Sharif says ``You cannot put a Muslim name on a product and not expect the core customers to be Muslim". With Tesco targeting the ethnic foods, changes this marketing strategy.

Qibla Cola: The brand has a presence as far as England, Canada, Pakistan and Africa. Since Qibla is an Islamic word used to describe the direction in which Muslims face to pray, one could think that the cola is aimed at Muslims. However, according to the producer the target is everyone who wants to make a conscious decision to buy an ethical brand.

Quakers: Quakers don't have a set of rules about anything including nutrition. Their principle is moderation in all things.

Rosacrucis: Lacto-vegetable, renunciation of alcohol.

Not to be mistaken by A.M.O.R.C. Antiquus Misticus Ordae Rosae Cruzis who smoke, drink alcohol, all forms of nutrition are allowed.

Sikhs: Meat of bovines and alcohol are not allowed.

Weight Reduction

Daily Intake of Energy

The only way to treat overweight is to bring the daily intake of energy down to the level of the daily output of energy. None of the above mentioned wonder diets have brought a durable weight reduction. "Eat half of what you eat now" can reduce intake of calories to an acceptable amount.

Formula Diets: Formula diets such as Cambridge-diet, Day-fit, Slimfastor Herbalife according to DGE (Deutsche Gesellschaft für Ernährung) are expensive, reduce life quality and destroy environment.

Formula diets in Germany have to be in accordance to the Diet-directrix which prescribes the concentration of nutritional components. The amount of dietary fibres of formula-diet is often to low, so fibres and pellets of peelings and hull of cereals are added.

FORMULA DIETS FOR WEIGHT REDUCTION ACCORDING TO CODEX ALIMENTARIUS

Formula Foods for weight reduction diets are foods which are ready to serve or must be prepared according to instructions and are intended to replace one or more meals of the day.

Formula foods to replace all daily meals. They should have at least 800 kcal(3.350 kJ) and not more than 1.200 kcal (5020 kJ). for a day, divided in three or four meals with equal amount of calories.

Formula foods to replace one or more meals. To replace one or more meals they should have at least 200 kcal (835 kJ) and not more than 400 kcal (1.670 kJ) for each meal.

If the formula foods are claimed to replace main meals they should not have more than 1.200 kcal (5.020 kJ). The formula diet system is not a safe system to reduce body weight. As soon as one comes back to former nutritional habits the overweight returns. This is called Jo-Jo-effect.

Publicity campaigns using words like flavour and delicious meals were prohibited in relation to formula diets because of their monotonous flavour which becomes disgusting being used for a long period.

To reduce body weight the DGE says to return to normal balanced nutritional habits.

There should be no struggle with the body.

A permanent bad conscience leads to stress. A good feeling is to achieve having no feeling of guilt.

As an orientation about the amount of energy which is necessary in normal life a table of the daily required energy is given below. This table does not replace weighing. It is not possible to calculate the real daily intake of energy and there is not possible to determinate the ideal intake of energy because each individual has its own basal metabolism and has different jobs and do different sports requiring different amount of energy.

The determination of nutritive value of carbohydrates and proteins in relation to their content in calories are calculated using calorie tables when recipes are known.

If recipes are not available the content of fat by means of solvent extraction are determined. Proteins are measured by means of the Kjeldahl method using the factor of 6,25 for conversion of nitrogen to protein. The content of fibres and water are determined at 105 C. Carbohydrates are calculated as being the rest of it. The energy of 100 g of food is calculated using the following values:

Ingredient	kJ	kcal
1 g protein	17 kJ	4 kcal
1 g fat	37kJ	9 kcal
1 g carbohydrate	17 kJ	4 kcal

Calorimetry: Calorimetry burning the food in a closed system and measuring the rise of temperature is a method which is seldom used.

Age	kCal/day (man/women)	cJoules/day (man/women)
0 to 2 month	550	2.200
2 to 5 month	750	3.100
6 to 11 month	850	3.600
1 to 3 years	1.100	4.500
4 to 6 years	1.500	6.500
7 to 9 years	1.900	8.000
10 to 12 years	2.300/2.200	9.500/9.000
13 to 14 years	2.700/2.500	11.500/10.500
15 to 18 years	3.000/2.400	12.500/10.000
19 to 35 years	2.600/2.000	11.000/9.000
36 to 50 years	2.400/2.000	10.000/8.500
51 to 65 years	2.200/1.800	9.000/7.500
65 years		
1.900/1.700	8.000/7.000	
Pregnancy	+ 300	+ 1.200
Breath-feeding	+ 700	+ 3.000

This table is made for people with normal activities. For hard workers please add:

- For moderate hard workers add 2.500 kJ (600 kcal)
- For very hard workers add 5.000 kJ (1.200 kcal
- For super hard workers add 6.700 kJ (1.600 kcal)

Drugs to Fight Bodyweight

The classic diets and fasting are seldom long lasting. The pharmaceutical industry is conscious of the growing market of drugs to reduce weight without changing once life habits.

H. HAUNER writes: "For the moment being there are no convincing drugs for treatment of overweight. The majority of authorized Drugs act on the neurotransmitter noradrenalin or serotonin. Suppressant of appetite like derivates of amphetamines should be used very seldom because of their side reactions (such as rise of heart beat frequency and rise of blood pressure, insomnia, pulmonary hypertension), their short time of activity and the danger of habit formation. A long-time effect every overweight therapy are disappointing. Only less than one third of patients can hold their weight after a diet."

Xenical, the Antifat Drug

Xenical is a drug containing the substance orlistat. It can reduce bodyweight up to 10% without serious side effects.

Xenical can help when used for a long period together with a change of life habits. Its activity takes place in the intestines. It reduces the absorption of fat up to 30 percent. Xenical is being produced by Hoffmann la Roche, Grenzach, Swiss.

Orlistat: Orlistat is a synthetic substance resulted from the research regarding lipstatin which had been found in bacteria which live in the soil of Mallorca, the Island in the Mediterranean Sea. Lipstatin was found to slow down the absorbtion of fat. This took the research of Roche to the discovery of orlistat. Xenical was liberated on the European market in august 1998.

Reductil: Reductil is being sold in the USA under the name of MERIDIA. It acts in the brain reducing appetite. The active substance of Reductil is sibutramin Reductil is being produced by BASF-Knoll (Badische Anilin und Soda Fabrik). The drug has been liberated by the FDA (Food and Drug Administration)in USA only after a long time. A similar drug, the appetite suppressant REDUX with its active part the dexfenfluramin presented dangerous secondary reactions. In Germany and in Austria Redux had been sold under the name of Isomeride. Redux has caused damage of cardiac valves as well as pulmonary hypertension. After many tests it has been proved that Reductil does not have these side reactions.

Amphetamines: Amphetamines were used in war to keep soldiers awake during combat.Later amphetamines were found to act as appetite suppressant and being sold as such. Very soon the selling was canceled because of heart complaints, Angina-pectoris tremble and nervosity.

Phentermin and Norephedrine: Phentermine is the active substance of Adipex N and norephedrine was used in Antidiapositum X 112 Fugoa N and Regenon. They are appetite suppressant. They have. the same side reactions noted by amphetamines. Phentermin was prohibited in Germany because of the high blood pressure of the pulmonary artery. In Austria it is still being sold under the name Adipex.

Aminorex: Aminorex was used as active substance of the drug Menocil. Its selling was canceled because of irreparable high pressure at the pulmonary artery.

Phenfluramine: Phenfluramine is an appetite suppressant which stimulates serotonin presenting the same side reactions described above as well as depressions.

Sesame seed and oil and control of high blood pressure: Researches at the Osaka University of Pharmaceutical Sciences and Taiwanese researchers have demonstrated vasodepressing properties which help to control high blood pressure.

Sesamin, a supplement made from sesame exerts action on nitric oxide production and its ability to inhibit ET-1 production from endothelial cells. ET-1 constricts blood vessels.

James R Marshall and Zhao Chen argue that epidemiologic patterns of disease-exposure associations must be interpreted in light of the profound imprecision of exposure assessment that characterizes nutritional epidemiology. The authors highlight the imposition of publication bias: the failure of researchers to submit and of editors to publish findings that do not fit well with the their own understanding. The information extracted from assays of associations between exposure and disease is always estimated with serious imprecision or bias.

Physiology of Hunger

Hunger has different phases:

Phase 1: The seat of the centre of hunger is located in the hipothalamus. Tiny sensors situated on the walls of the stomach and intestines communicate with the hipothalamus. They send informations about quantity of food filling the stomach and the intestines.

Other biochemical sensors control the concentration of the different substances such as glucose, the amino acids and the concentration of fatty acids in blood. These informations are also send to the hipothalamus.

When the level of glucose drops the hipothalamus sends signals to the brain where old habits related to the search for food are located.

Phase 2: If the body does not react on these signals the hipothalamus intensifies the signals of hunger.

Phase 3: If these strong signals of hunger does not work the hipothalamus changes his tactic and starts to burn fatty acids, situated in the centres of reserve.

Phase 4: If this phase is also overcome the hipothalamus erases the signals of hunger.

Hunger artists and Fakirs can overcome long periods of hunger. These people report that hunger vanishes after 2 to 3 days of starving being replaced by a feeling of wellnes which may escalate to euphoria.

Appetite to Specific Foods

The body can show unspecific hunger but also increase the desire to specific foods, for example:

Noradrenalin, insulin and the neuropeptide Y are responsible for the desire to eat bread or noodles.

Galanin is responsible for the desire to fatty food. As serotonin rises the desire for carbohydrates decreases increases the appetite to food rich in proteins such as fried meat. After a meal rich in proteins the blood level of serotonin decreases. The next meal will then be rich in carbohydrates.

Well-fed: The feeling of well-fed comes slowly. The first signals come from the walls of the stomach and intestines indicating the stretch of these organs. These informations are centralized in the brain.

The feeling of well-fed depends not only from the amount of food which had been eaten but also from the quality of food. One litre of water does not kill hunger.

The seat of the feeling of well-fed is located in the hipothalamus controlling also the level of nutrient substances in blood.

Noradrenalin and cholecystokinin are responsible for the informations of sufficient quantity of energy being stored. Other substances such as serotonin modulate the informations with emotions.

Serotonin is being produced in the brain and transported along the spinal cord to the neurons where it produces the feeling of well-fed.

Reductil, a suppressant of appetite: Reductil or Plenty makes serotonin stay for a longer time between the neurons. By this mean the appetite is suppressed. The neurotransmitter serotonin transmits the feeling of well-fed in the sinapsis from one neuron to another. after some time serotonin is slowly catabolized and partially reabsorbed by the neurons.

Reductil with sibutramin closes the way which exists in the cell membrane of the neurons in the region of the sinapsis avoiding serotonin being absorbed. Serotonin can therefore transmit for a longer time the feeling of well-fed.

At the end of the decade of the 80 the WHO (World Health Organization) had obesity declared as being a worldwide epidemic.

The FDA (Food and Drug Administration) being conscious of the gravity of the problem had speeded the registration and the approval of weight reducing substances. This caused a flood of new drugs, fibres to fill the stomach, laxatives, teas, special diets and appetite suppressants. All these products don't work or have serious side reactions.

Xenical, The Fight against Fat

Digestion of fat takes place with help of bilear acids and pancreatic lipases, which hydrolyzes the fat molecules enables thus the absorbtion by the gastric mucose.

Xenical by means of its active substance orlistat blocs the lipases of pancreas avoiding 30% of fat to be hydrolysed in smaller parts. Fat which is not hydrolysed cannot be absobed by the gastric mucous. It remains in the faeces causing diarrhea when to much fat is consumed. This causes an educational effect which lead to a reduced intake of foods rich in fat.

Xenical acts slowly. It is necessary to take the drug for a long period. It helps only in combination with a diet, together with a change of its nutritional habits towards a healthy composition: much fruits and vegetables, little meat, less fat accompanied by physical activities such as sport or garden work. One cannot escape the following overweight equation:

(Absorbed energy)-(Basal metabolism energy
+ physical activities energy) = Body fat

To reduce body weight it is necessary to eat less, to reduce fat intake, and practice more physical activities.

All efforts to reduce overweight with drugs, even surgery of the adipose tissue are not lasting when they are not accompanied by a change of the nutritional habits.

Basal Metabolic Rate: The Basal Metabolic Rate (BMR) is the number of calories burned in a 24 hours period while lying down, but not sleeping in a comfortably warm environment.

Active Metabolic Rate: The Active Metabolic Rate (AMR) is estimated by adding the caloric cost of all activities throughout the day to the BMR. A person should not eat less than their BMR but not more then their ANR.

SEROTONIN

Serotonin is a neurotransmitter which together with more than 100 other substances are active in the brain where nerve cells (neurons) link. Serotonin is 5-Hydroxytryptamine. Besides its biochemical activities in the neurophysiology it is also active as biogenic amine produced by bacteria. Serotonin is part of the blood clotting, being released by the trombocytes. Serotonin causes a strong contraction of blood vessels resulting in an increase of blood pressure.

Tryptophane is basis for serotonin. It is broken down by monoamineoxidase The Institute of Technology of Massachusetts discovered that a high level of serotonin provides good mood and avoids uncontrolled hunger and continuous desire to sweet food. Serotonin is therefore also known as " Good mood hormone". Serotonin should be present in a steady concentration of about 10 mg. Some foods are rich in serotonin such as pineapple, banana, tomatoes. Other foods are rich in trytophan which can be used by the body to synthetize serotonin. These foods should therefore build the basis for a long lasting diet to reduce overweight.

Foods rich in serotonin and/or Tryptophan:

Fruits: Pineapple,avocado, banana, date, fig, papaya.

Vegetable: Lamb's lettuce, carrot, round lettuce, leek, parsley, beetroot, spinach, tomato, onion.

Meat: Chicken, veal, beef, pork, turkey breast.

Seafood: Perch, catfish, trout, shrimp, herring, codfish, carp, salmon, spiny lobster, mackerel, mussel, sardine, haddock, plaice, pollack, sole, tuna.

Cereals: Rolled oats, rice, rye bread, white bread, rusk.

Milk and Eggs: Buttermilk, eggs, fresh cheese, yoghurt, low fat curd cheese, milk.

Nuts: Cashewkernel, peanuts, hazelnut, almond, Brazil nut, walnut.

Food with Reduced Fat

Curd cheese can be used in place of butter or margarine as bread spread.

Avoid all white sauces like mayonnaise, use vinegar or sauces made with diluted yoghurt. Be careful not to use Sauces with yoghurt from the supermarket. they contain small amount of yoghurt together with a lot of oil in order to increase self life. Avoid peanuts, sunflower nuts and other nuts. They contain much oil.

Avoid fried potatoes and all fast food.

Medical prescription of Xenical in case of BMI 30 to 40.

In Germany Xenical is being sold only with medical prescription. The BMI must be at least 30 (obesity degree I and higher).

Use of Xenical in case of BMI over 40: In case of overweight with a BMI over 40 the use of Xenical should not be used. The loss of weight would be to slow. In these cases the use of the Optifast program is indicated or even a surgical reduction of the stomach.

Xenical, the drug of the rich society: The use of Xenical is very expensive. The medication of one month with Xenical costs 200 Dm in Germany and 300 Reais in Brasil. The use of Xenical for two years costs 2.400 Dm.

Dexfenfluramin: Dexfenfluramin acts on the brain reducing appetite. It was recalled from market because of serious side reactions such as coronary problems. Dexfenfluramin had been sold under the name of Redux and is an example of serious side effects which are noted only after years of use. One of such horrible markers of the history of pharmacy Contergan which produced anatomical modifications on unborn. Other drugs which are being studied as possible weight reduction are leptin, neuropeptide Y inhibitor, and CCK hormone. CCK hormone is produced by the small intestine and acts as message substance telling the brain that there is enough food which has been taken in.

Instead of praising a new era of wellness-drugs (Viagra from Pfizer, Prozac from Eli Lilly an antidepressant, Propecia from Merck Sharp and Dohme for better hairs, Xenical from BASF to fight overweight and Reductil from Roche an appetite suppressant) one should come back to the real values of life.

Spices and Obesity: Magriet Westerterp-Plantenga and colleagues found that consumption of spiced foods or herbal drinks leads to greater thermogenesis (heat generation) and in some cases to greater satiety. In this regard, capsaicin, black pepper, ginger, mixed spices, green tea, black tea and caffeine are relevant examples.

The authors conclude that thermogenic ingredients may be considered as functional agents that could help in preventing a positive energy balance and obesity.

Active Capsaicin of red chilli pepper boosts heat generation by the body. More energy is therefore burned, reducing fat deposition.

Gingerols and shogaols of ginger have thermogenic properties.

Mixtures of of black pepper, red chilli, turmeric, cumin, ginger and other spices could therefore become interesting to help against obesity.

Piperine of black pepper, is said to bind to so-called Transient Receptor Potential Vanilloid (TRPV1)receptors in the brain and other parts of the nervous system.

Transient receptor potential or TRP:The phrase Transient receptor potential or TRP is appended to at least three classes of ion channels which mediate the response of a cell to external stimuli (electrical charge, substances, and forces) by increasing or decreasing its selective permeability to particular ions. The effect of this change is to modify the potential difference between inside and outside of the cell. Hence "receptor," for sensitivity to the environment, and "potential" for this difference. TRPV1 to TRPV4 can basically be seen as thermometers on a molecular level, and are activated by various means. When TRPV1 gets activated, it turns up the heat by boosting heat production by the body. TRPV1 is activated by noxious heat, acidic pH and capsaicin.

These new findings should not lead to a higher consumption of chilli con carne. Obesity is the result of many biochemical psychological and environmental occurrences. Seasoning could be a small contribution to tackle the obesity problem.

Rising childhood obesity were highlighted at the Conference trying to find out how additional increases in obesity could be prevented.

Matthew Gillman, MD, Harvard Medical School, Boston, Massachusetts, pointed out some of the highlights of the conference: factors in foetal development and the first six month of life:

- Preconception: Maternal prepregnancy body mass index (BMI) may determine pregnancy glucose and insulin levels in the mother and fetus, with high levels increasing newborn weight.
- Postnatal: The feeding of the newborn, infant, and child can determine the rate of growth and influence the timing and magnitude of the adiposity rebound seen in childhood

According to Dr. Gillman differences in birth weight as well as subsequent BMI may be determined by some the prenatal and postnatal environments In addition, genes that cause birth-weight differences may also determine BMI differences.

Alterations in the foetal environment: Transfer of fatty acids, leptin, and other hormones, foetal hyperinsulinemia, and the functioning of the foetal/placental unit are here included.

Other speakers pointed out: Breastfeeding is protective against obesity and should be encouraged to be practiced during the first year of life.

Foods and beverages that are energy dense and nutrient poor like soda and french fries should not be fed to infants as young as 7 months of age as they alter taste preferences.

Authoritative versus permissive parenting styles and their role in childhood obesity should be subject of further research.

Relationship of Birth Weight and Childhood

According to Dr S. Kramer from the McGill University, Montreal, Quebec, like the United States, Canada is experiencing an epidemic of obesity, not only among 6-to 17-year-old individuals but even in the toddler and preschool periods.

During the course of life, exposures that determine obesity may be attributable to environmental, social, behavioural, or biological factors.

He examined relationship of birth weight to weight in childhood data from the Special Supplemental Nutrition Program for Women, Infants, and Children (WIC) in Tennessee, and found that the 3.0-to 3.5-kg birth-weight grouping most closely approximated that value at 5 years of age. The lightest infants (1.0-1.5 kg) and the heaviest infants (4.5-5.0 kg) had the most extreme weight-for-age and height-for-age scores initially but moved to less extreme values within about 12 months.

Overweight status at 7 years of age tended to increase as birth weight increased, with the greatest increase in prevalence in the highest birth-weight (3.61-5.56 kg).

Obesity during Pregnancy Linked to High Birth Weight

Dr. Kramer examined a Swedish study linking women's weight in early pregnancy and their own birth weights. There was a statistically significant increased risk of having a BMI of over 25 during pregnancy among women who were born large for gestional age.

The effect of high birth weight may become more important as birth-weight distributions move toward higher weights.

Breathfeeding and Obesity

The relationship between breastfeeding and obesity data was also discussed by Dr Kramer. He found that high maternal BMI is associated with reduced breastfeeding initiation and duration. Therefore, the higher weight status of bottle-fed infants could be attributable to selection of children of higher-weight mothers, who were both less likely to have breastfed and more likely to have higher-weight children.

In addition, highly controlling bottle feeding practices at 18 month may interfere with the child's ability to self-regulate energy intake, an effect that may be long-lasting.

Dr Kramer concluded that there is probably a small protective effect of breastfeeding on child obesity but is not of major public health importance. Neither birth-weight changes nor breastfeeding explains the obesity epidemic.

Decreased Physical Activity as Key Role to the Obesity Epidemic

Dr Kramer believes that a decrease in physical activity to be the main reason for the obesity epidemic and less the higher energy intake.

Influences on the Nutritional behaviour of Children

Barbara Devaney, PhD, Mathematica Policy Research, Princeton, New Jersey According to Dr Devaney reported energy intakes of infants and toddlers are exceeding estimated requirements. The transition in infant feeding from true infant foods to more adult foods occurs during a long period but begins mostly at 9 to 11 months. As infants start to make the transition, the adult diet has a significant influence on what children eat. With the importance of table foods in the diets of children through the second year, changing what toddlers are eating may require changing what adults and older siblings are eating.

Nutritional and Flavour Programming Early in Life

According to Dr. Julie Menella, of the Chemical Senses Center, Philadelphia, Pennsylvaniathe eating preferences of children are guided by their senses and not cognitive decisions. These senses are well developed in utero but continue to change during development. There is mounting evidence of nutritional and flavour programming early in life.

Infants can detect a diversity of flavours in amniotic fluid and mother's milk. They accept new foods, such as cereals, more readily if they are prepared with their mother's milk. The flavour profile of human milk reflects the mother's diet and the culture in which the infant is born and is similar to the flavour profile experienced in utero.

These findings are the first experimental demonstration that prenatal and early postnatal exposure to a flavour enhances the acceptance and enjoyment of that flavour during weaning. Dr. Menella concludes that the more varied the mother's diet is during pregnancy and lactation, the more likely it is that the infant will accept new flavours, and that these very early flavour experiences may provide the foundation for cultural and ethnic differences in cuisine. Understanding both the causes of and likely solutions to poor food habits and choices requires attention to the complex interactions of our genes, experiences, and lifestyles. Parental feeding styles and children's eating and weight.

Dr Jane Wardle of the University College, London, presented an overview about the relationships between parental feeding styles and children's eating and weight, and came to the conclusion that greater control is probably associated with slightly lower weight and lower weight gain.

Breathfeeding and the Time of Introduction of Solids

Dr Andrew Ness, from the University of Bristol, Bristol, England, presented results from the Avon Longitudinal Study of Parents and Children (ALSPAC).

The associations of breastfeeding and introduction of solids with obesity risk were examined. Breastfeeding appeared to be protective against obesity in unadjusted models, but these associations did not remain after adjustment. Some models examined the effect of the timing of the introduction of solids. There was a suggestion in the unadjusted odds that the later introduction of solids reduced the risk of obesity, but this was not the case after adjustment.

Family Characteristics

Dr. Ness found that for children whose mother's BMI was 30, there was a 4.5-fold increase in obesity risk, which was reduced to 4.2-fold after adjustment. For children whose father's BMI was 30, there was a nearly 3-fold increase in obesity risk, which was reduced to 2.7-fold after adjustment. If both parents had BMIs of 30, then the child's risk was increased 11.7-fold. Children with no siblings had an increased risk of obesity, with an OR that increased to 2.2 and became statistically significant with adjustment. None of the other family factors was a significant predictor of obesity risk.

Effects of activity, several characteristics of children's lifestyles: Dr. Ness noted that the effect of activity measured at 38 month showed that watching television more than 8 hours/week increased obesity risk, compared with less than 4 hours/week. Obesity risk was increased if less time was spent asleep overnight. More active children sleep better in opposition to those who are sitting and eating in front of the television.

Defining obesity: Obesity is defined according to sex-and age-specific BMI cut-off points proposed by the International Obesity Task Force and Dietary Recommendations for Children and Adolescents.

Meal frequency and obesity cite Toschke meal frequency André Michael Toschke from the Ludwig-Maximilians-University Munich, Germany and colleagues assessed the relationship between meal frequency and childhood obesity. An inverse association between meal frequency and the prevalence of obesity in adulthood had been related in previous studies.

The scientists found that prevalence of obesity decreased by number of daily meals: three or fewer meals, 4.2%; four meals, 2.8%; and 5 or more meals, 1.7%.

They concluded that the protective effect of an increased daily meal frequency on obesity in children appeared to be independent of other risk factors for childhood obesity, and might be due to a modulation of the response of hormones such as insulin.

Breath feeding and intelligence: Several studies suggest a positive association between breastfeeding and intellectual development in childhood.

Mortensen and colleagues noted in a study published in 2003, that test scores suggested a dose-response relationship for breastfeeding during the first nine months of life and adult intelligence. The researchers found a significant positive association between duration of breastfeeding and intelligence. They conclude that duration of breastfeeding may correlate with maternal intelligence and with the quality of mother-child interaction, and that nutrients in breastmilk may have long-term positive effects on cognitive and intellectual development.

Height, predictors of C-peptide and cancer risk in men Giovannucci and colleagues in a study, found that excessive energy intake tends to increase circulating levels of insulin and free insulin-like growth factor-1 (IGF-I), which may increase risk of some cancers that are common in Western countries. Greater body mass index, lower physical activity, and a Western dietary pattern were independent predictors of higher plasma C-peptide levels. A C-peptide score, based on these variables, was positively related to risk of Western-related cancers, but not to other cancer types. Height was also only related to Western-related cancers.

The authors concluded that maximal growth in the pre-adult period and hyperinsulinaemia during adulthood may largely underlie the excess risk of some cancers that are common in Western populations. A substantial proportion of these cancers may be modifiable in adulthood, through alterations in body weight, sedentary behaviour, and dietary patterns that stimulate hyperinsulinaemia. The risk for Western cancers could be cut by about 50% if the entire population had an adult height and C-peptide score comparable to those values seen in the lowest decile of the population.

A classification and regression trees analysis on risk factors for childhood overweight (CART analysis)

André Michael Toschke and colleagues used high weight gain, parental overweight and obesity, lack of breastfeeding, parental education under 10 years, high birth weight, having older siblings, ethnic affiliation, and maternal smoking in pregnancy as predictors for later overweight or obesity. The classification and regression trees (CART) was used as predictive analytical method. They found that identifying children at high risk for overweight at school entry by means of predictors detectable at 2 years of age the authors found that the Weight gain 10,000 grams and obese parents accounted for the best reliable positive predictive value of 40%. In this subgroup of 4% of the entire population, two of five children will be overweight at school entry. These results reflect an improved but still insufficient identification of high-risk children even with an optimal set of of predictors. Toschke came to the conclusion that positive predictive values might be insufficient to allow for decision-making regarding specific interventions targeted at high-risk children: most children would undergo an unnecessary intervention with potential side effects if intervention were based on the sets of predictors assessed in this study.

Classification and Regression Trees (CART): Predictive analytics is an area of statistical analysis that deals with extracting information from data and using it to predict future trends and behaviour patterns. The core of predictive analytics relies on capturing relationships between explanatory variables and the predicted variables from past occurrences, and exploiting it to predict future outcomes. Such predictions rarely take the form of absolute statements, and are more likely to be expressed as numbers that correspond to the odds of a particular event or behaviour taking place in the future.

Classification and regression trees (CART) CART is a non-parametric technique that produces either classification or regression trees, depending on whether the dependent variable is categorical or numeric, respectively.

Predictive values are essential for objective evaluation of the predictive potential of tests under consideration for the general population or test results on the individual level. Furthermore, decision trees provide a useful and precise tool for decision-making in the physician's daily routine by simple visual assessment of disease probability without the need of any calculations.

Dietary Fibre

Dietary fibre are a variety of carbohydrates which are not hydrolysed by the digestive system of the small intestine. They comprise polysaccharides which are not starch, Oligosaccharides and lignin. They are found in vegetables, fruits, wheat bran, oat bran, sugar beet pulp, Guar gum, locust bean gum, gum arabic, Psyllium, carrageenan,gum tragacanth (Astragalus spec., alginic acid, xanthan gum, dextran, lactulose, karaya gum (Sterculia urens). Dietary fibre have great nutritional values for intestinal bacteria in the colon.

Dietary fibre have influence in the metabolism of the carbohydrates, lipids and minerals they act protective against colon cancer.

Recommended daily intake of dietary fibre: at least 30 g/ day.

European and other industrial countries daily intake of dietary fibre is around 20 g/day. The intake of food rich in dietary fibre should therefore be increased.

Recommended composition of the dietary fibre:

-20 g macromolecular dietary fibre of polysaccharides of not starch type. 5 g of them should be insoluble.

-15 g of resistant starch

-3-4 g oligofructose

Mango Dietary Fibre

Interest in dietary fibre has been increasing with scientific studies linking increased intake to reduced risks of cancers such as colorectal, and cardiovascular disease. According to the Columbia University showed the average intake in the US was about 12.5 grams a day, instead of 32 grams recommended by the US National Fibre Council.

According to Nely Vergara-Valencia from the Centro de Desarrollo de Productos Bioticos del IPN Mango dietary fibre might be an alternative for development of products with balanced dietary fibre components and low glycaemic response, aimed to people with special carbohydrate/energy requirements. Unripe mangoes have promising chemical composition, soluble and insoluble fibre content, antioxidant activity and of extractable polyphenols. The concentrated extract of mango was tested in cookies and bread with a better balance of soluble and insoluble dietary fibre compared to control bakery products.

The new products had higher total dietary fibre that respective controls, and the products maintained significant antioxidant capacity associated to their extractable polyphenols.

Pectin

Pectin can:

- Bind and help the excretion of steroid compounds reducing thus blood level of LDL-cholesterol.

- It increases viscosity and reduces the availability of nutritional energy.
- It reduces the peak of glucose after meals.
- It binds water and increases volume of faecis.
- Pectin has anionic groups which can be used as a transport medium of special drugs which should act in colon. On the other side it should always taken under consideration if medication should be taken during meals or between meals as the in some cases important parts of the drug may be absorbed by pectin and other dietary fibre.
- Pectin can cause modification of the mucosa. Increase of the weight of ileum and colon of mice was found by Schmehl.

Low esterified pectin had great activity. Even with no limits established by food law the use of pectin should be kept in a reasonable level as the high viscosity may reduce resorption of important food components.

Dietary Fibre and Inflammation

C-reactive protein (CRP) is produced in the liver and is a known marker for inflammation. Increased levels of CRP are a good predictor for the onset of both type-2 diabetes and cardiovascular disease.

Yunsheng Ma and colleagues suggest that a diet high in fibre may play a role in reducing inflammation and, thus, the risk of cardiovascular disease and diabetes, and that dietary fibre is protective against high CRP. 20 to 35 grams of fibre per day, including both soluble and insoluble fibre are being recommended.

It was suggested that dietary fibre could reduce the oxidation of fats and that soluble fibre act as prebiotics improving gut health diminishing inflammatory conditions.

Dietary Natural Agents and Cancer

Lupeol from Fruits and Vegetables: Lupeol, a triterpene present in fruits and vegetables is being studied as dietary natural agent to slow tumour progression in prostate cancer. Lupeol treatment resulted in significant inhibition of cell viability in a dose-dependent manner and caused apoptotic death of prostate cancer cells. Among all death receptor targets examined, Lupeol specifically caused a significant increase in the expression of Fas receptor.

The small interfering RNA-mediated silencing of the Fas gene and inhibition of caspase-6, caspase-8, and caspase-9 by their specific inhibitors confirmed that Lupeol specifically activates the Fas receptor-mediated apoptotic pathway in androgen-sensitive prostate cancer cells.

The treatment of cells with a combination of anti-Fas monoclonal antibody and Lupeol resulted in higher cell death compared with the additive effect of the two compounds alone, suggesting a synergistic effect. Because early clinical prostate cancer growth is an androgen-dependent response, the results of the present study suggest that Lupeol may have a potential to be an effective agent against prostate cancer.

Green Tea: Green tea polyphenols, a mixture of various polyphenols inhibit the growth and progression of prostate cancer in TRAMP mice. Epidemiologic reports support that green tea may reduce prostate cancer risk in humans. During the course of prostate cancer development and progression the effectiveness of green tea is not yet certain in humans. However, based on the study, it is suggested that green tea in general and polyphenols present therein may prove to be a useful supplement in the prevention or slower progress of prostate cancer in humans. The IGF-I/IGFBP-3 signalling pathway is a prime pathway for green tea polyphenol mediated inhibition of prostate cancer that limits the progression of cancer through inhibition of angiogenesis and metastasis.

Chemopreventive and chemotherapeutic activity of C3G compound from blackberry: Min Ding an colleagues say that epidemiological data suggest that consumption of fruits and vegetables has been associated with a lower incidence of cancer. Cyanidin-3-glucoside (C3G), a compound found in blackberry and other food products, was shown to possess chemopreventive and chemotherapeutic activity in the present study.

They conclude that a purified compound of anthocyanin inhibits tumor promoter-induced carcinogenesis and tumor metastasis in vivo.

Genistein: Studies in vitro suggest that osteopontin (OPN), an extracellular matrix protein secreted by macrophages infiltrating prostate tumours, and by tumour cells, may have a role in the transition from clinically insignificant tumours to metastatic prostate cancer.

Studies are consistent with the possibility that dietary genistein may delay the progression from benign to malignant tumours by inhibiting OPN expression. Our earlier studies in Transgenic Mouse Prostate adenocarcinoma (TRAMP) mice showed that genistein, an isoflavone found in soybeans, lowered the incidence of advanced PC. This suggested that lower intake of dietary soy may be one possible cause for higher incidence of advanced prostate carcinome in Western men.

Green Tea Reducing Cancer Risk

Green tea is supposed to reduced risks of breast, lung, prostate and ovarian cancer. Black tea does not present cancer protective effect.

The meta-analysis of Can-Lan Sun and colleges from the Cancer Center of the University of Minnesota indicates a lower risk for breast cancer with green tea consumption. Available data suggest a possible late-stage, promotional effect of black tea on breast carcinogenesis.

Administration of green tea to SKH-1 mice, via the drinking fluid, was found to significantly reduce the incidence and volume of ultraviolet B (UVB) radiation-induced skin tumors in a study by leading author Q Liu.

Epigallocatechin Gallate is an anti-oxidant polyphenol flavonoid isolated from green tea. Its possible benefit as a nutritional chemopreventive agent for cancer, atherosclerosis, and neurodegenerative diseases is generating increased scientific interest.

The protection from breast cancer by tea is related specifically to the catechin content, specifically epillocatechin.

According to Joshua D. Lambert and Chung S. Yang a typical cup of brewed green tea contains, by dry weight, 30-40% catechins including epicatechin, epigallocatechin, epicatechin-3-gallate, and epigallocatechin-3-gallate. Through fermentation, a large percentage of the catechins are converted to oligomeric theaflavins and polymeric thearubigins in black tea. The resulting brewed black tea contains 3-10% catechins, 2-6% theaflavins and 20% thearubigins.

The catechins have been demonstrated to undergo considerable biotransformation and to have low bioavailability. The theaflavins are even less bioavailable. This poor availability confounds attempts to correlate in vitro findings with cancer prevention in animal models. Cell line studies typically require concentrations of compound in the 5-100-micro mol/L range. Such concentrations are typically not observed systemically. Dietary supplementation with green tea extract, epigallocatechin gallate EGCG as a contribution to anti-diabetic nutritional strategies.

Swen Wolfram and colleagues in a study found that dietary supplementation of epigallocatechin gallate (high purity green tea leaf extract) resulted in improved oral glucose tolerance, blood glucoses levels, lower free fatty acid plasma concentrations, as well as increasing plasma insulin concentrations in mice and rats. The researchers wrote that EGCG downregulated genes involved in gluconeogenesis, as well as genes involved in the synthesis of fatty acids, triacylgycerol, and cholesterol.

The authors conclude that EGCG beneficially modifies glucose and lipid metabolism in H4IIE cells and markedly enhances glucose tolerance in diabetic rodents. Dietary supplementation with EGCG could potentially contribute to nutritional strategies for the prevention and treatment of type 2 diabetes mellitus if the findings can be translated to humans.

Bamboo Leaves Extract: The active compounds, include flavone, phenolic acid, lactone, polyose, amino acid, and microelements of bamboo extract and are, according to Carol Cheow from Cactus Botanics, linked to protection of blood vessels, the liver, improving sleep quality, protection against cancer, and anti-age, having positive impacts on the health and longevity of human beings.

Green Tea and Cognitive Function: According to Kuriyama from the Tohoku University Graduate School of Medicine, Japan, considerable experimental and animal evidence shows that green tea may possess potent activities of neuroprotection, neurorescue, and amyloid precursor protein processing that may lead to cognitive enhancement, no human data are available. That is why Kuriyama analysed the consumption of green tea, black tea, oolong tea and coffee)

Green tea is a rich source of catechins, compounds suggested to play a beneficial role in weight loss, cardiovascular and oral health, such as epigallocatechin gallate which is said to be brain permeable. Its protection of the brain is proposed to be due to mechanisms other than its antioxidant and iron-chelating properties. Modulation of cell survival and cell cycle genes and promotion of neurite overgrowth activity are cited as possible mechanism.

This may be the reason why Kuriyama found that drinking more than two cups of green tea a day could cut the risk of dementia by half in elderly Japanese subjects. Kuriyama concluded that a higher consumption of green tea is associated with a lower prevalence of cognitive impairment in humans.

Kuriyama found only a weak or null relation between consumption of black or oolong tea or coffee and cognitive impairment.

The authors, however point out the limitations of the study noting that healthier and more active individuals might have more opportunities to consume green tea which might promote higher cognitive function.

Reduction of Risk of Age-related Neurodegenerative Pathologies

Beta-amyloid deleterious role in the Alzheimer's disease. Bastianetto and colleagues found that green and black tea extracts and flavan-3-ols were neuroprotective active against toxicity induced by beta-amyloid-derived peptides.

Strong Activity: Strong active flavan-3-ol were found to be gallic acid, epicatechin gallate (ECG) and epigallocatechin gallate (EGCG) being the strongest of them.

Ineffective: Bastianetto and colleagues found epicatechin and epigallocatechin ineffective in the same range of concentrations. According to this study the catechin gallates (through the galloyl moiety) contribute to the neuroprotective effects of both green and black teas, reducing age-related neurodegenerative diseases, such as Alzheimer disease. The content of catechins of green tea is about 70 mg per 100 mL. Black tea contains only about 15 mg per 100 mL. Green tea should therefore be given preference.

Increased intake of folate by diet and supplements may may decrease risk of Alzheimer's disease.

Luchsinger and colleagues studied the role of higher intake of folate, vitamins B (pyridoxine hydrochloride) and B (cyanocobalamin) in decreasing the risk of Alzheimer disease (AD) through the lowering of homocysteine levels.

The authors concluded that higher folate intake from both dietary and supplements decrease the risk of Alzheimers's disease about 50%, and that the effect of folate was independent of other risk factors and levels of s B and B. The authors point out that dietary folate nor supplements alone were significantly linked to Alzheimer's disease risk; only the two in combination appeared to produce an effect, and that vitamin B and B levels were not associated with Alzheimer's disease risk.

Lower homocysteine levels were found in the group of higher folate intake. Homocystein is involved in the accumulation of amyloid proteins in the brains causing Alzheimer disease.

The authors call for clinical studies before the decision to increase folate intake to prevent Alzheimer's disease can be made. The results of the ongoing "B-Vitamin Treatment Trialist's Collaboration" addressing the link between B-vitamins, homocysteine levels, and cognitive function should be waited for.

The Role of Tea in wound Healing, Cardiovascular-related Diseases and Cancer

Restricted oxygen supply (hypoxia) such as found in altitude sickness when oxygen supply to tissue or the whole body is restricted apoptosis takes place meaning that cells die. According to Hae Jeong Park, it is an important factor in wound healing, cardiovascular-related disease and certain cancers. EGCG was found to have a beneficial effect against hypoxia-induced apoptosis for human haematoma cells.

According to Park EGCG probably prevents the expression of a certain enzyme called caspase 3, which plays a important role in programmed cell death.

FDA Report on Possible Anti-cancer Effect of Green Tea

The origin, risk factors, diagnosis, and treatment for each type of cancer are unique. Since each form of cancer is a unique disease based on organ site, risk factors, treatment options, and mortality risk, each form of cancer must be individually evaluated in a health claim petition.

As a result, the agency considered whether the studies supported the potential substance-disease relationship for any type of cancer.

Two studies do not show that drinking green tea reduces the risk of breast cancer in women, but one weaker, more limited study suggests that drinking green tea may reduce this risk. According to FDA it is, therefore, highly unlikely that green tea reduces the risk of breast cancer and concludes that existing evidence does not support qualified health claims for green tea consumption and a reduced risk of any other type of cancer.

Cannabinoids

Cannabinoids are the active components of Cannabis sativa Linnacus (marijuana) and their derivatives. Cannabinoids received renewed interest in pharmacology in recent years due to their diverse activities such as cell growth inhibition, anti-inflammatory effects and tumour regression.

Results of studies suggest that WIN-55,212-2 or other non-habit-forming cannabinoid receptor antagonists could be developed as novel therapeutic agents for the treatment of prostate cancer.

Black Tea and Post-stress Recovery

Andrew Steptoe and colleagues in a study concerning black tea, found that 6 weeks of tea consumption leads to lower post-stress cortisol and greater subjective relaxation, together with reduced platelet activation. Black tea may have health benefits in part by aiding stress recovery. Speeding the recovery following acute stress may reduce risk of chronic illnesses such as coronary heart disease.

50 minutes after a stress situation, lower cortisol levels, a lower blood platelet activation, and a greater degree of relaxation in the recovery period were found in a tea drinking group, compared with a not drinking tea group.

Because of the complex composition of tea comprising catechins, polyphenols, flavonoids and amino acids, no compound, either independently or acting in synergistic could be identified to be responsible for these positive effects,

Benefits of Mediterranean diet: Studies published in 2006 suggest that Mediterranean diet, rich in fruit, vegetables and olive and sparing in red meat and dairy products has been associated with a lower risk for several diseases and risk factors, including cancer, obesity, high cholesterol, high blood pressure and problems with processing glucose that may lead to diabetes, coronary heart disease, reduction of the risk of Alzheimer disease. According to the studies, the diet should contain turmeric and omega-3 fatty acids.

VEGETARIAN NUTRITION

Vegetarian nutrition may lead to undersupply of iron, proteins, calcium, vitamin D and vitamin B12. Iron can be got from wholemeal bread and green vegetable such as broccoli or kale (Brassica oleracea sabellica). Proteins are get from vegetables wholemeal bread, cereals, legumes, nuts, milk, cheese and yoghurt. Calcium, vitamin D and vitamin B12 can be supplied by milk and milk products.

Calcium supplementation is usually found in vitamin and mineral supplement formulas as calcium hydrogen phosphate. Gadot Biochemical company, however, offers a citrate based calcium compound, designed to supplement liquid food products conveniently with a readily absorbable form of calcium. The company claims the product to be suitable for soy milk and other soy based products, rice milk and other dairy alternative beverages fortification. According to Gadot specification it is free of raw materials from bovine origin and any food allergens according to annex 3a of EU directive 2003/89.

Although soymilk is recognized as a nutritious beverage, it contains much less calcium than cowmilk (20-30 mg/100 ml vs. 100-120 mg/100 ml), so fortification is essential.

Potassium, the major intracellular cation in the body, is required for normal cellular function. Severe potassium deficiency is characterized by hypokalemia. Moderate potassium deficiency, which typically occurs without hypokalemia, is characterized by increased blood pressure, increased salt sensitivity, an increased risk of kidney stones, and increased bone turnover (as indicated by greater urinary calcium excretion and biochemical evidence of reduced bone formation and increased bone resorption).

An inadequate intake of dietary potassium may also increase the risk of cardiovascular disease, particularly stroke. On the basis of available data, an Adequate Intake (AI) for potassium is set at 4.7 g (120 mmol)/day for all adults. This level of dietary intake (i.e., from foods) should maintain lower blood pressure levels, reduce the adverse effects of sodium chloride intake on blood pressure, reduce the risk of recurrent kidney stones, and possibly decrease bone loss. It is generally agreed that the bioavailability of Organic Calcium is much higher than Inorganic Calcium. From the litreature it appears that the bioavailability of Organic Calcium is 2 to 5 times higher than Calcium Carbonate. On the other hand, the various organic forms of calcium show more or less the same bioavailability with slight advantage to Calcium Citrate. In addition, potassium/calcium combination may enhance calcium absorption. GADOCAL K contains therefore 15 % calcium and 6 % potassium.

Conversion Salt and Sodium

Sodium is responsible for elevated blood pressure, heart diseases and stroke.

UK Food Standards Agency recommends not to eat more than 6g salt a day and provides a salt calculator.

In 1994, the Committee on Medical Aspects of Food and Nutrition Policy (COMA) recommended reducing the average salt intake of the population from 9g to 6g a day because of the link between high salt intake and high blood pressure.

National guidance regarding salt varies in Europe. Belgium recommends less than 8.75 grams a day. Portgual recommends less than 5g and countries such as Greece and Hungary advice people to avoid salt and foods rich in salt.

The WHO Intake Goal: It is less than 5g per day and is contained in the joint WHO/FAO report on diet, nutrition, and the prevention of chronic diseases.

The Expert Report's specific recommendations on diet include limiting fat to between 15 and 30 percent of total daily energy intake and saturated fats to less than 10 percent of this total. Carbohydrates, the report suggests, should provide the bulk of energy requirements-between 55 and 75 percent of daily intake and free sugars should remain beneath 10 percent. Protein should make up a further 10-15 percent of calorie intake and salt should be restricted to less than 5 grams a day. Intake of fruit and vegetables should be plumped up to reach at least 400 grams a day. Australia, New Zealand, Canada and U.S. have a guidance of less than 6g salt intake/day.

Singapore recommends less than 5g/day and Japan has a guidance of less than 10g salt/day. Brazil has a guidance of less than 5g salt intake/day all other countries of South America have no guidance on this matter, remaining a lot of work to be done by WHO to convince these countries to tackle the problem of salt-reduction.

Consensus Action on Salt and Health: This organization urges consumers to boycott foods that contain either more than 1.25g of salt (0.5g of sodium) per 100g or more than 2.4g of salt per serving, forcing manufacturers to reformulate excessively salty foods. World Action on Salt and Health (WASH) was established in 2005 and is a global group with the mission to improve the health of populations throughout the world by achieving a gradual reduction in salt intake.

Labels

Sodium is usually listed in the nutritional information on food labels. If salt is listed, sodium chloride is meant.

Conversion Salt to sodium and sodium to salt

- Salt = sodium X 2.5
- Sodium = salt X 0,4

Conversion Potassium chloride and potassium Salt replacer

- Potassium chloride = potassium X 2
- Potassium = potassium chloride X 0,5

Blends of KCl (potassium chloride), sugar, yeast extract, and flavours are being developed to hide the bitterness of potassium chloride,with salty perception but does not work against the active yeast of a dough system.

Gender/Age	Fibre, g	Sodium, mg	Potassium, mg
1-3 y	19	1500	3000
4-8 y			
Female	25	1900	3800
Male	25	1900	3800
9-13 y			
Female	26	2200	4500
Male	31	2200	4500
14-18 y			
Female	29	2300	4700
Male	38	2300	4700

Dietary fibre recent studies on colorectal cancer: Denis Burkitt proposed in 1971 the link between colorectal cancer and dietary fibre. Inconsistent results of studies could not back this theory.

A new study of Elizabeth Jacobs from the Arizona Cancer Center, however considered the sex of the participants and found a significant benefit of fibre for men, but not for women. This may explain the discrepant results of the Wheat Bran Fibre Trial and the Polyp Prevention Trial.

The Wheat Bran Fibre Trial assessed the effect of a high wheat bran fibre supplement against a low wheat bran fibre supplement men and women, randomly assigned to the supplements. The Polyp Prevention Trial studied the effect of a low-fat, high fibre diet, rich in fruit and vegetables on the recurrence of pre-cancerous polyps in the colon and rectum.

Both studies reported that the high-fibre diets had no effect of the recurrence of colorectal polyps.

The Arizona researchers from the Arizona Cancer Center re-evaluating the data of both studies observed statistically significant reduced odds of recurrence for men, but no significant association for women.

The recently published results of the Women's Health Initiative (WHI) trial also reported no link between a diet low in fat, and high in fruit, vegetables and whole-grain intake. This study was restricted to women and appears to agree with the results from Arizona. Poor compliance with the dietary intervention in the WHI trial do, however, raise questions about the validity of these results.

Limitations of the two studies (Wheat Bran Fibre Trial and the Polyp Prevention Trial): 1.-Both had very short follow-up periods of only two to four years The latency period of the cancer is between 10 and 20 years, 2.-The use of polyps as a marker for actual cancer was criticized as questionable by Dr. Arasaradnam from Northern General Hospital in Sheffield in 2004.

Concorde Grape: Vitis labrusca (Fox grape) is a specific grape native in the northeast of the United States. It is the source of many grape cultivars, including concord grapes. The characteristic "foxy" musk of V. labrusca is inherited by the Concorde grape.

A study performed by lead author Barbara Shukitt-Hale the Human Nutrition Research Center on Aging at Tufts University relate improved results on behavioural tests and enhanced motor performance on rats fed with Concorde grape juice, which is rich in polyphenoles. The study suggests that the effects of Concorde grape juice may be more effective than any one single Hopes are rising that component of grape juice may reverse brain aging. Concord grapes may have many health benefits such as reducing hypertension and the negative effects of second-hand smoking, but these results are tentative.

Cardiovascular Protection of Red Wine and White Wine

M. Falchi and colleagues found that the flesh of grapes are equally cardioprotective as skin, and antioxidant potential of skin and flesh of grapes are comparable with each other despite of the fact that flesh does not possess any anthocyanin activities.

Recent studies have documented that grapes and grape juices are equally cardioprotective as red wine. despite vastly differing polyphenol content.

Several studies have linked regular consumption of red wine to reduced risk of heart disease. The skin of red grapes is a rich source of red coloured anthocianine. Red grapes are usually crushed whole, meaning the anthocyanines are transferred to resulting wine and juice, on the contrary, most white wine or white grape juices are prepared by discarding the grape skin, nourishing the belief that red wines and red grape juice are healthier than white.

M. Falchi fed three groups of rats with water only (control), grape skin extract, or grape flesh extract. The increase of malondialdehyde (MDA), a reactive carbonyl compound related to oxidative stress, was measured under ischemic and myocardial infarction conditions.

No difference was observed between the flesh and skin extracts, both groups had significantly reduced heart attack size compared with water control group.

Quantification of the polyphenol content confirmed that, while the skins had anthocyanin concentrations of about 128 milligrams per 100 grams, the flesh contained no such compounds.

However, the radical scavenging abilities of both the flesh and skin extracts were found to be the same. The flesh of the grapes did contain polyphenols but not of the anthocyanin type of grape skin. Furthermore caffeic acid, caftaric acid, and coutaric acid have been reported which are also present in white grape varieties.

Red Wine and Reduction of Atherosclerosis

Tony Hayek and colleagues studied the effect of consuming red wine, or its major polyphenol constituents catechin or quercetin, on the development of atherosclerotic lesions, in relation to the susceptibility of plasma LDL to oxidation and to aggregation in mice.

They found that the inhibition of LDL oxidation by polyphenols could be related, at least in part, to a direct effect of the polyphenols on the LDL, since both quercetin and catechin were found to bind to the LDL particle via the formation of an ether bond.

The authors conclude that dietary consumption of red wine or its polyphenolic flavonoids quercetin and, to a lesser extent, catechin leads to attenuation in the development of the atherosclerotic lesion, and this effect is associated with reduced susceptibility of their LDL to oxidation and aggregation.

Concentrated Red Grape Juice Reduces Risk of Cardiovascular Disease

The aim of the study was to study the effects of dietary supplementation with concentrated red grape juice, a source of polyphenols, on lipoprotein profile, antioxidant capacity, LDL oxidation, and inflammatory biomarkers. The authors concluded that dietary supplementation with concentrated red grape juice improves the lipoprotein profile, reduces plasma concentrations of inflammatory biomarkers and oxidized LDL, and may favor a reduction in cardiovascular disease risk.

Nutrition Claims in the Philippines

The US company Procter & Gambler has launched on the Philippines market a concentrated orange powder "NutriDelight". This orange juice in form of a dehydrated powder is enriched with vitamin A, iron and iodine.

This product is claimed to " let children grow stronger, taller, and smarter.

According to P&G director Durk Jager the undersupply of these three elements is one of the most outstanding problem of worldwide nutrition. The "Nutridelight" according to Jager has been developed in cooperation with Health departments and UNICEF and was tested in Tanzania. This product may have importance in the nutrition of a wide population in case of undersupply during catastrophes where international associations try to feed people of a limited region to overcome a short period of calamity. It not suitable for the nutrition at normal times. The population which has no money to buy a balanced natural nutrition will certainly have not the possibility to achieve orange juice powder enriched with food supplements from Procter & Gambler.

Health authorities should try to get the population educated in a way to get a well balanced nutrition with local fruits,vegetables, fish and meat.

Getting back to the elementary balanced nutrition helps although the local industry, fishery and agriculture bringing jobs and the most important of all: It gives thousand and thousand all other components which are necessary to our nutrition avoiding synthetic food from pills and pharmacy.

Complete Low Caloric Servings

Low caloric serving "pro figur" are servings of 250 g of yoghurt enriched with vitamins, pineapple, cereals vitamins and minerals. The servings are to small to avoid hunger. Artificial sweetener are used not being in consent to an organic food. The amount of cereals should be increased. the flavouring of the product is very intensive turning it very soon to be felt awful. Intensive flavouring should always be avoided in products which are supposed to be used over a long time.

It is advisable to go back to the recommendations of the health departments and associations like the DGE in order to reduce or to avoid overweight:

1. Increase the amount of vegetables and fruits.
2. Reduce fat
3. Eat fish
4. Practice sport to burn excessive calories.

These recommendations lead to normal weight without synthetic modified foods. The main goal which Nestlé tries to achieve with "profigur" is to boost sails taking out sails from drugstores where low caloric ready servings are well sold. However even there these servings have proven to bring no success on lasting weight reduction.

Low Fat Nutrition

Low fat nutrition has proved to be suitable to reduce body weight.

The Ernärungsphychologische Forschungsstelle in Göttingen (Nutrition Psychology Research Center in Göttingen) has made a study related to body weight reducing diet changing from high fat to low fat nutrition. High fat sausages and cheese types were exchanged by low fat foods. Milk and yoghurt with 1,5 % fat were taken in the nutrition plan. Whipped-cream gateau was exchanged with fruit tart with a bottom of yeast pastry. Foods based on carbohydrates such as vegetables and fruits were unlimited allowed.

The result of this study was successful. In 8 weeks weight reduction of 1,5 up to 2,9 Kg took place. This nutrition should be used to body weight reduction instead of pills or special foods which cannot be consumed a whole life.

The low fat nutrition keeping the old nutrition habits can be followed for an unlimited period. It is therefore an alternative to the reduction diets which can be followed only during short time ending in the jo-jo effect.

Recommended Dietary Allowance (RDA) and Dietary Reference Intakes (DRI)

History of RDA

The RDA was developed during World War II by lydia J. Roberts, Hazel K. Stiebeling and Helen S. Mitchel under the auspices of the National Research Council. The National Research Council determined that a set of dietary standards were needed, especially given the possibility that rations would be needed during the war.

The standards would be used for nutrition recommendations for the armed forces, for civilians, and for overseas population who might need food relief. Roberts, Stiebeling, and Mitchell surveyed all available data, created a tentative set of allowances, and submitted them to experts for review. The final set of allowances were accepted in 1941. The allowances were meant to provide superior nutrition for civilians and military personnel, so they included a "margin of safety."

The RDA was established by the Food and Nutrition Board of the (US) National Academy of Sciences.

In 1997 at the suggestion of the Institute of Medicine of the National Academy RDA became one part of a broader set of dietary guidelines called the Dietary Reference Intake used by both the United States and Canada.

RDA inclusion in DRI family: The Recommended Dietary Allowances (RDAs) had been valid from 1941 until 1989, the RDAs to evaluate and plan menus that would meet the nutrient requirements of groups as well as other applications such as interpreting food consumption records of populations, establishing standards for food assistance programs, establishing guidelines for nutrition labelling, to name a few. The RDAs were created to prevent nutrient deficiencies. They were not intended to evaluate the diets of individuals.

Dietary Reference Intakes (DRIs) family In 1997, the Food and Nutrition Board of the National Academy of Sciences created the Dietary Reference Intakes (DRIs) after a extensive revision of the RDAs. The new family of nutrient reference values is organized in four types of DRI reference values:

1. *Estimated Average Requirement (EAR):* A daily nutrient intake value that is estimated to meet the requirement of half of the healthy individuals in a life stage and gender group. EAR is used to assess dietary adequacy and as the basis for the RDA.
2. *Recommended Dietary Allowance (RDA):* The average daily dietary intake level that is sufficient to meet the nutrient requirement of nearly all (97 to 98%) healthy individuals in a particular life stage and gender group.
3. *Adequate Intake (AI):* A recommended intake value based on observed or experimentally determined approximations or estimates of nutrient intake by a group

(or groups) of healthy people, that are assumed to be adequate. AI is used when an RDA cannot be determined.

4. *Tolerable Upper Intake Level (UL):* The highest level of daily nutrient intake that is likely to pose no risk of adverse health effects for almost all individuals in the general population. As intake increase above the UL, the potential risk of adverse effects increases.

These dietary reference values were intended to prevent nutrient deficiencies and to reduce the risk of chronic diseases such as osteoporosis, cancer, and cardiovascular disease.

Critical Issues in the Application of Dietary Reference Intakes

Dr. George Beaton, University of Toronto, examining application of the Dietary Reference Intakes (DRI) among individuals and groups comes to the conclusion that the RDA lacks an acceptable scientific basis and suggests that dietary advice for both groups should be achieved through critical DRI reference values.

According to Beaton, tradition and the DRI reports themselves have created an erroneous impression that the Recommended Dietary Allowance (RDA) is intended for use with individuals, while the Estimated Average Requirement (EAR) is to be used with populations.

He concludes that the median requirement and Tolerable Upper Limit (UL) are the critical reference values for both individuals and populations. The RDA is both unneeded and lacking a sound scientific basis.

Defending RDA

According to Murphy, Barr, and Yates, Dietary each DRI category has specific uses in dietary assessment and/or planning for groups or individuals. For example, the RDA is "intended to be used as a goal for daily intake by individuals as this value estimates an intake level that has a high probability of meeting the requirement of a randomly chosen individual." The DRI paradigm is being used as a model for nutrient standards worldwide. The authors argue in favour of keeping the present thinking about it the uses of nutrients. Beaton replied that we now live in an era of increasing demand for evidence-based nutrition and stresses the necessity of revising previous thinking and approaches as it becomes apparent that they lack evidence of validity. Actual dietary references set from US Food and Drug Administration FDA.

DVs (Daily Values): The use of Dvs on the food label started in 1994, following the US Nutrition Labelling and Education Act of 1990.

It is made up of two sets of references, DRVs and RDIs. But, according to Paula Kurtzweil from FDA, these two sets are "behind the scenes" in food labelling; only the Daily Value term will appear on the label to make label reading less confusing.

The labelling act from 1990 requires nutrition label information to be conveyed in a way that enables the public to observe and comprehend the information readily and to understand its relative significance in the context of a total daily diet.

According to Christine Lewis from FDA's Office of Food Labelling, the DV does that in two ways: First, it serves as a basis for declaring on the label the percent of the Daily Value for each nutrient that a serving of the food provides.

For example, the Daily Value for fat, based on a 2,000-calorie diet, is 65 grams (g). A food that has 13 g of fat per serving would state on the label that the "percent Daily Value" for fat is 20 percent. Second, it provides a basis for thresholds that define descriptive words for nutrient content, called descriptors, such as "high fibre" and "low fat." For example, the descriptor "high fibre" can be used if a serving of food provides 20 percent or more of the Daily Value for fibre-that is, 5 g or more.

URLs (Daily Reference Values): A set of dietary references that applies to fat, saturated fat, cholesterol, carbohydrate, protein, fibre, sodium, and potassium.

RDIs (Reference Daily Intakes): A set of dietary references based on the Recommended Dietary Allowances for essential vitamins and minerals and, in selected groups, protein. The name "RDI" replaces the term "U.S. RDA."

RDAs (Recommended Dietary Allowances): A set of estimated nutrient allowances established by the National Academy of Sciences. It is updated periodically to reflect current scientific knowledge.

Vitamins and Essential Elements

The WHO (World health Organization of the United Nations) has recommended the Daily Allowance(RDA) of vitamins and minerals given in the table below.

Linus Pauling and a group of his followers claim higher doses.

The table draws a comparison between WHO and other recommended doses.

The recommendations of WHO should be followed as the doses marked ***are likely to be considered as overdose when used for long time.

You may find the table of RDA useful to compare with the labeling of your food complements.

Vitamin or mineral	RDA	minimum	daily	maximum
		***	***	***
Vitamin C (ascorbic acid)	60 mg	500	2000	10.000
Vitamin E (d-alfa tocopherol)	10 I.U.	400	600	1.000
Beta carotene		0 mg	15	15
Vitamin B1 (thiamine)	1,0-1,4 mg	10	50	100
Vitamin B2 (riboflavin)	1,2-1,7 mg	10	50	100
Vitamin B3 (niacinamide)	18 mg	10	50	100
Vitamin B6 (pyridoxine)	2,2 mg	10	50	50
Pantothenic acid	4-7 mg	50	100	200
Folic acid		400 mu	1.000	5.000
Biotin	100-200 mu g	0	300	3ßß
Vitamin D	200-300 I.U.	0	200	400

Contd...

Vitamin or mineral	RDA	minimum ***	daily ***	maximum ***
Vitamin K	70-120 mu g	0	0	120
Selenium		100 mu g	150	200
Chrome picolinate		200 mu g	200	400
Zinc		15 mg	15	30
Calcium		500 mg	1.000	1.500
Magnesium		200mg	400	600
Iodine	150 g	150	150	300
Bioflavonoid		0	200mg	1.000
Garlic		0	600 mg	900
Concentrated fish oil		0	1.000 mg	2000
Glutathione		0	50 mg	100
Glutamine		0	2.000 mg	8.000
Coenzyme Q-10		0	30 mg	240
Ginkgo Bilobe Egb 761		0	120 mg	120
Iron	0-18 mg	0	0	5
Copper	2-3 mg	0	2	3
Manganese	2,5-5,0 mg	0	2,5	5,0
Molybdenum	0,15-0,5 mg	0	0,15	0,5
Fluor		0mg	0	0

Vitamin B6 Overdose

Heavy overdose of vitamin B6 (pyridoxine can cause alterations of mobility, psychological alterations and reactions like those of Contergan in new born.

The Committee on Toxicity of Chemicals in Food Consumer Products and the Environment (COT) gives the advice not to exceed daily 10 mg. Supplier of vitamin B6 are meat, fish, eggs, cereals and some vegetables.

Some food complements contain dose up to 100 mg. COT tries to establish a voluntary limit of vitamin B6 in food complements between manufacturers and include more informations on the label. The commission has great concern with possible about damages of the nervous System in case of over dose.

Other Components of Nutrition

The Nutritional Value of Fats

Oils and fats have high nutritional value as they are rich in energy and act as transport medium of liposoluble vitamins. Some fatty acids cannot be synthetize by human body, they are called essential fatty acids (arachidonic acid, linoleic acid and linolenic and linolenic acid). They are important parts of the synthesis of the hormone prostaglandin and are part of the structure of cell membrane.

The intake of fat, however is to high. Adults should reduce the intake of fat

There is a connection between the amount of fat consumed and arterial diseases, as well as duodenal cancer and mammal cancer.

It is advisable to reduce fat an to chose fat with high amount of polyunsaturated fatty acids.

Daily Intake of Fat

The European population has a daily intake of 130 to 150 gram/person/day. This should be reduced to 60 gram with maximum of 90 gram.

Recommended Composition of Fats

According to the DGE (Deutsche Gesellschaft für Ernährung) and WHO the intake of fat should be constituted by on third of saturated fatty acids, one third of monounsaturated fatty acids and one third of polyunsaturated fatty acids. (This rule is called "The one third rule".

The amount of saturated fatty acids in nutrition is to high.

The main source of saturated fatty acids is found in meat, sausages milk product, cakes and biscuits. This should be reduced.

Total fat intake: should not be over 30% of total energy by people with light manual work, and not over 35% of total energy by people for people with heavy manual work.

Long chain saturated fatty acids: should not be over 10% of total energy.

Polyunsaturated fatty acids: should be about 7% of total energy and up to 10% when the amount of saturated fatty acids lies over 10%.

Relation between linoleic acid (n-6) and linolenic acid (n-3): the relation should be 5:1. Monounsaturated fatty acids: can fill up to the total amount of total energy. Trans-fatty acids: should be less than 1% of total energy.

Recommended intake of Cholesterol

The European daily intake is 500 to 800 mg/person/day. This should be reduced to a maximum of 300 mg/day.

Every health organization supports the theory of an excess of animal food rich in cholesterol and saturated fatty acids being the main cause of high levels of blood fats and arteriosclerosis.

Saturated fatty acids rise thae blood cholesterol, accelerating the formation of arteriosclerosis.

Polyunsaturated fatty acids may help to reduce blood cholesterol.

Blood Levels of Cholesterol

- HDL cholesterol should be at least 45 mg/dl for females and 35 mg/dl for male.

The maximum of cholesterol for adults allowed is 200 mg.

- Values of cholesterol between 200 and 250 mg/dl have to be controlled. They can be tolerated if the bad LDL is low and the good HDL is high and there are no secondary risks (high arterial pressure, smoke, diabetes, excessive body weight, no sports are made and continuous stress). The higher secondary risks are more cholesterol values have to be reduced. According Lancet

1996 every third person with more then 40 years, smoking, with high arterial pressure and cholesterol over 230 mg/dl of blood will suffer an infarct. In Germany 261000 persons die of infarct each year.

- Values of cholesterol over 250 md/dl are always coronary risks. Everyone should know his values of blood cholesterol. Values over 200 mg/dl should be reason enough to change the way of life, the nutrition and the physical constitution.

With a modification of nutrition indicated by a dietician blood cholesterol may be reduced by 20%. (250 mg/dl may be brought down to 200 mg/dl without medication.)

It is therefore important to stop smoking, to have a healthy nutrition and practice sports.

According to the WHO healthy nutrition should have 45 to 55% complex carbohydrates, 30% of oils and fats having more than half of her fatty acids unsaturated. (Some say 10% saturated, 10% monounsaturated and 10% polyunsaturated fatty acids.) The intake of cholesterol should be under 300 mg/day and less than 5 gram of salt/day. This means nutrition rich in pasta, fish, olive oil, vegetables and fruits. The daily sport should be 30 minutes biking or walking. Infarct risk and diabetes II can so be reduced significantly. It is important to consider the fat intake not in percentage of calories but as grams of fat.

Salt Intake, Recommendations of the American Heart Association

According to the American Heart Association physicians recommend keeping salt intake below 2,300 milligrams sodium (mg)(one teaspoon of salt) per day. for people with heart failure, recommended sodium intake is no more than 2,000 mg per day.

Sodium is present not alone in salt also in sodium alginate, sodium sulfite, sodium caseinate, disodium phosphate, sodium benzoate, sodium hydroxide, monosodium glutamate, sodium citrate and other ingredients.

High salt intake is the major reason of raising blood pressure, responsible for strokes and heart attacks.

Current intake in Europe varies between 10 and 15 grams/ day,WHO which recommends no more than 5 grams of salt intake per day for every adult in the world.

The Consensus Action on Salt and Health, together with the UK's Specialist Advisory Committee on Nutrition, which advises the FSA, say that consumers should reduce their consumption to 6g a day.

About 80 per cent of salt is consumed through the consumption of processed food. Salt makes the product cheap, tasteless food edible, and more water to products can be added because it acts as a binder.

Robert Speiser, director of EuSalt, however, says that there is scientific evidence to suggest that reducing salt may not necessarily be in the interests of all consumers.

He says that two recent studies that concluded that there was no need to reduce salt among healthy people were neglected by regulators. According to Speiser the UK Food Standards Agency (FSA) is the only official authority to propose a signposting initiative that says it is necessary to reduce salt. The scientific evidence for this doesn't exist. Salt intake should remain determined by the needs of the individual. The National Health and Nutrition Examination Surveys (NHANES)1960 to 1994 shows that the intake of fat in percent has decreased but the average body weight has increased. This was caused by a steady increase of all other components of food.

The NHANES paper shows that lowering fat intake lowers total cholesterol, lowers low density lipoprotein (LDL) cholesterol, reducing cardiovascular risks, but it also reduces the high density lipoprotein (HDL) cholesterol, increasing cardiovascular risk if it drops below 35 mg/decilitre. Trevor Smith says that a blanket condemnation of saturated fats is unwise. It has been shown by Scott Grundy that stearates (saturated fatty acids) does not raise blood cholesterol. Lowering fat intake often lowers HDL cholesterol.

According to Trevor Smith it is sufficient to limit the fat intake to an average of one gram per kilogram of body weight, or target body weight per day. There is no need to count calories having a normal balanced diet. In addition one should limit animal fat intake avoid hydrogenated fats entirely, pefer olive and rapeseed oil, increase the consumption of fruits, vegetables, whole grains and prevention of excessive weight increasing physical activity like walking three miles a day at least five days a week, or an hour a day.

Salt Consumption

The UK Food Standards Agency recommends for adults not to eat more than 6 gram salt a day. The daily recommended maximum for children depends on their age:

- 1 to 3 years-2 g salt a day (0.8g sodium)
- 4 to 6 years-3g salt a day (1.2g sodium)
- 7 to 10 years-5g salt a day (2g sodium)
- 11 and over-6g salt a day (2.5g sodium)

These are the recommended maximums for children. It is better for them to have less.

The Agency advises to look at the nutritional information on the label:

High salted foods have 1.25g salt or more per 100g (0.5g sodium or more per 100g).

Low salted foods have 0.25g salt or less per 100g (0.1g sodium or less per 100g.

The FSA classifies foods between high and low, as moderate salted foods.

EFFECT OF DIETARY FATTY ACIDS ON ATHEROGENESIS

According to many studies saturated fat from foods, such as meat products, hard cheese, cream and palm oil, increase serum cholesterol.

Studying the effect of dietary fatty acids on atherogenesis lead researcher, Dr. David CelermajerStephen, J. Nicholls and colleagues found that consumption of a saturated fat reduces the anti-inflammatory potential of HDL and impairs arterial endothelial function. In contrast, the anti-inflammatory activity of HDL improves after consumption of polyunsaturated fat. They found mechanisms by which different dietary fatty acids may influence key atherogenic processes due to anti-inflammatory properties of high-density lipoproteins (HDL) and vascular function.

Raised levels Intercellular adhesion molecule-1 (ICAM-1) and vascular cell adhesion molecule-1 (VCAM-1) were found to be a response of the immune system which results in inflammation of the vascular endothelian.

A saturated fat meal made HDL-cholesterol to be less effective at inhibiting the expression of both ICAM-1 and VCAM-1 and polyunsaturated meal caused HDL to have increased inhibitory activity compared HDL from fasting plasma.

Labelling of the content of saturated fat and trans fatty acids could help to reduce the risk of heart disease by choosing products with reduced content of saturated fatty acids. Depression and lower levels of omega-3 fatty acids. In order to examine whether depression was associated with lower levels of omega-3 FAs in serum phospholipids cancer patients were divided in three groups: major depression group a minor depression group and a nondepression group.

There were no differences between the major depression group and nondepression group in any FAs. The minor depression group had higher mean levels of docosahexaenoic acid. These results suggested that serum FAs are associated with minor, but not major, depression in lung cancer patients.

Omega 3 fats and prostate cancer. The Omega-6 poly-unsaturated fatty acid, Arachidonic acid, has been shown to enhance the proliferation of malignant prostate epithelial cells and increase the risk of advanced prostate cancer.

Invasion of the human bone marrow takes place. This invasion is mediated by the arachidonic acid metabolite prostaglandin E.

Mick Brown and colleagues found, however, when Omega-3 poly-unsaturated fatty acids eicosapentaenoic acid and docosahexaenoic acid at a ratio of 1: 2 Omega-3: Omega-6 were present the spread of cancer cells was stopped.

N-3 polyunsaturated fatty acids and reduction of mortality due to myocardial infarction

A meta-analysis of Heiner Bucher and colleagues suggests that dietary and nondietary intake of n-3 polyunsaturated fatty acids reduces overall mortality, mortality due to myocardial infarction, and sudden death in patients with coronary heart disease. Lack of benefit of dietary advice concerning fruits and oily fish. In this study 3114 patients with angina were distributed in four groups:

1. advised to eat two portions of oily fish each week, or to take three fish oil capsules daily;
2. advised to eat more fruit, vegetables and oats;
3. given both the above types of advice;
4. and given no specific dietary advice.

A study of Burr and colleagues found that the advice to eat more fruit resulted in no detectable effect on mortality. Men advised to eat oily fish, and particularly those supplied with fish oil capsules, had a higher risk of cardiac death. The result is unexplained, but caused a high repercussion in non-medical press like "Der Spiegel" denying any protection again cancer and are of no help against depression.

Long Chain and Shorter Chain Omega 3 Fats Discredited

Hooper and colleagues, in a meta-analysis of randomised control trials and cohort studies concluded that long chain and shorter chain omega 3 fats do not have a clear effect on total mortality, combined cardiovascular events, or cancer. Trial results were inconsistent and showed no strong evidence of reduced mortality or cardiovascular events in participants taking additional omega 3 fats.

It is not clear whether long chain or short chain omega 3 fats (together or separately) reduce or increase total mortality, cardiovascular events, cancer, or strokes. The findings do not rule out an important effect of omega-3 fats on total mortality, as robust trials at low risk of bias reported few deaths. There is no evidence that the source (dietary or supplemental) and dose of omega-3 fats affected the effectiveness of long chain omega-3 fats. Hooper looked for an explanation why the study by Burr et al contradict the other large studies by not suggesting a benefit of omega-3. The authors examined the harmful cumulative effects of methylmercury in the long Burry trial, the fact that a specific angina patient group was chosen, and if oily fish could have a different effect as fish oil supplements, but no explanation was found. It is therefore not clear why the results of Burr et al differ from the other large studies on fish based omega-3. The authors conclude that the effect of omega 3 fats on cardiovascular disease is smaller than previously thought, or that its beneficial effect is limited to a specific group not represented in the study by Burr et al.

The authors add as final recommendation that UK guidelines encourage the general public to eat more oily fish, and higher amounts are advised after myocardial infarction (supported by trials after myocardial infarction). This advice should continue at present but the evidence should be reviewed regularly. It is probably not appropriate to recommend a high intake of omega 3 fats for people who have angina but have not had a myocardial infarction.

Health Recommendations Conflict Concerning Oily Fish and Omega-3 Fat Supplements

In an editorial in 2006 Brunner states that for the general public some omega-3 fat is good for health. Long chain omega 3 fatty acids are structural components of neuronal and other cell membranes, and they modulate the production of eicosanoids and inflammatory cytokines.

Whether omega-3 fat prevents cognitive impairment and dementia is currently being tested in trials. Extreme nutritional deficiency of these fats results in a neuropathy that can be reversed with rapeseed oil or other vegetable oils containing alfa-linolenic acid (18:3 omega 3). Alfa-Linolenic acid is a precursor of long chain omega-3, but endogenous conversion to eicosapentaenoic acid (20:5 omega-3) and docosahexaenoic acid (22:6 omega-3) is limited and inefficient.

Benefits of Omega Fatty Acids Supplementation Outweighs any likely Hazard of Fish Oils

Hooper et al. address the risks and benefits of omega-3 fats mentioning contaminants such as methylmercury, dioxins and dioxin like polychlorinated biphenyls (PCBs).

Michael J. James and colleagues analysed the anti-inflammatory effects of fish oil advising patients to take 15mls fish oil daily on juice (equivalent to 14 standard capsules daily) Third party analysis showed dioxins and indicator PCBs, which can be reduced by molecular distillation during processing of fish oil, to be below the level of detection and mercury present at 0.006mg/kg. Analysing mercury levels in both urine and blood in patients who had taken fish oil 15ml/day for at least 3 years low levels within the normal reference range and in most cases at or below the limit of detection were found.

In evaluating the risks of fish oil one needs to consider the hazards of treatments it displaces. This collateral damage clearly outweighs any likely hazards associated with fish oil use.

High Yields of DHA (docosahexaenoic acid) from Microalgae

With the introduction of Advanced BioNutritions DHA from microalgae rather than from fish meal and oil, there is the added benefit of the fish fed with these microalgae to bee a completely renewable and contaminant-free resource which can be certified as organic.

The fermentation process for the production of plant DHA uses the microalgae Crypthecodinium cohnii as well as some other microalgae.

DHA and ARA are used infant formulas. The best source of DHA, an omega-3 fatty acid, has traditionally been fish oil.

DHA from microalgae avoids mercury contamination of fish oil. Other vegetarian sources such as flax oil are considerably less bioavailable.

Omega-3 Fatty Acids Levels in Fresh beef from Feedlots

A feedlot or feedyard is a type of concentrated animal feeding operation (also known as factory farming) which is used for fattening livestock, notably beef cattle, prior to slaughter. Aside from ethical and environmental concerns, feedlots have come under criticism for human health reasons. The tissues of feedlot-raised cattle have far more saturated fat than that of grass-fed cattle, some sources say up to 500 percent more.

Feedlot-raised beef may after long periods on feed have reduced healthy omega-3 fatty acids because of the corn-and-grain diets of the cattle.

Maddock and colleagues assessed the effects of flax addition and flax processing on feedlot performance and carcass characteristics. The researchers found that feeding 8% flax to feedlot heifers increased gain and efficiency, and processing flax increased available energy and resulted in increased efficiency of gain and increased levels of n-3 fatty acids in fresh beef.

Importance of n-3 Fatty Acids in Health and Disease

William E. Connor in a supplement in 2000 states that n-3 Fatty acids favorably affect atherosclerosis, coronary heart disease, inflammatory disease, and perhaps even behavioural disorders.

Omega-3 Fatty Acids and Biomarkers of Inflammation and Endothelian Activation in Women

Lopez-Garcia and colleagues found in 2004 that the intake of alfa-linolenic acid was inversely related to plasma concentrations of C-reactive protein (CRP), and E-selectin. (n-3) fatty acids (eicosapentaenoic and docosahexaenoic) were inversely related to soluble intracellular adhesion molecule (sICAM-1) and soluble vascular adhesion molecule (sVCAM-1). Total (n-3) fatty acids had an inverse relation with CRP, E-selectin, sICAM-1, and sVCAM-1.

The researchers conclude that dietary (n-3) fatty acids are associated with levels of these biomarkers reflecting lower levels of inflammation and endothelial activation, which might explain in part the effect of these fatty acids in preventing cardiovascular disease.

The Effects of Diet on Inflammation

Giugliano in a review in 2006, states that the incidence of coronary heart disease may be reduced with a diet comprising adequate omega-3 fatty acids intake, reduction of saturated and trans-fats, and consumption of a diet high in fruits, vegetables, nuts, and whole grains and low in refined grains.

Prudent dietary patterns may reduce inflammation associated with the metabolic syndrome.

Omega-3 Fatty Acids and Serum C-reactive Protein

The intake of n-3 polyunsaturated fatty acids or fish is inversely associated with serum C-reactive protein (CRP) concentrations.

K. Niu and colleagues, studying in 2006 the effect of high intake of of omega-3 fatty acids from a diet rich in marine products, found that greater intake of n-3 PUFAs was independently related to a lower prevalence of high C-reactive protein concentrations in an older Japanese population with a diet rich in marine products, suggesting that even very high intakes of n-3 PUFAs may lower serum C-reactive protein concentrations.

n-3 Fatty Acids and Cardiovascular Disease

Jan L. Bleslow in 2006 writes that fish oil containing the fatty acids eicosapentaenoic acid (EPA) and docosahexaenoic acid (DHA) is associated with decreased cardiovascular death, whereas consumption of the vegetable oilderived n-3 fatty acid alfa-linolenic acid is not as effective.

At doses 3 g/d, EPA plus DHA can improve cardiovascular disease risk factors, including decreasing plasma triacylglycerols, blood pressure, platelet aggregation, and inflammation, while improving vascular reactivity. The American Heart Association recommends that everyone eat oily fish twice per week and that those with coronary heart disease eat 1 g/d of EPA plus DHA from oily fish or supplements.

Fish Consumption and Cognitive Decline

In a prospective cohort study Morris and colleagues examined whether intakes of fish and the omega-3 fatty acids protect against age-related cognitive decline.

The results of the study were a 10% and 13% slower decline among persons who consumed 1 fish meal per week and 2 or more fish meals per week, respectively, compared with the cognitive decline of persons who consumed fish less than weekly.

The authors concluded that fish consumption may be associated with slower cognitive decline with age. Further study is needed to determine whether fat composition is the relevant dietary constituent, as there were little evidence that the omega-3 polyunsaturated fatty acids were associated with cognitive change.

Balancing Benefits and Risks of Seafood Study 2006

The 2006 study Seafood Choices: Balancing Benefits and Risks sponsored by the National Oceanic and Atmospheric Administration's (NOAA) Marine Fisheries Service and the FDA, supports public health guidelines.

According to this study the contamination coming from seafood counts only for only 9 per cent of the PCBs in the diet. The rest come from meat and dairy. According to this study, which was conducted by the US National Academies of Science, Institutes of Medicine, the levels of dioxins and polychlorinated biphenyls are low, and potential cardiovascular and other effects are outweighed by potential benefits of fish intake.

The findings of the study is backed up by the results of the study of Dariush Mozaffarian and Eric B. Rimm

Fish Intake, the Risks and the Benefits

Searching reports published through April 2006, Dariush Mozaffarian, and Eric B. Rimm found evidences that modest consumption of fish (eg, 1-2 servings/wk), especially species higher in the n-3 fatty acids eicosapentaenoic acid (EPA) and docosahexaenoic acid (DHA), reduces risk of coronary death by 36% and total mortality by 17% and may favourably affect other clinical outcomes. Intake of 250 mg/d of EPA and DHA appears sufficient for primary prevention.

Women of childbearing age and nursing mothers should consume 2 seafood servings/wk, limiting intake of selected species.

A variety of seafood should be consumed; individuals with very high consumption (5 servings/wk) should limit intake of species highest in mercury levels. Levels of dioxins and polychlorinated biphenyls in fish are low, and potential carcinogenic and other effects are outweighed by potential benefits of fish intake.

Recommendations of the National Heart Foundation

Reduce saturated fat (SF) (and-fatty acids) to reduce CVD risk. Replace SF and trans-fatty acids with polyunsaturated fatty acids (PUFAs), and monunsaturated fatty acids (MUFAs).

Identify food sources of different fats i.e. SF (and trans fats), mono and poly. Promote consumption of at least 2 fish meals per week.

Australian Regulations for Mercury in Fish

The Australia New Zealand Food Standards Code prescribes maximum level for mercury of 1.0 mg mercury/kg for swordfish, southern bluefin tuna, barramundi, ling, orange roughy, rays and shark. and a level of 0.5 mg/kg for all other species of fish, crustacea and molluscs.

The U.S. Environmental Protection Agency (EPA) has issued two major reports on mercury the Mercury Study Report to Congress (1997) and the Utility Hazardous Air Pollutant Report to Congress (1998). In those reports, fossil-fuel power plants, especially coal-fired utility boilers, were identified as the source category that generates the greatest Hg emissions, releasing approximately 40 tons annually in the United States.

Methylmercury

The major pathway for human exposure to methylmercury is consumption of contaminated fish. Dietary methylmercury is almost completely absorbed into the blood and is distributed to all tissues including the brain; it also readily passes through the placenta to the foetus and foetal brain.

Major Health Effects of MethylmercuryEpidemics of mercury poisoning following high-dose exposures to methylmercury in Japan and Iraq demonstrated that neurotoxicity is the health effect of greatest concern, such as effects on the foetal nervous system, mental retardation, cerebral palsy, deafness, blindness, and dysarthria in utero and in sensory and motor impairment in adults.

The studies in the Seychelles Islands, New Zealand, and the Faroe Islands were designed to evaluate childhood development and neurotoxicity in relation to foetal exposures to methylmercury in fish-consuming populations. No adverse effects were reported from the Seychelles Islands study, but children in the Faroe Islands exhibited subtle developmental dose-related deficits at 7 years of age. These effects include abnormalities in memory, attention, and language. In the New Zealand prospective study, children at 4 and 6 years of age exhibited deficiencies in a number of neuropsychological tests.

Other studies were conducted in the Amazon; Ecuador; French Guiana; Madeira; Mancora, Peru; northern Quebec; and Germany. Effects of methylmercury on the nervous system were reported in all but the Peruvian population. The EPATissue Residue Criterion is 0.3 mg methylmercury/kg fish. This is the concentration in fish tissue that should not be exceeded based on a total fish and shellfish consumption-weighted rate of 0.0175 kg fish/day. The risks posed by pollutants such a methylmercury, and polychlorinated biphenols (PCBs) is outweighed by the benefits of fish consumption, like omega-3, protein,mineral content, and essential vitamins such as vitamin D where a 150 g serve of fish will supply around 3 micrograms of vitamin D.

EPA is proposed to function by increasing blood flow in the body, to affect hormones and the immune system, and is involved in the membrane of ion channels in the brain, making it easier for them to change shape and transit electrical signals. Outstanding publications on this matter are:

The Pregnancy Outcome and Community Health (POUCH) StudyA diet high in ocean fish poses risk of premature birth.

A study leaded by Fei Xuein and published in 2006, reinforced previous findings suggesting that fish consumption is a major source of mercury exposure for pregnant women. The greatest fish source for mercury exposure appeared to be canned fish, both because it was consumed more and, per meal, it was among the fish categories associated with the highest levels of mercury in maternal hair. The observed relationship between elevated mercury levels and increased risk of very preterm delivery is a new finding and requires caution in interpretation. Major strengths of the present study include the large number of pregnant women participating, the prospective design, and the use of hair as an index of methylmercury exposure. Hair levels of total mercury represent a longer window of exposure than those of blood levels. Mercury levels in hair ranged from 0.01 to 2.50 ppm (mean = 0.29 ppm, median = 0.23 ppm). The study is the first to report an association between delivery at less than 35 weeksâ gestation and maternal hair mercury levels at or above 0.55 ppm

The Seychelles Islands Study Finds no Threat Coming from Diet high in Ocean Fish

Philip W. Davidson and colleagues in a ten-year study of over 700 children in the Seychelles Islands found that the mean maternal hair total mercury level was 6.8 ppm and the mean child hair total mercury level at age 66 months was 6.5 ppm. No adverse outcomes at 66 months were associated with either prenatal or postnatal MeHg exposure. The authors concluded that consumption of a diet high in ocean fish appears to pose no threat to developmental outcomes through 66 months of age. The Seychelles Islands study is significant as the studied population eats 12 fish meals a week, There is no home made mercury pollution.

Omega-3 Fatty Acid Function of Brain Neurons

Docosahexaenoic acid (22:6n-3), one of the main structural lipids in the mammalian brain, plays crucial roles in the development and function of brain neurons. The function of DHA in neurogenesis and learning was examined in a study conducted by Kawakita, Hashimoto and Shido Ohese. The researchers demonstrated that docosahexaenoic acid effectively promotes neurogenesis both in vitro and in vivo, suggesting that it has the new property of modulating hippocampal function regulated by neurogenesis. Maintaining brain DHA concentrations may be an important part of prevention of neurodegeneration with ageing.

Fish Advisories in United States

Each state sets its own criteria and decides which bodies of water to monitor. Fish advisories are voluntary state recommendations and are not governed by federal regulations.

Frequently, when a fish advisory is issued it is because of pollutants that have lingered in the environment for long periods, sometimes decades, even though they are no longer used or their use has been significantly curtailed. These pollutants include PCB's, chlordane, DDT, mercury and dioxin.

EPA has made considerable progress toward reducing the occurrence of these contaminants in the environment: EPA issued first-ever regulations to control mercury emissions from the power sector by 70 percent, the Clean Air Mercury Rule. Production of PCBs for use ceased in 1977; chlordane was banned in 1988; DDT was banned in 1972; and known and quantifiable industrial emissions of dioxin in the United States are estimated to have been reduced by approximately 90 percent from 1987 levels.

General Dietary Advice: FDA recommends that consumers eat a balanced diet, choosing a variety of foods including fruits and vegetables, foods that are low in trans fat and saturated fat, as well as foods rich in high fibre grains and nutrients. Fish and shellfish can be an important part of this diet.

WHO Guidelines for Mercury in Fish

The World Health Organization's guidelines maintain that the lowest level that could possibly be harmful to humans is 5 parts per million (ppm).This level is based on scientific results from the 1960s that placed the level at which risk begins at 50 ppm for most people; WHO then applied a safety factor of 10, deciding that a level of 5 or less is safe for even the most vulnerable populations.

EPA has recommended that a person ingest no more than 30 micrograms of mercury per day. Based on estimates of U.S. fish consumption, FDA recommended that only commercial fish with less than 1 ppm of mercury be sold. Later on the EPA recommended to Congress that the tolerable daily intake of mercury be dropped to just one-fifth the current allowable level, to about 6 micrograms per day.

The FDA supports statements that it is safe to eat fish and shellfish twice a week and that one should always eat a variety of species.

Morrissey stresses that pregnant women should stick with current FDA recommendations of about 12 ounces (340 grams) per week. Do not eat shark, swordfish, King Mackerel, Tilefish. The rest of the population should be eating fish four to seven times per week. EPA and FDA fish consumption advice for pregnant women and young children.

EPA and FDA Advice not Eat: Shark, Swordfish, King Mackerel, Tilefish. They contain high levels of mercury. EPA and FDA recommend to eat up to 12 ounces (2 average meals) a week of a variety of fish and shellfish that are lower in mercury. Five of the most commonly eaten fish that are low in mercury are shrimp, canned light tuna, salmon, pollock, and catfish. EPA and FDA says to be carefully with albacore tuna which has more mercury than canned light tuna. No more than 6 ounces (one average meal) of albacore tuna fish from local lakes, rivers, and coastal areas. per week should be eaten and no other fish during that week.

EWG Recommendation in Addition to FDA citeEWG Brain Food : Recommendation of the Environmental Working Group (EWG) and the U.S. Public Interest Research Group (U.S. PIRG) published in Brain Food: What Women Should Know About Mercury Contamination of Fish:

- Pregnant women, nursing mothers and all women of childbearing age, should not eat tuna steaks, sea bass, oysters from the Gulf Coast, marlin, halibut, pike, walleye, white croaker, and largemouth bass. These are in addition to FDA's recommendation to entirely avoid shark, swordfish, king mackerel and tilefish.
- These women should eat no more than one meal per month combined of canned tuna, mahi-mahi, blue mussel, Eastern oyster, cod, pollock, salmon from the Great Lakes, blue crab from the Gulf of Mexico, wild channel catfish and lake whitefish.
- The following fish are safer choices for avoiding mercury exposure: farmed trout or catfish, shrimp, fish sticks, flounder, wild Pacific salmon, croaker, haddock, and blue crab from the mid-Atlantic.

Mercury Levels in High-End Consumers of Fish Jane M. Hightower and Dan Moore tested mercury levels in blood and hair of frequent fish eaters. They found mercury levels ranging from 2.0 to 89.5 g/L for the 89 subjects. The mean for 66 women was 15 g/L, and for 23 men was 13 g/L.

- (Environmental Protection Agency (U.S. EPA) and the National Academy of Sciences recommend keeping the whole blood mercury level 5.0 g/L or the hair level 1.0 g/g. This corresponds to a reference dose (RfD) of 0.1 g/kg body weight per day.)

The authors concluded that high blood levels of mercury could be reduced by abstaining from eating fish for more than 21 weeks. Mercury levels in tested women averaged in this study 10 times the levels recommended by the U.S. Environmental Protection Agency and the National Academy of Sciences. Levels in men were close behind, while some of the children tested were found to have levels 40 times those recommended. Nearly 90% of those tested were above the recommended levels.

Environment and Power Plants

Concern over mercury contamination has led government agencies to warn consumers not to eat bass, trout and other sport fish caught in over a thousand lakes and streams across 40 U.S. states. Coal-burning power plants are the single largest source of mercury pollution, and the only major source the government does not regulate. Mercury is an extremely volatile metal that can be transported great distances after spewed into the atmosphere. Once it reaches an aquatic environment, mercury is transformed into methylmercury, a potent neurotoxin, which accumulates in top predator fish and the people and wildlife who eat them. When ingested by pregnant women, methylmercury readily crosses placenta and targets the developing brain and central nervous system. Even relative tiny amounts can produce serious developmental delays in walking, talking hearing and writing. Infants can also be exposed to high levels of methylmercury during breastfeeding.

Mercury emissions from the power sector was reduced by 70 percent, following the EPA Clean Air Mercury Rule of 2005.

9

Fatty Acids with Trans Configuration

Most of the unsaturated fatty acids in nature have a cis configuration. The trans configuration results mainly during chemical hydrogenation of polyunsaturated fatty acids.

In February 1995 the first part of the Euromic-Study was published in The Lancet. This part of the study was mainly concerned with trans fatty acids and diseases of the coronary vessels. The second part of the study was related to intake of TFA and cancer.

Approximately 2 to 3% of the fat of the milk and derivates have a cis configuration being elaidinic acid (C18:1 trans) responsible for most of the trans fatty acids of milk.

In some cases the amount of trans fatty acids in milk and derivates can be as high as 5%. Therefore the International Federation of Margarine Association (IFMA) and the IMACE (Association of Margarine Industry of the EC Countries) index Association of the Margarine Industry of the EC Countries (IMACE) recommended to lower the amount of TFA (Trans Fatty Acids) in margarine to a maximum of 5% of fat.

Margarine to be used as spread or cooking should have less than 1%.

The trans fatty acids can be reduced during refining by reducing the temperature of the process. This however means a longer time the oil or fat has to spend in the system an therefore higher operation costs. The increased costs should be accepted in change of a healthy product.

The deodorization of vegetable oils during refining using temperatures over 230 C results more than 3% of trans fatty acids. Using temperatures under 230 C a maximum of 0,5% trans fatty acids are formed. This can be tolerated. A real great amount of trans fatty acids are formed by partial hydrogenation of soy oil.

A melting point of 36 to 37 C of soya oil very commonly used in the production of margarine as well as deep frying fat and products for bakery results in up to 50% of trans fatty acids.

Trans fatty acids are therefore hidden in cakes, cookies, creams and margarine and all kind of fried product. In USA partially hydrogenated oil is used almost everywhere. The trans fatty acids represents therefore a great menace to health because they act as saturated fatty acids and may cause arteriosclerosis. Trans fatty acids can be avoided during industrial processing of oil using entirely hydrogenated oil.

If all double and triple bindings of the molecule of the fatty acids are saturated the trans stereoisometric configuration ceases to exist and there is no negative physiological activity left. To obtain the same consistence of partially hydrogenated oil it is necessary to add more liquid oil and esterified the whole compound.

This implies in higher production cost. All efforts to get healthy products should however be made, including the acceptance of a small increase of price of the final product in order to get margarine, fats, creams and bakery products having less than 5% of their fatty acids in trans configuration.

FATS AND MARGARINE FOR BAKERY

Fats and margarine for bakery must have special stability, structure and melting point. Therefore special hydrogenated oils and fats are needed.

Palm oil, hydrogenated melting point 45/46 C	40%
Soybean oil, hydrogenated melting point 36/38 C	35%
Rapeseed oil, liquid melting point 5 C	25%

This fat blend has a content of trans-fatty acids of 20 to 25%.

Melting Points of Fats Found in Nature: Coconut fat melting point 24-28 C Palm oil melting point 37-39 C Palmkernel oil melting point 26-30 C These melting points are to low for the production of pastry margarine.

To avoid hydrogenated oils and fats for bakery it is possible to fractionate fats leaving it at specific temperature to permit the hard components (stearin) to crystallize. Filtration separates the low melting components (olein).

Industry still uses hydration instead of fractionated fats because of the the higher prices of fractionated fats. For the sake of health the higher price should be accepted by the consumer in order to get healthy food.

Bakery products bear a lot of hidden fats and are a great source of trans fatty acids with arteriosclerotic and carcinogenic activity.

PHYSIOLOGY OF TRANS FATTY ACIDS

The fatty acids in cis form have the property to reduce blood cholesterol, meanwhile the trans configuration being consumed about 30 to 40 gram a day make the total blood cholesterol and LDL cholesterol to rise. HDL cholesterol is reduced by trans fatty acids.

In countries with high consume of partially hardened soya oil like USA there is an increase of heart diseases like heart infarct.

Industrial manufactured oils and fats cannot avoid completely trans fatty acids. By using proper technologies the content of trans fatty acids however can be reduced to a tolerable amount of maximum 5%.

A daily intake of 4 to 6 gram of trans fatty acids are told to be harmless. All effort should be made by the industry to reduce the amount of trans fatty acids.

TRANS FAT CLAIMS, FDA PROPOSAL

In its November 1999 proposal, FDA proposed a definition for the nutrient content claim "trans fat free" and proposed limits on the amounts of trans fat wherever saturated fat limits are placed on nutrient content claims, health claims, or disclosure and disqualifying levels.

With regard to the specific definitions, FDA proposed that "trans fat free" and "saturated fat free" should be defined as less than 0.5 g trans fat and less than 0.5 g saturated fat per reference amount and per labelled serving; "low saturated fat" as 1 g or less of saturated fat and less than 0.5 g of trans fat per reference amount and not more than 15 percent of calories from saturated fat and trans fat combined; "reduced saturated fat" as at least 25 percent less saturated fat and at least 25 percent less saturated fat and trans fat combined; "lean" as 4.5 g or less of saturated fat and trans fat combined; and "extra lean" as less than 2 g of saturated fat and trans fat combined.

In addition, cholesterol claims were allowed only on foods containing 2 g or less of saturated fat and trans fat combined, and disqualifying and disclosure levels were set at 4 g or less of saturated fat and trans fat combined. FDA did not propose to define "low trans fat."

Quantitative Declaration of Trans Fat in the Nutrition Facts Panel

The Food and Drug Administration (FDA) amended its regulations on nutrition labelling to require that trans fatty acids be declared in the nutrition label of conventional foods and dietary supplements on a separate line immediately under the line for the declaration of saturated fatty acids.

FDA is revised Sec. 101.9(c) by adding paragraph Sec. 101.9(c)(2)(ii) to require the quantitative declaration of trans fat in the Nutrition Facts panel. This new paragraph requires the listing of trans fat on a separate line under the statement for saturated fat.

As is the case for all subcomponents of total fat, it is to be indented and separated by a hairline, with the amount expressed as grams per serving to the nearest 0.5 g increment below 5 g and to the nearest gram increment above 5 g. If the serving contains less than 0.5 g, the content must be expressed as 0, except when the statement "Not a significant source of trans fat" is used. In addition, the agency is clarifying that the word "trans" may be italicized to indicate its Latin origin.

Not a significant source of...

Section 101.9(c) requires that information on mandatory nutrients, such as saturated fat and trans fat, be included in all nutrition labelling unless otherwise excepted from such labelling as provided for in specified paragraphs.

Special provisions within Sec. 101.9(c) allow for shortened formats that provide manufacturers flexibility to omit noncore nutrients (i.e., mandatory nutrients other than calories, total fat, sodium, total carbohydrate, and protein) that are present in insignificant amounts from the list of nutrients and group them in a summary statement at the bottom of the label that states-Not a significant source of------(see 58 FR 2079 at 2083, Comment 8, January 6, 1993).

These special provisions are found in Sec. 101.9(c)(1)(ii) for calories from fat, Sec. 101.9(c)(2)(i) for saturated fat, Sec. 101.9(c)(3) for cholesterol, Sec. 101.9(c)(6)(i) for dietary fibre, Sec. 101.9(c)(6)(ii) for sugars, and Sec. 101.9(c)(8)(iii) for vitamin A, vitamin C, calcium, or iron. For consistency with the labelling scheme for these other noncore mandatory nutrients, new Sec. 101.9(c)(2)(ii) provides that if the trans fat content is not required and, as a result, not declared, the statement-Not a significant source of trans fat-must be placed at the bottom of the table of nutrient values.

PHYSIOLOGY OF SATURATED FATTY ACIDS

Saturated fatty acids rise the blood level of LDL cholesterol.

U.S. Food and Drug Administration has approved to label foods containing at least 6,25 grams of soy protein per serving touting a link between eating soy and lower risk of heart disease.

6,25 grams of soy proteins are one-fourth of the 25 grams of soy protein daily which are supposed to be needed to show a significant cholesterol-lowering effect.

The claim was requested by Protein Technologies International, a subsidiary of DuPont Co, which is a manufacturer of isolated soybean protein. Foods which may be qualified for this claim are soy beverages, tofu, soy-based meat alternatives and some baked goods.

OMEGA-3 FATTY ACIDS CLAIMS

The major source of omega-3 fatty acids is dietary intake of fish, fish oil, vegetable oils (principally canola and soybean), some nuts such as walnuts, and, dietary supplements.

The Oxfor-Durham Study Concerning Omega-3 Fatty Acids and DCD

Alexandra J. Richardson and colleagues studied the effect of dietary supplementation with omega-3 and omega-6 fatty acids on children with developmental coordination disorder (DCD). This disorder affects 5% of school-aged children. They present deficits in motor function associated with difficulties in learning, behaviour, and psychosocial adjustment.

The authors found significant improvements in reading, spelling, and behaviour, however, no effect of treatment on motor skills was apparent. They concluded that fatty acid supplementation may offer a safe efficacious treatment option for educational and behavioural problems among children with DCD.

The British company Dairy Crest relying on these results claimed that her omega enriched milk could enhance children's ability to concentrate and learn. The Britain's Advertising Standards Authority requested to stop this claim alleging that children would have to drink more than five litres of that milk every day to get the same amount of omega-3, being thus misleading.

Britain's Joint Health Claims Initiative (JHCI) has approved a generic health claim that foods containing omega-3 benefit heart health, but not learning ability or concentration. The JHCI offers pre-market advice and a code of practice for the food industry, enforcers and consumers, to ensure that health claims on foods are both scientifically truthful and legally acceptable.

UK Food Standards Agency, concerning omega fatty acids said that there is insufficient quality evidence to reach firm conclusions on the effect of nutrition and dietary changes on learning, education or performance for all schoolchildren. The Agency maintains their advice to a diet lower in fat, sate and sugar but high in fruits, vegetables and complex carbohydrates, in addition to being physically active.

Omega-3 Fatty Acids and Brain Function

Omega-3 fatty acids were proposed as having an important role in mental health, because up to 60% of the adult brain is composed of lipids (dry weight). Thirty five percent of the lipids are phospholipids comprised of unsaturated fatty acid such as docosahexaenoic acid (an omega-3 fatty acid) and arachidonic acid (an omega-6 fatty acid) acids.

Omega 3 and Psychiatric Disorders

Disorders of mental health are becoming increasingly common in the US. It is estimated that in a given year, 22%, or one in five American adults, suffers from a diagnosable mental health disorder.

These disorders, including major depression, bipolar disorder, schizophrenia, and obsessive-compulsive disorder, account for four of the ten leading causes of disability in the US and other developed countries. Many people suffer from more than one mental disorder at a given time.

Schachter, and colleagues co authors of the Oxford-Durham study write that overall, other than for the topics of schizophrenia and depression, few efficacy or safety studies were identified.

Only with respect to the supplemental treatment of schizophrenia is the evidence even somewhat suggestive of omega-3 fatty acidsâ potential as short-term intervention. Additional research might reveal the short-term or long-term therapeutic value of omega-3 fatty acids.

One study demonstrating a significant clinical effect related to 1 g/d E-EPA given over 12 weeks to 17 patients with depressive symptoms cannot be taken to support the view of the utility of this exposure as a supplemental treatment for depressive symptomatology or disorders.

Nothing can yet be concluded concerning the clinical utility of omega-3 fatty acids as supplemental treatment for any other psychiatric disorder or condition, or as a primary treatment for all psychiatric disorders or conditions examined in the review. Primary treatment studies were rare.

Much more research is needed before the possible utility of (foods or supplements containing) omega-3 fatty acids as primary prevention for psychiatric disorders or conditions can be ascertained. Studies of omega-3 fatty acidsâ□™ primary protective potential in mental health could be œpiggybacked onto longitudinal studies of their impact on general health and development.

FSA Systematic review of the effect of nutrition, diet and dietary change on learning, education and performance of school children carried out by the University of Teeside

The UK's Food Standards Agency has published the results of a systematic review of the effect of nutrition, diet and dietary change on learning, education and performance of school children aged 4-18 years, covering already published studies.

The Government and those involved in education are committed to improving learning and raising standards in schools, as well as meeting the needs of individual pupils.

There is widespread belief that nutrition and diet may have a part to play in this process; however, there is a degree of uncertainty as to what interventions or supplements work.

Much of the available evidence is confusing and contradictory. In essence those charged with supporting and delivering education are seeking clear guidance for both individuals and groups of children, so as to be able to identify what probably works, what might work and what probably does not work.

The authors conclude that there is insufficient evidence to identify any effect of nutrition, diet and dietary change on learning, education or performance of school aged children from the developed world. Further research is required in settings of relevance to the UK and must be of high quality, representative of all populations, undertaken for longer durations and use universal standardised measures of educational attainment.

However, challenges in terms of interpreting the results of such studies within the context of confounders such as family and community context, poverty, disease and the rate of individual maturation and neurodevelopment will remain.

Whilst the importance of diet in educational attainment remains under investigation, the evidence for promotion of lower fat, salt and sugar diets, high in fruits, vegetables and complex carbohydrates, as well as promotion of physical activity remains unequivocal in terms of health outcomes for all school children.

Omega-3 Fatty Acids from Diet or Supplements and Depression

Omega-3 fatty acid supplementation have been linked with behavioural improvements of children with learning difficulties, behavioural problems or Attention Deficit Hyperactivity Disorder (ADHD).

According to the phospholipid hypothesis the decreased omega-3 fatty acid intake could be responsible for the disease.

According to the US Department of Health and Human Services 3% of children and 12% of adolescents may suffer from clinical depression.

Professor Haim Belmaker and colleagues treated for one month children aged between 6 and 12 with a combination of eicosapentaenoic acid (EPA) and docosahexaenoic acid (DHA), an omega-3 supplement commonly available at drugstores.

The researchers found significant depression reductions in the omega-3 treated group, concluding that Omega-3 fatty acids may have therapeutic benefits in childhood depression.

Cognitive function seems to benefit from DHA which is involved in the membrane of ion channels in the brain, making it easier for them to change shape and transit electrical signals. EPA may influence brain function directly increasing blood flow in the body, affecting hormones and the immune system.

Belmaker and colleagues concluded that omega-3 fatty acids may have therapeutic benefits in childhood depression.

Omega-3 Polyunsaturated Essential Fatty Acid Status as a Predictor of Future Suicide Risk

Low levels of docosahexaenoic acid, a polyunsaturated fatty acid, and elevated ratios of omega-6/omega-3 fatty acids are associated with major depression and, possibly, suicidal behaviour.

M. Elizabeth Sublette and colleagues found in a study that a low docosahexaenoic acid percentage and low omega-3 proportions of lipid profile predicted risk of suicidal behaviour among depressed patients over the 2-year period. If confirmed, this finding would have implications for the neurobiology of suicide and reduction of suicide risk.

Omega-3 Fatty Acids and Mood Disorders

In an overview of epidemiological and treatment studies concerning deficits in dietary-based omega-3 polyunsaturated fatty acids, resulting mood disorders and their therapy with omega-3 fatty acids supplementation Gordon and colleaugues found that according to the different authors reviewed eicosapentaenoic acid (EPA) or docosahexaenoic acid (DHA), is likely to provide the greatest benefit.

More studies studies clarifying the efficacy of omega-3 supplementation for unipolar and bipolar depressive disorders are needed.

Mood gene D4DR The gene, called D4DR (fourth dopamine receptor gene) and located on the 11th chromosome, is said to be responsible for 10 percent of people's novelty-seeking or adventurous behaviour. The D4DR gene was discovered in the United States in 1991.

Its functioning is expressed in the limbic part of the brain-the section involved in emotions-and binds with high affinity to clozapine, a drug used to treat schizophrenia. Doctors at Soroka Hospital and the Beersheva Mental Health Center and at Jerusalem's Herzog Memorial-Ezrat Nashim Hospital, who tested 124 healthy Israelis, made the discovery. Doctors from the U.S. National Cancer Institute also pinpointed the gene on 300 people of various ethnic groups at the University of Maryland.

People who score low on the novelty-seeking test tend to be exploratory, fickle, excitable, quick tempered, and extravagant, while those who score high are more stoic, loyal, reflective, frugal, rigid, and even-tempered.

An U.S. team, which included Dr. Jonathan Benjamin of Soroka, backed up the Israeli findings.

Changing Nutritional Habits Regarding Omega Fatty Acids

Nutritional habits have changed from whole grains, beans and other seeds, and seafood high in omega-3 fatty acids to prepared foods containing corn oil, safflower oil, cottonseed oil, peanut oil, soybean oil and red meat, which are high in omega-6.

EM Berrry says omega-6 fatty acids are essential for normal growth, development and health, and so extreme care is necessary before deciding that they are harmful. The relation n-6: n-3 changed from 3:1 towards 1:20

n-6 function cannot be considered in isolation but needs to be seen as part of the complex of nutrient interactions with n-3 fatty acids (which compete for the same enzymatic pathways) and antioxidants.

Insulin sensitivity might be the common factor relating disease to fatty acid metabolism both within and between the fatty acid pathways. High linoleate to arachidonate concentrations have been observed in insulin resistance, diabetic complications and some tumours, but these are multifactorial processes that include many lifestyle determinants and it is therefore wrong to condemn only n-6 fatty acids in their etiology.

Omega-6 and Prostate Cancer

New research, leaded by Professor William Aronson found that changing the ration of omega-3 to omega-6 in the typical

Western diet might reduce prostate cancer tumor growth rates and prostate specific antigen PSA levels. PSA is a marker for the risk of prostate cancer.

Omega-3 fatty acids(eicosapentaenoic acid (EPA) and docosahexaenoic acid (DHA)) and the omega-6 acid (arachidonic acid) compete to be converted by cyclooxgenase enzymes (COX-1 and COX-2) into prostaglandins, which can become either pro-inflammatory and increase tumour growth, or anti-inflammatory and reduce growth. Aronson and colleagues found that levels of the pro-inflammatory prostaglandin (PGE-2) were 83 per cent lower in tumours in the omega-3 group than in mice on the predominantly omega-6 fatty acid diet.

According to this study higher levels omega-3 fatty acids may lead to development of more anti-inflammatory prostaglandins. The authors conclude that eating a healthier ratio of these two types of fatty acids may make a difference in reducing prostate cancer growth.

The Role of Fat and Cardiovascular Diseases

The Women Health Initiative Randomized Controlled Dietary Modification Trial leaded by Barbara Howard found that dietary changes like eating less fat and more vegetables has no effect on the risk of cardiovascular disease.

This study is inconsistent with earlier studies which associate dietary fat intake and a lowered risk of cardiovascular disease, focusing on wholegrain, fish oil and omega-3 fatty acids. The authors, however, find it possible that a diet specifically lower in saturated and trans fat combined with increased intakes of vegetables, fruits, and grains might have led to a decrease in cardiovascular disease risk.

According to Cheryl Anderson and Lawrence Appel The Women's Health Initiative study had not considered current dietary guidelines to cut CVD risk, such as less salt and more potassium, the DASH (Dietary Approach to Stop Hypertension) diet, and weight loss. Current policies towards fruit, vegetables and wholegrain would probably be unaffected.

The study, however, may indicate that saturated fat levels should be lowered from 10 per cent to seven per cent of total energy intake. The possibility that the effect might have been greater in men or if the diet had been initiated at younger ages cannot be ruled out.

Reduction of fat level in fried fish: Three hydrocolloid coating materials were tested in reducing fat uptake in battered fish products. Camden and Chorleywood Food Research Association Group coatings such as alginate, pectin, gellan gum, methyl cellulose, and hydroxypropyl methyl cellulose.

Fish fillets were coated with alginate, pectin and gellan gum and then fried. All three coated battered fish fillets with either water or one of the three hydrocolloids showed reduced fat level in the final product.

These findings could help to reduce total lipid intake by the population as fried fish is an important constituent of the average population.

The authors suggest that the reduction of fat was due to the waterbinding ability of the coatings. In fully fried products, the reduction in fat uptake was less marked, although an effect was still seen.

It is likely that the longer frying times compromised the integrity of the coatings, emphasising the need to consider the requirements of both product and process when applying edible films.

Green Paper: Promoting Healthy Diets and Physical Activity

The obesity crisis:The Green Paper of the Commission of the European Communities entitled" Promoting healthy diets and physical activity: towards a European strategy for the prevention of overweight, obesity and chronic diseases" opens the discussion on the obesity crisis, focusing on the factor of food for the prevention of chronic diseases, overweight and obesity

Improving the health of Europeans through better diets and greater physical activity is crucial to preventing a range of non-communicable diseases and improving quality of life for millions of people.

According to the Confederation of Food and Drink Industry of the EU a greater understanding of all obesity-related factors is needed, calling for improved public health education on nutrition and healthy lifestyles. This would enable consumers to take responsibility for making healthy choices. It will be also be the basis for understanding and making use of product information provided by the industry.

Strategies should include the determinants that affect food choice, factors that lead to insufficient physical activity in every-day life, and not just food products themselves.

The Green Paper considers industry self-regulation the best way of dealing with the problem. According to the CIAA, however, a broader approach is needed to meet all factors involved, such as:

- It should be clear that each consumer is responsible for ensuring that his or her own lifestyle is a healthy one.
- Parents have a similar responsibility for their children.
- Increase of level of physical activity in children, adolescents and adults, in particular in the school environment.

The European Vending Association (EVA) questions the scientific data of the Green Paper regarding the excessive intake of energy-dense snacks and sugar-sweetened soft drinks:

EVA says the "notion of excessive intake" is vague and very subjective, and it is unclear how it impacts directly on the Body Mass Index. EVA calls for other factors such as energy out determining if intake is excessive or not.

NEW DISCUSSION CONNECTING HIGH FRUCTOSE SYRUP WITH OBESITY

High fructose corn syrup (HFCS) was introduced in the 1970s. Food industry, particularly the soft drink industry, uses fructose syrup in excess. Removing fructose from soft beverages could help to reduce obesity, as a possible mechanism is suggested which may explain the link between rising obesity and sweetened beverages.

Three important studies report that high fructose corn syrup is an important factor in the rising obesity epidemic:

According to Hella S. Jürgens and colleagues (2005), from the Department of Pharmacology, German Institute of Human Nutrition, Potsdam-Rehbruecke, exposure to fructose water increased adiposity, whereas increased fat mass after consumption of soft drinks or diet soft drinks did not reach statistical significance. Total intake of energy was unaltered, because mice proportionally reduced their caloric intake from chow. The researchers found that fructose also produced a hepatic lipid accumulation with a characteristic pericentral pattern.

Jürgens conclude that a high intake of fructose selectively enhances adipogenesis, possibly through a shift of substrate use to lipogenesis.

Swiss researcher Kim-Anne Le and colleagues report in December 2006 that moderate fructose supplementation over 4 weeks increases plasma triacylglycerol and glucose concentrations without causing ectopic lipid deposition or insulin resistance in healthy humans.

In February 27, 2007 Juan Carlos Laguna and colleagues wrote that liquid fructose changes the metabolism of fat in the liver by impacting a specific nuclear receptor called PPAR-alpha, leading to a reduction in the liver's ability to degrade the sugar.

According to the authors, this would partly explain the link between increased consumption of fructose and widening epidemics of obesity and metabolic syndrome. In their article the authors conclude that hypertriglyceridemia and the retention of fat in liver induced by fructose ingestion result from a reduction in the hepatic catabolism of fatty acids driven by a state of leptin resistance.

According to this research, the fructose increased fat synthesis in the liver and also acted on the PPAR-alpha receptor(which controls the oxidation of fatty acids) to reduce the degradation of the fructose, and reduces the activity of the hormone leptin which is engaged in the metabolism of faty acids in liver.

ANTIOXIDANTS IN HUMAN NUTRITION

Formation of Radicals

Free radicals are told to start cancinogenic reactions in vivo. Oxygen is the main source of free radicals such as Singulett-O2, superoxydation and the hydroxilradical.

In small amounts the radicals are used in many biochemical reactions. The amount of free radicals being however to high the benefit of the radicals turn out to be dangerous to the physiology of the cell ending in Arteriosclerosis and cancer.

The organism protects itself from free radicals with the building of an own free radical defence system helped by external antioxidant vitamins.

Antioxidant vitamins	Protective function against free radicals
Carotenoids (provitamin A)	Singulett-O2 quencher.
Tocopherols (vitamin E)	Act as radical receiver in lipid layers together with vitamin C mainly to protect polyunsaturated fatty acids. Tocopherols also protects beta-carotene and vitamin A from autoxidation in cells.
Vitamin C	Act as radical receiver in the cytoplasm together with vitamin E. It also regenerates tocopherol from tocopheryl radicals which were originated during the antioxidant function. Aspirin can triple the rate of excretion of vitamin C
Selenium, Zinc, copper, manganese	As elements being found as traces in enzyme system of the cells. An undersupply of these elements reduces the efficiency of vitamins, therefore they are here included
Magnesium	Magnesium is a light metal which can burn in presence of oxygen, being used as torch but also in metal alloys in aeronautic. It is present in minerals, seawater and mineral water, in plants as chlorophyll and wheat bran 590 mg/100g, slim cocoa powder 500 mg/100g, sunflower seed kernel 20 mg/1000g, sesame seed 350 mg/100g, cashew nut 270 mg/100g peanuts 163 mg/100g, oat flakes instant 140 mg/100g dried figs 70 mg/100g, Edam cheese 45% 59 mg/100g cooked spinach 50 mg/

Contd...

Antioxidant vitamins	Protective function against free radicals
	100g, wholemeal bread 92 mg/100g white bread 19 mg/100g. A balanced diet supplies sufficient magnesium It is an important biological element for animals and humans. It is a physiological antagonist of calcium. Values of serum are 0,65-1,03 mmol/l Magnesium is very important for many enzymatic reactions (it activates all reactions where ATP is present. Important for undisturbed building of bones, It acts relaxing. It is being told that magnesium improves the connections of the synapsis of nerve cells having therefore anti stress function, however there is no scientific evidence for it. According to D. Hötze, C. Küpper and A. Zittermann research has been done relating a permanent effect of the streß hormones catecholamine and cortisol. The result of this research was that there is a loss of magnesium. Other findings say there is an improving of the stress situation with supplementation of magnesium working in very laud places. An undersupply of Magnesium may be an additional factor of the origin of arteriosclerosis Undersupply of Magnesium electrolyte syndrome caused by undersupply of magnesium due to unbalanced diet, infusion therapy, chronic diarrhea, special diets, excessive alcoholism. laxatives, inflammation of the pancreas, diseases of the intestinal tract. faulty absorption syndrome, magnesium loss through urine with diuretica therapy. chemotherapy, Diabetes mellitus Syndromes of undersupply of magnesium are: Loss of appetite, nausea, vomiting,lack of drive, weakness. Course tremor, cramps, cramp in the leg during the night. Tetanic contractions.
Selenium	Aside of its function in enzymes selenium is known acting by itself as an antioxidant and probably protecting from cancer. All other inorganic elements have not been found with antioxidant properties.

RDI of Vitamin C

The recommended daily intake of the vitamin C in Europe is 60 mg. In the US, men are recommended to consume 90 mg per day, and women 75 mg per day.

To provide data for the RDA of vitamin C, Mark Levine and colleagues conducted an in-hospital depletion-repletion study. They found that bioavailability was complete for 200 mg of vitamin C as a single dose. No vitamin C was excreted in urine of six of seven volunteers until the 100-mg dose. At single doses of 500 mg and higher, bioavailability declined and the absorbed amount was excreted.

Oxalate and urate excretion were elevated at 1000 mg of vitamin C daily compared to lower doses. Based on these data and Institute of Medicine criteria, the current RDA of 60 mg daily should be increased to 200 mg daily, which can be obtained from fruits and vegetables. Safe doses of vitamin C are less than 1000 mg daily, and vitamin C daily doses above 400 mg have no evident value.

Antiinflammatory effects of Vitamin C

Blood levels of C-reactive protein (CRP) and tissue plasminogen activator (t-PA), known as markers linked to inflammation were found inversely associated with Plasma vitamin C, fruit intake, and dietary vitamin C.

Goya Wannamethee and colleagues from the Royal Free and University College Medical School, London concluded that vitamin C has antiinflammatory effects and is associated with lower endothelial dysfunction in men with no history of cardiovascular disease or diabetes.

The authors found that the high blood levels of vitamin C were associated with a 45 per cent reduced risk of inflammation (with respect to CRP levels), and high fruit intake was related to a 25 per cent reduced risk of inflammation.

Plasma (but not dietary) vitamin C also showed inverse associations with both fibrinogen concentrations and blood viscosity. No associations were seen with von Willebrand factor or factor VIII.

Critics on the Wannamethee Study

Previous clinical trials (with diabetics, smokers and healthy men) had not reported an anti-inflammatory effect from vitamin C supplementation.

In contrast, intravenous vitamin C trials did report an improvement in endothelial function.

Ishwarlal Jialal and Uma Singh from the University of California Davis Medical Center, writes in an editorial that in respect to the antiinflammatory effects of vitamin C, the article of Wannamethee does not allow the drawing of any valid conclusions. Much further research in a dose-response structure is required to ascertain whether oral vitamin C supplementation is antiinflammatory and whether it improves endothelial dysfunction. Until such studies have been conducted, it is safe to adhere to the guidelines of national organizations to consume e 5 or more daily servings of fruit and vegetables.

Other shortcomings of the article of Wannamethee are cited in this editorial:

The study was only focused on elderly white men and thus could not be generalized for other groups.

The use of t-PA as a measure of endothelial inflammation is being questioned.

Previous clinical trials (with diabetics, smokers and healthy men) had not reported an anti-inflammatory effect from vitamin C supplementation.

Intravenous vitamin C trials did report an improvement in endothelial function.

The authors call for more research in a dose-response to ascertain whether oral vitamin C supplementation is anti-inflammatory and whether it improves endothelial dysfunction.

Different Forms of Vitamin E

There are eight forms of vitamin E: Tocopherols: alpha, beta, gamma, delta. Alpha-tocopherol is found in supplements and in the European diet, and gamma-tocopherol is found in the American diet.

Tocotrienols: alpha, beta, gamma, delta. They are found in palmoil, cereal grains and rice bran.

Tocotrienols Stopping the Spread of Cancer Cells

Yoshiyuki Mizushina from the Kobe-Gakuin University, leading author studied the effects of all eight forms of vitamin E on the inhibition of mammalian DNA polymerase, the enzyme that assists DNA replication. He found that tocotrienols could stop the spread of cancer cells.

The four tocopherols did not influence the activities of mammalian polymerases and had no effect on the spread of cancer cells.

Alpha-and delta-tocotrienols inhibited polymerase lambda activity, and inhibited the spread of cancer cells, and angiogenesis (the growth of new blood vessels) is inhibited and the spread of the cancer to other parts of the body is hindered reducing risk of metastasis.

Other Study by Chandon Sen, Savita Khanna and Sashwati Roy support identical claims for tocotrienols, including neuroprotection, reduction of cholesterol, as an antioxidant, and other anti-cancer studies.

ACTIVITY OF POLYPHENOLS

These substances interrupt the radical chain reaction in lipids of the cell membrane avoiding the formation of oxidized LDL which starts ateriosclerotic diseases.

They have reducing properties. Flavonoids may also act as antimutagenic and anticarcinogenic.

Some activities of flavonoids in human are studied but are not confirmed yet:

Inhibition of enzymes with carcinogenic activity.

Inhibition of proteolytic enzymes.

Polyphenoles of these groups are found in many fruits and vegetables.

That is why more fruits and vegetables and less meat, fat and alcoholics should be consumed.

Tea is the main source of catechins. According to the Rotterdam-Study the consumption of tea protects against heavy aorta ateriosclerosis in particular in women.

Important varieties and their content of polyphenoles are:

Camellia sinensis var. assamica:

- High content of catechins and coffein
- High activity of Phenoloxidase activity resulting in dark brown colour of black tea

Camellia sinensis var. sinensis:

- Lower content of catechins and caffeine as noted in assamica
- Lower activity of Phenoloxidase activity which makes it suitabler for the production of green tea

Protective effect of green tea and soy intake in relation to breath cancer risk

There is substantial in vitro and in vivo evidence implicating tea polyphenols as chemopreventive agents against various cancers.

However, epidemic data collected by researchers of the Department of Preventive Medicine, University of Southern California, Keck School of Medicine, Los Angeles are not supportive of a protective role of tea, mainly black tea, in the aetiology of breast cancer.

The case study showed that both green tea and soy intake had significant, independent protective effects on breast cancer risk The results of this case study point to an important role of both green tea and soy intake in relation to breast cancer risk.

Anticancer Effects of Green Tea

Shaun K. Rodriguez et col. suggest a novel mechanism for green tea catechin, epigallocatechin-3-gallate anticancer effects where epigallocatechin gallate can abrogate vascular endothelial growth factor signalling by interfering with the formation of a receptor complex, resulting in attenuated mitogenic and angiogenic signalling.

Bitter chocolate has high levels of catechins (53,3 mg/100g chocolate). Milk chocolate has only 15,9 mg catechins/100g chocolate. Catechines are situated in the cocoa part of the cocoa beans (Theobroma cacao), that is why bitter chocolate with high cocoa is rich in catechines.

Analytical test for total polyphenols is the Folin-Ciocalteau. Due to the reducing activity of the polyphenols a strong blue colour is created which can be be measured.

Specific polyphenols are measured with aid of HPLC or capyllary electrophoresis.

In order to act reducing it is necessary have at least one of the following structures:

1. 3', 4'-Dihydrofunction at the B ring. This makes the turnover of a proton building thus an aryloxy-radical.
2. OH-A group in position 5 and 7 at the A ring.
3. A doublebound in 2-3 position in conjugation with the 4-Oxo-function and the 3-OH group at the ring C turning possible the delocalization of the electrons of the B ring.

Quercentine has all three structures turning out to be an excelent antioxydant in water solution.

Flavonols in Chocolate

A 15 years follow up study made by Brian Buijsse and colleges indicate that cocoa-containing foods improve endothelial function and reduce blood pressure. In a cohort of elderly men Brian Buijsse and colleges found that cocoa intake is inversely associated with blood pressure and 15-year cardiovascular and all-cause mortality, confirming previous studies which have linked flavanols (Flavan-3-ols) to improved cardiovascular health.

The cocoa-containing foods from this study included chocolate confectionery, cocoa sandwich filling, cocoa desserts, cocoa drinks, and dietary supplements.

The men who consumed the most cocoa (more than 2.3 grams per day) had lower systolic diastolic blood pressures (3.7 mmHg and 2.1 mmHg, respectively) than those who consumed the least cocoa (less than 0.36 grams per day).

Several previous studies have shown that flavonol consumption increased blood vessel vasodilation, and improve endothelial function.

However, Cathy Ross, of the British Heart Foundation, said that here is some evidence that when eaten in small quantities, dark chocolate might have some beneficial effects on blood vessels and lowering blood pressure, but as yet no study has investigated the long-terms clinical effects.

People would have to eat about 100 grams of dark chocolate a day with 500 calories and 30 % of fat to get an effective amount of flavanols. According to Cathy Ross there are much better ways of improving heart health like products with increased flavonol content.

LEGUMIN AND HOMOLOGOUS PROTEINS

Legumin in Maize

Legumin is a member of a family of storage proteins (11S globulins) found in the Leguminaceae and other higher plants.

It is a histidine-and glutamine-rich polypeptide of 50â□"55 kDa with a peptide bond joining the C-terminus of the alfa-subunit (always asparagine) and the N-terminus of the beta-subunit (almost always glycine)

Yamagata and colleagues found that a legumin does exist in maize, that it is uncleaved, that it appears to be localized to small protein bodies essentially identical to those found in legumes, and that it is more abundant in wild type (W64A), than in sweet corn or opaque-2 maize. The authors discuss the phylogenetic relations between maize legumin and 7S globulin (vicilins).

Convicilin in Pisum and Faba Beans

Boulter and colleagues found in Pisum and faba beans two major families of storage proteins, legumin and vicilin. Legumins are hexameric proteins comprising of 6M gama 60 000 subunits. Vicilins are a less well-defined group of proteins consisting largely ofM gama 50 000 subunits. Boulter found a third storage protein, convicilin, a vicilin-type protein with vicilin immunological determinants.

According to Boulter proteins homologous to legumin have been found in Arachis, Glycine,Vigna unguiculata, Lupinus, Cicer, Lens and Lathyrus. Equivalent vicilin-type proteins occur in Phaseolus vulgaris, Glycine, Arachis and Vigna unguiculata.

Legumin Type Protein in Almond

According to Shridhar and colleagues the almond major storage protein, amandin,Amandin is a legumin type protein. Amandin is composed of two major types of polypeptides-linked via disulfide bonds. Amandin is a storage protein-Amandin is not a glycoprotein. Amandin-1, amandin-2, and amandin-3 are antigenically related and have similar biochemical properties. Shiddhar found that methionine is the first essential limiting amino acid in amandin followed by lysine and threonine.

Western Blot Legumin Protein

The classical three-step procedure of Western Blot (blocking, primary antibody-binding and secondary antibody-binding) takes about 4.5 hrs. GenScript developed the One-Step Western which performs Western blot or Dot blot to detect any protein including Legumin protein and related proteins within an hour. After the proteins are transferred from a gel to the membrane, the membrane is incubated in Pretreatment Solution for 5 minutes and in WB solution with primary antibody added for 40 min, the membrane is washed three times for 5 min each and the blots are develop using either Chemiluminescent substrate or TMB.

10

THE PHARMACOLOGY OF NUTRITION

AYURVEDA: AN INTRODUCTION

Ayurveda is a Sanskrit word derived from two roots: *ayur*, which means life; and *veda*, which means knowledge. It has its roots in ancient vedic literature.

Ayurveda, a system of diet, healing and health maintenance, is probably the oldest science of life, just like the science of Yoga.

Ayurveda includes all aspects of daily life like:

- Maintenance of health
- Prevention of disease
- Harmonization of body and mind
- Natural treatments
- Holistic and complimentary healing techniques

Ayurveda combines yoga, meditation, food, natural preparations, cleansing and regenerative treatments. The overall effect is physical strength, better health, mental clarity, inner peace and calmness.

Ayurveda is a science of life so to know more about it, we must know what is life. Life, according to Ayurveda, is a combination of senses, mind, body and soul. It is clear from this definition of life that Ayurveda is not only limited to body or physical symptoms but also gives a comprehensive knowledge about spiritual, mental and social health.

ROLE OF AYURVEDA

Ayurveda teaches us to understand our body; our particular nature; and our individual mixture of elements at a deep physical, mental and emotional level. With that knowledge we are able to identify activities, conditions, herbs and foods that either keep us healthy and in balance, or make us ill and throw us out of balance.

AYURVEDA AND HEALTH

Ayurveda forms an integral part of the daily regimen of hundreds of millions of people worldwide. Its principles are utilized not only to treat persons who are ill but also to prepare a balanced meal and to construct a harmonious environment to live in. Ayurveda brings to life the concepts of preventive health care and health promotion.

The goal of Ayurveda is to help an individual discover the knowledge of living and health. Health is the state of harmonious chemical balance in a living organism. Our health depends on the chemical environments inside and outside our bodies. Food plays an important role in creating the internal chemical environment.

THE FIVE ELEMENTS

Our very existence is the interplay of different frequencies of vibrations, which have been classified into a system of five elements by the Ayurvedic seers and sages. These five elements are the agents of the primary inertia principle of consciousness and are the materialized form of the universal energy. Akasha, or Ether, evolved first and is the subtlest of the five elements. From it comes air, from air evolves fire, from fire evolves water and from water comes earth. The human body, which is composed of these elements, is also nourished and maintained by them.

THE DOSHAS

The starting point for many people into the ancient scientific art of Ayurveda is the relationship of the three Doshas: Vata, Pitta and Kapha.

Ayurveda sees life as a harmonic flow, a dynamic balance of those three fundamental forces:

- Vata ? (wind, air) the principle of movement and impulse
- Pitta ? (bile, fire) the principle of assimilation and transformation
- Kapha ? (mucus, water) the principle of stability

These forces act in everyone. When they are in balance they bring well-being and health, in imbalance they lead to feeling unwell and later disease. Everybody is unique and Ayurveda respects this uniqueness. That is why there are individual constitution types, Doshas, in the body.

Out of the three basic forces can seven categories be formed:

1. Wind dominated individuals (vata)
2. Bile dominated individuals (pitta)
3. Mucus dominated individuals (kapha)
4. Wind and Bile dominated individuals (vata and pitta)
5. Wind and Mucus dominated individuals (vata and kapha)
6. Bile and mucus dominated individuals (pitta and kapha)
7. Wind, bile and mucus dominated individuals (vata and pitta and kapha in equal proportion)

THE THREE CONSTITUTIONAL TYPES: THE GUNAS

There are three basic constitutional types. To live a long and healthy life, Ayurveda states it is necessary for us to recognize them in ourselves and be able to preserve their balance with nature. It is possible, though, to take a step back and study the mind as Ayurveda clearly tells us that we create what our minds dictate.

So do we have any control over our thoughts? Ayurveda says yes, but not in the sense of thought manipulation. We are told that the mind has three tendencies or qualities.

- Satva, the principle of contentment, joy, peace and harmony.

- Rajas, the principle of energy, of change, emotion and turbulence
- Tamas, the principle towards rest, dullness, inertia, depression and resistance

To progress thru life in a harmonious way, it is suggested that we increase Satva and keep a pinch of Rajas and Tamas to accommodate movement and rest.

All three Gunas enhance the qualities of the three Doshas.

- A mind tendency toward Satva will encourage the qualities of intelligence, perception and strong digestion found in the Pitta Dosha.
- If the mind of the Pitta type is Rajasic, restlessness, irritation, heat and anger will be dominant, and,
- eventually, through exhaustion, tipping over into dullness and depression. Which are the signs of Tamas.

To help ourselves live a joyful and fulfilled life, we can become aware of our lifestyle and use tools such as breathing techniques, asanas and meditation to calm and integrate the nervous system. Being with like-minded people helps, and of course will food play a significant role.

AYURVEDIC FOOD

The food is either satvic, rajasic or tamasic according to its character and effect upon the body and the mind. One can find out the nature or temperament of a man from the nature of the food he prefers.

Satvic Food

- Satvic foods are fresh, juicy, light, unctuous, nourishing, sweet and tasty.
- It increases the energy of the mind and produces cheerfulness, serenity and mental clarity.
- satvic food is highly conducive to good health.
- A satvic man relishes juicy food and other foods which are attractive in form, soft to touch and pleasant to

taste, which are small in bulk but great in nourishment like the words from the lips of a spiritual preceptor.

- Milk, butter, ghee (clarified butter), fresh ripe fruits, almonds, dates, green gram, sprouts, barley, wheat, cereals, tomatoes, plantains etc., are satvic.

Rajasic Food

- Rajasic foods are bitter, sour, salty, pungent, hot and dry.
- These foods create sensuality, sexuality, greed, jealousy, anger, delusion, fantasies, egotism and irreligious feelings.
- The rajasic man always plans to prepare various kinds of preparations to satisfy his palate. The palate remains unsatisfied until the stomach is completely filled with pungent things and till the tongue is burnt with chillies.
- Pungent condiments, meat, fish, eggs, sweets, fried bread, curd, egg plant, carrots, black gram, onions, garlic, lemon, red gram, tea, coffee, betel leaves, tobacco are rajasic articles of food.

Tamasic Food

- Tamasic food is stale, dry, bad smelling, distasteful or unpalatable.
- It increases pessimism, ignorance, lack of common sense, greed, laziness, criminal tendencies and doubt.
- The tamasic man will eat, in the afternoon, food which has been cooked on the previous day and also will like the food which is half-cooked or burnt.
- Foods that have been processed, canned or frozen are tamasic.
- Beef, fish, eggs, wine, garlic, onions and tobacco are tamasic foodstuffs.

Ayurveda places responsibility firmly on the individual to be aware of his or her relationship with nature and she gives us the tools to correct imbalances before they develop into full-blown disease.

Sri Kalki says that it is essential to have a healthy body free of mucus in order to attain the state of altered consciousness of enlightenment. A deeper knowledge about Ayurveda will help sincere seekers to understand their bodies and minds from the Annamaya Kosha's point of view so that it helps in the enlightenment process.

The science of Ayurveda, like the science of Yoga, was inspired and developed by the great masters and seers of ancient India. The origin of Ayurveda and Yoga are common to play a highly complimentary role in spiritual evolution and the maintenance of physical well-being and vitality.

Ayurveda is, perhaps, the oldest science of life, a system of diet, healing and health maintenance that is deeply spiritual in origin. Unlike traditional Western medicine, Ayurveda is not confined to healing of disease in a superficial treatment of symptoms. Instead, it evaluates the complete body mind of the individual.

Ayurveda sees medicine and diet as complementary rather than separate. No one can expect to retain vitality, recover from disease, or succeed in the practice of Yoga without the appropriate knowledge of the powerful effect diet has on physical health, mental clarity and spiritual progress.

Indeed, yogis place great emphasis on diet as an integral part of the successful practice of any spiritual discipline. Ayurveda addresses not only healing, but also prevention and maintenance of vitality, as crucial in the practice of Yoga. Ancient seers describe the human body and the body of the universe as composed of prana, the primal energy, vital for life and which manifests in the form of earth, water, fire, air and ether.

Any imbalance of these elements in our body is experienced in illness, discomfort or pain. These elements are kept in harmony by a healthy body that consumes them through breath, food, vegetables, seeds, beans, herbs and roots as vital carriers and balancers for the energy of prana in the body. The power of these foods manifests only when they are used in proper combinations and in complete coordination with unique conditions of each individual. This is where the profound effects of Ayurvedic food reveal themselves.

DISCOVERING YOUR CONSTITUTION

The particular combination of energies present when we enter this world at birth is known in Ayurveda as our innate constitution or prakruti. What we do with our constitution is up to us. It is the source for our health, vitality and well-being. It can also be the springboard toward difficulties, if we ignore its needs. The five elements come together to create the three basic constitutional types. They are Vata, Pitta and Kapha. If air and ether predominate in your constitution, you are Vata in nature. If fire and water take the lead in your physical make up, Pitta is the result. If water and earth hold ascendancy in your body at birth Kapha is your constitution.

What does understanding your constitution mean, practically? Each constitution has different needs. Meeting these needs assures balance and better chances for good health and peace of mind. It also offers you more informed choices in what health care methods are most appropriate for you.

How can you discover your constitution? Ideally, a skilled Ayurvedic physician can assess your pulse and give you information about your prakruti (constitution). From pulse examination he or she can ascertain what elements are in balance, what is out, and what needs to be done.

The pulse is utilised in Ayurveda in a way similar to Tibetan and Chinese medicine. Working with a talent Ayurvedic practitioner is an invaluable resource. But what if you live in Boise, Idaho, where there is no vaidya? Each constitution has certain characteristics physical, emotional and mental attributes, which let us know what elements are present.

THE THREE DOSHAS

When the three doshas exist harmoniously the result is a sense of balance and health; an imbalance, which might be caused by an excess (vriddhi) or deficiency (kshaya) of any or all of them, results in a sign or symptom of disease. Our physical constitution and our health both depend on the balance and interplay of the tridoshas.

The three doshas are known as Vata, Pitta and Kapha. Each dosha has its own part to play in the maintenance of the body. The rhythmic pattern of these humors fluctuates periodically, since the doshas are affected by place, climate, seasonal changes, diet and other factors.

Of the three doshas, Wind is the key. Bile and Mucus cannot move from their centres unless the air within the body carries them. If just one of these doshas is disturbed, the diseases produced are easily curable. Diseases produced by the disturbance of two doshas become comparatively chronic and require more time to heal. When diseases are caused by the disorder of all three, the condition is even worse.

Vata (Wind)

The literal meaning of the word vata is motion

- Creativity ? Enthusiasm ? Freedom ? Generosity ? Joy ? Vitality ? Air
- Vata is the most powerful of the doshas.
- Formed by the interaction of space and air, Vata is movement, the body in motion.
- Vata is the originator of all kinds of movements in the body. So activities like respiration, movement of food in the digestive tract, circulation of various fluids, excretion of wastes and nervous functions are mainly governed by vata.

If you have a vata constitution, you are likely to be artistic and creative with a good imagination, though you may have it hard to put your ideas into practice, as new ideas continually catch your imagination. Your memory may not be very good.

Vata is mobile and governs: All movements within the body, stimulation of nerves, tears, transmission of sensory stimuli, initiation of motor functions, creation of impulses and reflexes, maintenance of consciousness, inspiration and expiration, heartbeat, circulation of blood, oxygen, nutrients, thoughts, stimulation of digestive juices, peristalsis, normal elimination, normal transformation of tissues, ejaculation, delivery of fetus from womb, expression of emotion.

Factors Aggravating Vata

- Eating too much food that are similar in qualities to that of vata like cabbage, broccoli, cauliflower, cucumber, melons, potatoes, dry breads, fast foods and apples etc.
- Activities like too much travelling, staying awake till late night and watching too much television, exposure to high noise levels, eating while anxious or depressed.
- Indulging in too much sexual activity.

Your Constitution According to Vata

- Small, active, dark eyes.
- Usually of a thin frame.
- Creative thinker.
- Dark complexioned.
- Unstable in making decisions.
- Difficulty in gaining weight.
- Changeable moods and ideas.
- Cold hands and feet, little perspiration
- Brittle nails.
- Prefer warm climate, sunshine and moisture.
- Dark, rough, wiry or kinky hair.
- Like to snack, nibble.
- Like to stay physically active.
- Variable thirst.

Essential oils for vata: Angelica, basil, bergamot, clary sage, eucalyptus, lemon, myrtle, orange, pine, tangerine, chamomile, lavender, rosewood, corrct seed, frankincence, galbanum, ginger, spikenard, myrrh, rose.

Kapha (mucus): The literal or etymological meaning of kapha is to embrace, cohesion or that which holds things together.

- Caring, Centeredness, Compassion, Contentment, Faith, Fulfilment, Groundedness, Patience-Stability
- Kapha, in its role as a lubricant, combines the structural properties of earth with water.
- It builds the body and forms its structural skeleton, muscles, organs, ligaments, tendons and skin.
- Kapha lubricates the body, ensuring the smooth function of joints. With strength, stability, and solidity, Kapha is the body in repose.

If kapha predominates in your constitution, you will have a steady, reliable mind. You will take time to learn, and will remember what you have learned. There can sometimes be elements of dullness with a kapha mind: it is usually content not to seek fresh mental stimulation.

Kapha governs: Lubrication fluids and supply system, mucous membranes, synovial fluid in joints, binding, firmness, heaviness in the body, softness in the body, distribution of heat, strength and stamina, longevity of cells and thus the person, sleep, long-term memory, security.

Factors Aggravating Kapha

- Eating foods that are very cold, heavy, oily like fried food, sweets like sugars, fats, milk products, ice creams and meat.
- Activities like sleeping during the daytime, not doing much physical activity, living in cold and humid climate etc.

Your Constitution According to Kapha

- Medium and well-built frame.
- Gain weight easily, have a hard time to lose.

- Large, attractive eyes with thick eyelashes.
- Thick, wavy hair, a little oily, dark or light.
- Have ideas and opinions but not confident of the same.
- Work well with routine.
- Steady, reliable, slow to change

AYURVEDA: HEALING WATERS

Ayurveda is perhaps the oldest science of life and a system of diet, healing and health maintenance that is deeply spiritual in origin. In this article the healing properties of water will be presented.

Well water, pond water, rain water, there are many types of water described in ayurvedic texts, and each has a therapeutic value, just as food does. Water represents soma, the nourishing cooling quality that is associated with lunar energy. It helps with digestion, cools and balances Pitta dosha, supports Kapha and counteracts the dryness of Vata. It nurtures, lubricates and also detoxifies when it flows out of the body as urine. Water, when properly absorbed by the body, has several healing qualities.

1. Helps to remove fatigue (shramnashana)
2. Enhances glow of skin
3. Prevents constipation
4. Increase stamina
5. Provides satisfaction
6. Helps the heart
7. Helps digestion
8. Cooling
9. Always helpful to the body
10. Easy to assimilate
11. Life-giving
12. Antioxidant

The healing effects of water can be enhanced using ayurvedic methods.

Water for Cleansing: Sometimes people have dry skin and unquenchable thirst even though they drink lots of water. The deeper physiology is not getting enough moist. This occurs when the person's agni is low and mucus blocks the micro channels, which carry water to the cells. In order to cleanse the channels and enhance moisture absorption, ayurvedic texts recommend boiling the water for various lengths of time, creating therapeutic water called ushnodaka. Another method is to add spices or herbs to the water after boiling.

Why it Works: When the water boils, it gets charged with heat and becoming sharper in quality. This sharpness allows it to cleanse the channels and penetrate deeper levels of the physiology. Spice creates an added therapeutic effect by interacting with the water on the molecular level. Spices create different effects on the body through aroma and taste.

It becomes easier for the body to flush out toxins and impurities because of the sharpness of the agni (heat) in the water and because of the sharpness of the spices. Over time, it cleanses the channels so the water is unobstructed as it travels into the body to hydrate the tissues, and travels out carrying waste.

Ancient texts talk about the difference in the rate of absorption of regular water vs. boiled water:

1. Regular water ? takes about six hours if every channel is clear.
2. Boiled and cooled water ? takes about three hours to be absorbed, and helps open the channels
3. Hot herbalized water ? takes about 1 1/2 hours, due to sharpness of Agni, herbs and spices.

Water for Your Body Type: An ayurvedic expert can design a therapeutic water recipe to give a specific benefit. One water recipe might enhance immunity, another might cleanse the skin, and another might help with prostate imbalance. You can also choose a spice-water recipe for your body type of imbalances.

Vata Balancing Water: Boil two quarts of water for 5 minutes. Take it off the heat and add 3 leaves mint, 1/2 tsp ajwain (ajwain is also known as Bishop's Weed, relatid with cumin but tastes more like thyme with an astringent edge) and 1/4 tsp singhada flour. Place the water in a thermos. Sip it throughout the day at a warm but not hot temperature.

Pitta Balancing Water: Boil two quarts of water for 2 minutes. Take it off the heat and add 1/4 tsp ajwain, 2 rose buds and 1 clove. Store in hot in inside a thermos, but before drinking pour it into a cup and let it cool to room temperature in summer. In winter, it can be slightly warmer.

Kapha Balancing Water: Boil two quarts of water for 5 minutes. Take it off the heat and add 3 holy basil leaves (Tulsi), two thin slices of fresh ginger, 1/4 tsp of cumin and 1/2 tsp of ajwain. Place the water and spices in a thermos, and sip the water at a hot or warm temperature throughout the day.

How Much is Enough: How much water you should drink depends on your age, how much physical work or exercise you do, the weather, your diet, your stress levels, your herbal food supplements, and your body type. The warm Pitta types usually are thirstier than the watery Kapha types. Vata types are often constipated or have dry skin and thus need to drink more water.

We recommend making your spice water first thing in the morning and sipping it every fifteen minutes throughout the day. Drink plain water after 7:00 pm, as spice-water is too enlivening to drink right before sleeping. If you don't finish the spice-water by then, throw it out and start fresh in the morning.

You may want to drink some plain water during the day as well. If you have been exercising and need to drink a full glass of water, it's better to drink plain water rather than the spice-water.

AYURVEDIC VIEW ON EATING FOR ENERGY

When you need a high energy fix, do you reach for a power bar or power shake? Or do you resort to caffeine, chocolate, or high-sugar snacks when you feel that end of the day sag?

It may surprise you, but according to Ayurveda, the real energy-boosters are fresh fruits, vegetables, species, and whole grains. These are the foods that are rich in chetna, the healing and nurturing influence of nature.

They are so alive with nature's intelligence that fatigue-causing toxins cannot accumulate in the body when you eat them.

Grains for Power

Athletes have long relied on carbohydrates in grains for long-term endurance and energy. Yet not all carbohydrates are created alike. A croissant, for instance, is high in fat and low in nutrition.

The most nutritious carbohydrates are whole grains, which have been found to lower cholesterol inhibits cancer causing activity and harmful bacteria in the intestines, and lower blood glucose level. And these whole grains, ayuerveda considers rye, quinoa, amaranth and millet as the most nutritious, because they are especially high in protein and mineral.

They are also high in fibre, and thus have a detoxifying value. These are the same auspicious grains that re described in the Verdict texts and are used for Vedict ceremonies.

One-half cup of Dalia (measured dry), for instance, contains 14g. protein, 8mg. iron, and also magnesium and zine.The same amount of Rava contains 13g. of protein, 9.mg of iron and 3 mg. of zinc. Rye is also high in protein with one-half cup yielding 15 grams of protein and 4mg. of zine. Millet is a good source of B vitamins

All of these grains contain copper, which is an essential trace mineral that improves energy and immunity, and their zinc content also boosts ojas, the finest product of digestion that creates lightness, inner energy, immunity and bliss.

To prepare power grains, place two cups of water in a saucepan and bring it to a boil. Add a teaspoon a Ghee and 1/2 cup of grain. Boil for then lower to a simmer. Cook is important because otherwise grains create internal dryness.

ENERGIZING VEGETABLES AND FRUITS

Other high-energy foods include fresh vegetables, which should constitute forty percent of the meal. Green, leafy vegetables are especially high in mineral and fibre, so should be eaten often.

Fruits are also a source of energy. You can start the day with a stewed apple, and if you feel hungry in between meals, try snacking on a juicy pear. If you are feeling heavy and bloated after lunch, eat a fresh papaya, it contain enzymes aiding digestion.

If you have a strong digestion and more Pitta in your constitution, mangoes are a rich ojas-producing food, and half a mango contains 2 mg beta-carotene and is a rich source of Vitamin C. According to Ayurveda, Raisins are among the best of fruits because they enhance sattva (purity), pacify the mind and heart and increase the coordination between them.

They are also a rich source of iron and Vitamin B6, and provide magnesium, calcium, zinc and potassium. Raisins aid digestion and elimination when they are soaked in water overnight. One handful per person is a good amount. A Date-Milk Energy Shake is a nourishing way to end the day. Because it promotes sleep and calm both Pitta and Vata sleep imbalances.

Date-Milk Energy Shake

4-5 whole dates (Medjool dates are ideal)

1 cup whole organic milk (unhomogenized if possible)

1 pinch cinnamon powder

The important thing is to eat foods every day that boost your energy, rather than relying on artificial boosters when you feel your energy sag.

Boil the milk until creates foam. Turn off the heat and cool until the temperature is comfortable for drinking. Combine the milk with the other ingredients and blend until the dates are ground up. Drink it warm in winter and at room temperature is summer.

Beware of Energy-Draining Foods

Just as there is food to boost energy, other foods drain it. Any fast food, canned, frozen, packaged, leftover or old foods or foods laced with preservatives, chemicals, and additives-are difficult to digest and contain little nutritional content. If you do eat some of these foods, and you feel heavy after eating, Ayurveda advices drinking half a glass of water with 1/4 of a fresh lime squeezed into it.

But if you are feeling dull, sluggish, and drained of energy every day, it probably means that your diet contains too many energy-draining foods, which have clogged your micro channels with toxins. This mean that you need to overhaul your diet to include foods that create ojas and energy.

The important thing is to eat food every day that boost your energy, rather then relying on a artificial boosters when you feel your energy sag, because there will always be a negative side-effect.

FOOD AND CONCIOUSNESS

Attention Deficit Hyperactivity Disorder

What is ADHD?

ADHD is a diagnosis characterized by behaviours showing inappropriate levels of inattention, impulsivity and hyperactivity. These behaviours appear in school, at home and in social situations, and typically become worse in situations where sustained attention is required (eg. doing seat-work, studying, listening to people talk). The behaviours associated with ADHD usually become apparent before the age of four, but are frequently not recognized until the child commences school. It is reported that up to 6 percent of children may show symptoms of ADHD, with males outnumbering females approximately three-to-one.

Cautions:

- many of the behaviours/characteristics of ADHD are present in all children to some degree and at particular ages;

- the behaviours are not abnormal in themselves-only when excessive for the child's age.
- what characterizes ADHD is the intensity,persistence, and patterning of the behaviours which significantly impairs social, academic, and work activities.

Behaviours Associated with ADHD

1. Inattention:
   - often fails to give close attention to details; makes careless mistakes in schoolwork and other activities
   - often has difficulty sustaining attention in tasks or play activities
   - often does not seem to listen when spoken to directly
   - often does not follow through on instructions and fails to finish schoolwork, chores, or other duties
   - often has difficulty organizing tasks and activities
   - often avoids, dislikes, or is reluctant to engage in tasks that require sustained mental effort (such as schoolwork or homework)
   - often loses things necessary for tasks or activities (e.g. toys, school assignments, pencil, books, or tools)
   - often easily distracted by extraneous stimuli
   - often forgetful in daily activities
2. Impulsivity:
   - often blurts out answers before questions have been completed
   - often has difficulty awaiting turn
   - often interrupts or intrudes on others
3. Hyperactivity:
   - often fidgets with hands or feet or squirms in seat
   - often leaves seat in the classroom or wherever remaining seated is expected

- often runs about or climbs excessively in situations where it is inappropriate
- often has difficulty playing or engaging in leisure activities quietly
- often "on the go" or often acts as if "driven by a motor"
- often talks excessively

Who can Diagnose ADHD?

Psychologists, psychological associates (with access to diagnosis) and physicians properly diagnose ADHD using criteria from the three characteristics of inattention, impulsivity and hyperactivity.

A child must show a significant number of the characteristic behaviours more frequently than expected for a child that age, in at least two different environments, and for at least six consecutive months. Onset of these behaviours should be before the age of seven. Since a child may show difficulties with sustaining attention for a variety of reasons, psychologists diagnosing ADHD will use a multidisciplinary approach involving parents, classroom teachers and other individuals who know the child.

How is ADHD Best Treated?

There is no single effective method for treating ADHD. Research in modifying children's environments; counselling; behaviour modification; medication and individualized academic programing all have shown promise. No one technique, nor single combination of techniques is effective with all children. In particular, treating ADHD with stimulant medication remains inconclusive.

There is little evidence that academic achievement improves with the use of medications such as Ritalin, Dexedrine and Cylert alone. Medication can and does increase the attention span of children. However, it is unclear that thinking, memory and academic skills are improved by simply helping children to attend and engage in learning activities for longer periods of time. Similarly, other treatment approaches to ADHD which emphasize specific diets, megavitamins, restrictions on food dyes and listening stimulation, have not been shown to have a significant effect on ADHD in well controlled research studies.

In the midst of all the uncertainty as to how to deal effectively with ADHD children, it appears that an eclectic or broad-based approach is best. A combination of behaviour modification, medication, and classroom and home management techniques has shown the most promising results. Only an individualized approach implemented by parents and teachers, under the direction and supervision of psychologists and physicians, will meet the special needs of children with ADHD.

Helpful Tips:

- only experienced psychologists and physicians can accurately diagnose ADHD.
- parents should be cautious not to diagnose their children after reading the characteristic behaviours of ADHD (be aware and concerned, but don't diagnose).
- seek advice from an experienced psychologist or physician for an accurate diagnosis and appropriate treatment plan.
- all methods of treatment should be closely monitored; be wary of the "take these pills and see me in six months" approach.

Facts and Figures about ADHD

According to the National Institutes of Mental Health (NIMH), "ADHD (Attention Deficit Hyperactivity Disorder) refers to a family of related chronic neurobiological disorders that interfere with the individual's capacity to regulate activity level (hyperactivity), inhibit behaviour (impulsivity), and attend to tasks (inattention) in developmentally appropriate ways."

ADHD, under different labels, has been recognized as a disorder from at least the 1940's. Far from being an "invented disease", it is well substantiated that ADHD is a disorder which involves a dysfunction in the prefrontal cortex of the brain. This is the area of the brain which is involved in higher-order planning skills, and which permits us to inhibit responding.

Using sophisticated neural imaging techniques, it has been discovered that there are structural differences in the brains of individuals with ADHD.

The parts of the brain responsible for controlling attention have been found to use less glucose (a major fuel source) in ADHD individuals compared to nonaffected individuals. In addition, evidence strongly suggests that ADHD individuals also demonstrate neurochemical differences, in particular less of a chemical neurotransmitter called dopamine which is needed in some areas of the brain to focus attention and to control impulsive responding.

There is very strong evidence of a genetic component in this disorder, again refuting suggestions that the condition is not real. At least 1/3 of fathers who were diagnosed as having ADHD as children have children who are also diagnosed with ADHD. Siblings of ADHD children are 5 to 7 times more likely to demonstrate the disorder than are children from unaffected families. Even more compelling, the majority of identical twins share the trait.

Nongenetic causes account for about 20 to 30 percent of ADHD cases, and include fetal distress, premature birth, maternal alcohol use during pregnancy, exposure to high levels of lead during early childhood, traumatic brain injury (especially injury of the frontal lobes) and sleep problems. There is no evidence that ADHD is caused by food allergies, by watching too much TV, by excess sugar, by poor home life, or by poor schooling.

Current data from the U.S. National Institutes of Mental Health (NIMH) estimate that about 5 to 6 percent of school age boys in the U.S. are diagnosed with this disorder. Boys with the disorder outnumber girls by a factor of 2 or 3. This translates into about 2 million children in the U.S. Similar percentages are reported for Canadian children.

There is no independent test for ADHD. This is a situation common to most psychiatric disorders, including schizophrenia and autism, due to their complexity and variability. Primary care and developmental pediatricians, family practitioners, child neurologists, psychologists and psychiatrists are the providers responsible for assessment, diagnosis and treatment of most children with ADHD. NIMH data indicate that family doctors diagnose more quickly and prescribe medication more frequently than psychiatrists and pediatricians.

Misdiagnosis can occur, as other disorders (learning disabilities, chronic ear infections, language delays, adjustment problems, substance abuse, personality disorders, epilepsy) can produce similar symptoms. In addition, a number of other disorders often accompany ADHD, including learning disabilities, fetal alcohol syndrome or effects, developmental delays, language disorders, anxiety disorders, mood disorders, conduct disorders and tic disorders, including Tourette's syndrome.

The more carefully the assessment is conducted, and the more information considered (e.g., medical, developmental, school, psychosocial and family histories, parent and teacher ratings, psychological testing) the lower the incidence is found to be for this disorder. Diagnosis should be based upon a thorough investigation of the child's life, in and outside of the home.

Many children do not "outgrow" ADHD: about 1/3 of individuals diagnosed as children still meet the formal criteria as adults. Hyperactive-impulsive symptoms generally decrease with age, but symptoms of inattention do not.

Without treatment, ADHD children are at significantly higher risk for a variety of negative life outcomes. They are more likely to be involved in accidents, especially motor vehicle accidents during adolescence, as well as tobacco use, early pregnancy and lower educational attainment. Almost half of ADHD children (mostly boys) exhibit symptoms of Oppositional Defiant Disorder, including stubbornness, bursts of temper, belligerent and defiant behaviour.

In some of these children, there is a progression into the much more serious behavioural problems associated with a diagnosis of Conduct Disorder. About 25 percent of these children experience anxiety or depression. Some develop antisocial personality disorder.

There are three types of stimulant most commonly prescribed for this disorder, and Ritalin has proved to be the most effective. Its clinical effects peak about one hour after each dose, and dissipate in about 4 hours. Ritalin appears to act by increasing the amount of dopamine at the synapses, addressing the deficiency which may underlie this disorder. Nine out of ten children with ADHD improve with the use of one of the three stimulant medications.

Ritalin has been prescribed for children since the 1970's and consequently has been well studied. Side effects do include sleep problems, appetite loss and, in rare cases, facial tics. There may be a negative effect on growth rate, although ultimate height does not appear to be affected. Interestingly, the NIMH study found that the highest level of side-effects was reported for children receiving the placebo ("sugar pill") rather than the actual stimulant medication.

Ritalin can be addictive when abused by adolescents and adults. However, long-term tolerance is rare as there is no need to increase the dosage to maintain clinical effects. Contrary to concerns about potential drug abuse, ADHD boys treated with stimulants are significantly less likely to abuse drugs and alcohol when older.

The NIMH and the US Department of Education recently published the results of the most comprehensive study of treatment effectiveness for ADHD ever undertaken. The Multimodal Treatment Study of Children with ADHD cost $11 million (US), and conclusively demonstrated that long-term combinations of psychosocial and stimulant treatments, as well as thorough and well-monitored medical management alone, were both significantly superior to intensive behavioural treatments alone and to treatments offered by most medical practitioners in the community.

Stimulants were found to have 3-fold greater benefit on behaviour ratings than on ratings of attention, and the best effect on academics and social behaviour were observed when medication was maintained for a year or more. In contrast, behavioural parent training and behavioural interventions in the classroom setting had limited effects on hyperactivity, but large effects in reducing oppositionality, defiance and aggression.

American statistics indicate that production of Ritalin has increased about 500 percent since 1990. Health Canada estimates that prescriptions for Ritalin have increased 637 percent over the same period. Current estimates place the number of Canadian children taking Ritalin at about 2 to 3 percent, which represents at most 145,000 children in the country. No one denies that misuse and abuse of this drug occur.

However, authorities agree that the increase in prescriptions primarily represents the fact that children with the inattentive type of this disorder (predominantly girls) are now being identified in addition to children with either the hyperactive-impulsive type and combined type, that children are being diagnosed earlier, and that they are staying on the drug for longer periods of time (often throughout adolescence and into adulthood).

There are a number of treatments for ADHD which have no proven effectiveness: allergy treatments, megavitamins, chiropractic adjustment, treatment for yeast infection, eye training, or the use of specially coloured glasses. Restricted diets have been found in some studies to only help about 5 percent of children with ADHD, primarily younger children or those with food allergies.

Both Efalex and pycnogenol have no scientifically documented effectiveness in helping children with ADHD, and their manufacturers have been recently prohibited from making any such claims by unanimous decisions of the US Federal Trade Commission. For parents, the message should be clear: it does not help to delay effective treatment while trying out unknown or unproven ones.

Families with ADHD kids have greater parental frustration, marital discord and rates of divorce. It is very hard to parent a child who is full of uncontrolled energy, who constantly leaves messes, throws tantrums and doesn't listen or follow instructions at a level appropriate for his/her age. If children do not develop age-appropriate attention and inhibitory control, they continue to encounter the same problems and to respond in the same ineffective ways, even though they may know better and try very hard to change. Discipline (reasoning, scolding and especially hitting) doesn't work, as the children are not choosing to act in these negative ways.

Children exposed to such an approach quickly label themselves as "bad", and come to experience scolding as virtually the only kind of attention that they get. As a result, they develop a cycle of frustration, blame and anger with their parents. In addition, research has demonstrated that children imitate or model such aggressive behaviour from their parents, and are more likely to try it with other children. In fact, recent data from the Canadian National Longitudinal Study of Children and Youth have indicated that children who experience hostile or ineffective parenting are nine times more likely to demonstrate behaviour problems than are children exposed to positive parenting approaches. The best approach consists of positive, consistent parenting, modest goals and flexible structure.

The poor prognosis for children with this disorder who fail to receive effective treatment underscores the importance of early identification and intervention for children with ADHD. The complex of hyperactivity, impulsivity and attentional problems is frequently observable in children as early as the preschool years. This combination of difficulties is strongly predictive of later behaviour problems.

However, inattention and impulsivity can follow from many kinds of problems at this age (e.g., language delays, recurrent ear infections), as well as from other sources such as natural rambunctiousness, or stressors such as divorce, neglect or inadequate child care. Consequently, diagnosis of ADHD in preschoolers should only be made cautiously by experts well trained in child neurobiological disorders. Medication for this very young age group is generally not recommended, as results of such treatment have not been thoroughly evaluated for effectiveness or safety. The NIMH study recommends that treatment should focus on structured play school, along with parent training and support.

Aggressive and anti-social behaviour has been found to consolidate between the ages of 6 and 10, suggesting that this age group is a particularly important one to screen for children with this disorder. Information should be collected from both parents and teachers, and ideally a multi-disciplinary approach should be implemented, involving both health-related and school-based assessments. Unfortunately, because of different legislative and funding structures, there is currently a "disconnect" between assessments conducted in these different settings.

In spite of its demonstrated effectiveness, medication alone is not necessarily the best treatment for all children. Treatment decisions should be based upon each child's individual needs, personal and medical history, research findings, and other relevant factors. Treatment combining medical management with behavioural approaches is more effective in addressing issues such as anxiety, academic performance, oppositionality, parent-child relationships and social skills. Children receiving combined treatments tend to require about 20 percent less medication.

The most common method of treatment for AD(H)D is the use of medication.

There are three types of medication used in the treatment of AD(H)D: stimulants-(Ritalin, Dexedrine, Cylert,) tricyclic antidepressants-(Tofranil, Janimine, Norpramin, Pertofrane.) and antihypertensive drugs.

Many books have been written on the subject reviewing the advantages and disadvantages as well as the contraindications for each of those medications. Talk to your doctor and stay informed.

Remember everyone is special and unique what works wonders on some children, or adults, may be devastating to others.

Bibliography

Angel, Bradley: *Toxic Threat to Indian Lands: A Greenpeace Report*, San Francisco, Greenpeace, 1991.

Ausubel, F.M.: *Current Protocols in Molecular Biology*, New York, John Wiley and Sons, 1989.

Bailey, Ronald: *Liberation Biology: The Scientific and Moral Case for the Biotech Revolution*, Amherst, Prometheus Books, 2005.

Baines, J: *Seasonal Factors Influencing Child Malnutrition on the Nembi Plateau*, New Guinea; Nembi, 1986.

Barlow K: *Ecology of Food and Nutrition*, Oceania, New Guinea, 1984.

Barnett, P.G.: *Survey of Research on the Impacts of Pesticides on Agricultural Workers and the Rural Environment*, Davis, CA: California Institute of Rural Studies, 1989.

Barnum, R.: *Biotechnology: An Introduction*, Belmont, Thomson/Brooks/Cole, 2005.

Bindon JR: *Food and Foodways*, Oceania, Samoa, 1988.

Burch, R. : *Human Ecology: An Environmental Approach*, Belmont, Duxbury Press, 1994.

Chrispeels, Maarten : *Plants, Genes and Crop Biotechnology*, Sudbury MA, Jones and Barlett Publishers, 2003.

Conton L: *Social, Economic and Ecological Parameters of Infant Feeding in Usino*, Oceania, New Guinea, 1985.

Crittendon R; : *Seasonal Factors Influencing Child Malnutrition on the Nembi Plateau*, New Guinea; Nembi, 1986.

Daubenmire, R. F.: *Plants and Environment*, New York, Wiley, 1947.

Dewey, K: *Cash Cropping, Subsistence Agriculture and Nutritional Status among Mothers of Children in Lowland*, Oceania, Papua New Guinea, 1990.

Dixon J: *The Changing Chicken: Chooks, Cooks and Culinary Culture*, University of New South Wales Press, Australia, 2002.

Ferro-Luzzi G: *Food Patterns and Nutrition in French Polynesia*, Oceania, Polynesia, 1962.

Fumento, Michael: *Bioevolution: How Biotechnology is Changing Our World*, San Francisco, California: Encounter Books, 2003.

Jenkins, C; : *Diet and Survival among the Hagahai of Papua New Guinea*, Papua New Guinea, Hagahai, 1993.

Kruvant, W.J.: *People, Energy, and Pollution*, Cambridge, Ballinger Publishing, 1975.

Manderson L: *Shared Wealth and Symbol: Food, Culture, and Society in Oceania*, Cambridge University Press, Oceania, 1986.

Metting, Jr., F.B.: *Soil Microbial Ecology: Applications in Agricultural and Environmental Management*, Marcel Dekker, New York, 1992.

Milton, K: *Diet and Survival among the Hagahai of Papua New Guinea*, Papua New Guinea, Hagahai, 1993.

Murton B: *The Cambridge World History of Food*, Cambridge University Press, Maori, 2000.

Nancy M. Brown: *Mendel in the Kitchen: A Scientist's View of Genetically Modified Foods*, Washington, Joseph Henry Press, 2004.

Nestle, M. : *Food Politics: How the Food Industry Influences Nutritional Health*, University of California Press, California, 2003.

Norcross, JC, : *Changing for Good*. Avon Books, NewYork, 1994.

Page LB: *The Solomon Island Project: A Long-Term Study of Health, Human Biology, and Culture Change*, Oxford University Press, Solomon Islands, 1987.

Peterson N: *The Nutrition of Aborigines in Relation to the Ecosystem of Central Australia*, Australia, Aborigines, 1978.

Pollock NJ: *The Concept of Food in Pacific Society: A Fijian Example*, Oceania, Fiji, 1985.

Powdermaker H: *Feast in New Ireland: The Social Function of Eating*, Oceania, New Ireland, 1932.

Prochaska, JO, : *Changing for Good.* Avon Books, NewYork, 1994.

Rappaport R: *The Flow of Energy in an Agricultural Society*, New Guinea, Tsembaga Maring, 1971.

Rody N: *Journal of Nutrition Education*, Oceania, Micronesia, 1978.

Shack, K; : *Cash Cropping, Subsistence Agriculture and Nutritional Status among Mothers of Children in Lowland*, Oceania, Papua New Guinea, 1990.

Shetty, Kalidas: *Food Biotechnology*, New York, Dekker/CRC Press, 2005.

Suchman, M.: *Envisioning Life on the Nano-Frontier*, Dordrecht, Kluwer, 2001.

Susan, R.: *Biotechnology: An Introduction*, Belmont, Thomson/ Brooks/Cole, 2005.

Walden, Richard: *Genetic Transformation in Plants*, England, Open University Press, 1988.

William, Jr.: *Human Ecology: An Environmental Approach*, Belmont, Duxbury Press, 1994.

INDEX

D

E

F

G

H

I

J

L

M

N

T

U

V

W

Y

❑❑❑